Editor: Anne Hardy

Senior Editors: Andrew Allentuck, Stan Garrod, Nicholas Macklem

Regional Editors: Penny Anderson, Rhonda Anderson, Steve Angelo, Jean Cook, Janet Goodall, Linda Greenaway, Grant Heckman, Christopher Knapper, Katherine LeButt, Carol Matthews, Mike Matthews, Paul Miller, Joan Polfuss, Ian Robertson, Ann Sherman

Contributing Editors: Carl Bird, Katie Bowden, Elaine Butcher, John Butcher, Roger Eaton, Sheila Gordon-Payne, Peter Gove, Judith Hardy, Elizabeth Macklem, Joan McCulloch, Brent McFadyen, Michael McKenna, Catherine McNair, Ian Mitchell, Katherine Hall Page, Ann Ripley, Don Saunderson, James Tyrrell, Alfred von Mirbach

Production: Michael Macklem

Anne Hardy

Where to Eat in Canada

FORTY-THIRD YEAR

13-14

ISBN 978 0 7780 1401 0

Cover photo by Rob Palmer, Mountain Press

Printed in Canada by Coach House Printing

PUBLISHED IN CANADA BY OBERON PRESS

HOW TO USE THIS GUIDE

The restaurants recommended in this guide have been arranged alphabetically by location, from Abbotsford in British Columbia to Yellowknife in the Northwest Territories. Each entry begins with the name of the city, town or village in which the restaurant is located, followed by the name and address of the restaurant and its telephone number. Next comes the entry itself, printed in roman type, followed by two or three lines, in italic type, indicating the hours during which the restaurant is open for business. The entry ends with a quantity of other useful information: does the restaurant have a full liquor licence or is it licensed for beer and wine only? What credit cards does it take? Is there an area for non-smokers or is it a smoking-only restaurant? Is smoking permitted anywhere on the premises? If the restaurant is in an urban centre, does it have free off-street parking? Do you need to book a table? Is there wheelchair access to the washrooms?

If you already know what restaurant you want to go to, look up the restaurant in the guide, selecting first the name of the centre and then the name of the restaurant. You will find a heading like this:

LAKE LOUISE, Alberta　　　　　　　　　**MAP 102**
THE POST HOTEL　　　　　　　　　　　☆☆☆
200 Pipestone Drive　　　　　　　　**$300 ($650)**
(800) 661-1586

At left, you will find the name, address and telephone number of the restaurant, all arranged under Lake Louise. The first line on the right means that Lake Louise is represented by Map Number 102. Look for Number 102 on the map of Alberta. Once you've found it, consult your road-map for the most convenient route to Lake Louise. Often a quick check of the entry in the guide will help you to find your way.

The second line indicates how many stars the restaurant has earned. The maximum is three, and there are

5

only twenty-four restaurants in the guide that have earned this rating. Eighty-one have earned two stars and 145 have earned one. We consider a further 114 restaurants to be good buys, which doesn't necessarily mean that they are unusually cheap, though it usually does. They are indicated by a pointing finger.

The third line indicates the price. The first (and often the only) figure indicates the average cost of dinner for two with a modest wine, applicable taxes and a tip of 15%. Dinner for two is taken to mean two appetizers, two main courses, one sweet, two coffees and three glasses of an open wine. Where a restaurant has earned two stars, the cost of half a bottle of wine is included. Where a restaurant has earned three stars, the cost of a full bottle is part of the estimated price. The wines chosen are not the cheapest the establishment has to offer, nor are they the most expensive. Where, as in the case of the Post Hotel, a second figure in parentheses follows the first, this second figure indicates the average cost of dinner, bed and breakfast. The presence of this figure means that we recommend not only dinner but also, if convenient, an overnight stay.

If you don't know where you want to go, turn to the maps. Find yourself on the map that shows the province you are in. Select the nearest number and then look it up in the Index. Under the number you'll find all the centres represented by that number. Let's suppose that the nearest number is 209, which stands for the city of Toronto. Look up Toronto in the Index to Southern Ontario and you'll find that there are three other centres with the same number, each enclosed in parentheses. This means that these centres are all in the immediate vicinity of Toronto, too close to be given a number of their own. They are: Nobleton, Port Credit and Whitby. Now look up Toronto in the main body of the guide, where you will find all 41 restaurants that we recommend in the city. If you then look up each of the other three centres, you will find three more restaurants in the area that are also recommended.

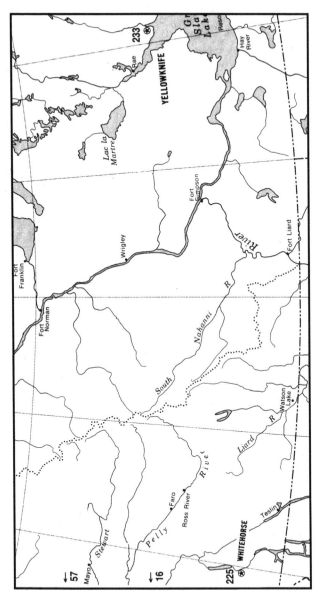

YUKON & NORTHWEST TERRITORIES

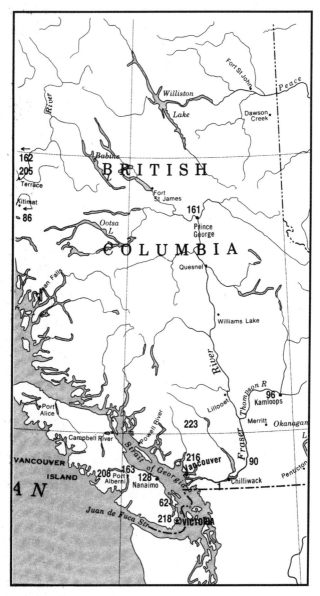

BRITISH COLUMBIA

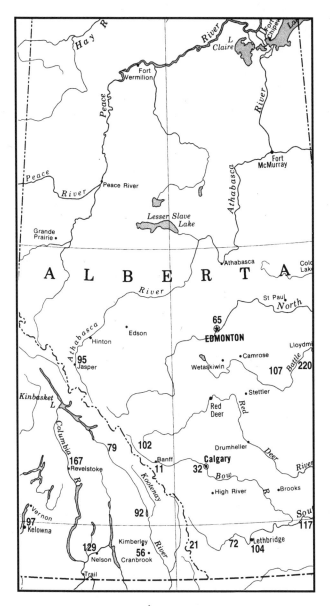

ALBERTA

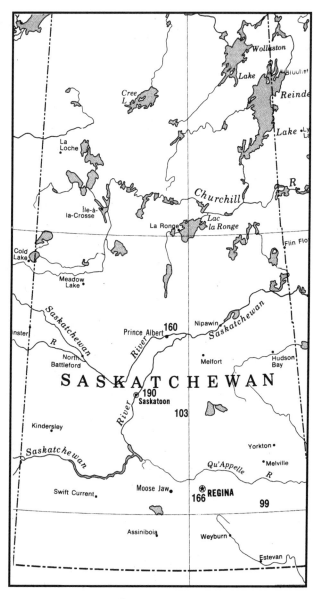

Wollaston

Lake

Brochet

Reinde

Cree
L.

Lake

Ly
La

La
Loche

R.

Île-à-
la-Crosse

Churchill

Flin Flo

Lac
la Ronge

La Ronge

Cold
Lake

Meadow
Lake

Saskatchewan

Saskatchewan

nster

R.

Prince Albert **160**

Nipawin

Hudson
Bay

North
Battleford

River

Melfort

S A S K A T C H E W A N

River

190
Saskatoon

103

Kindersley

Saskatchewan

Yorkton

Melville

Qu'Appelle

R.

Swift Current

Moose Jaw

166 REGINA

99

Assiniboia

Weyburn

Estevan

SASKATCHEWAN

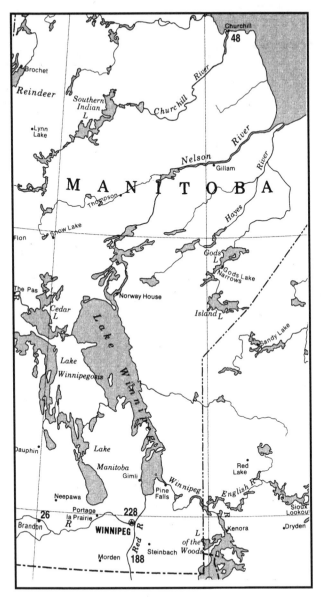

MANITOBA

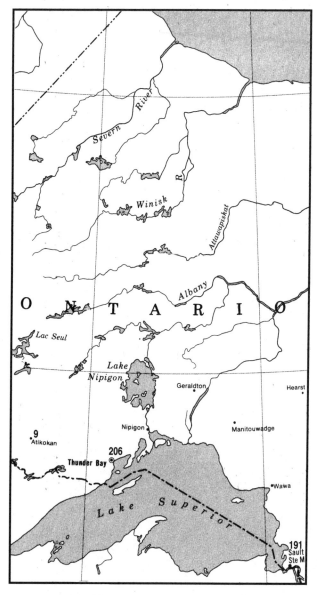

NORTHWESTERN ONTARIO

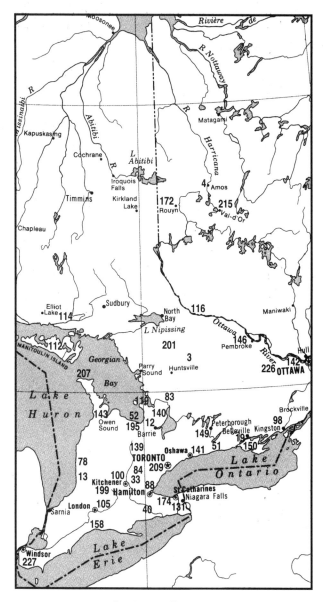

SOUTHERN ONTARIO

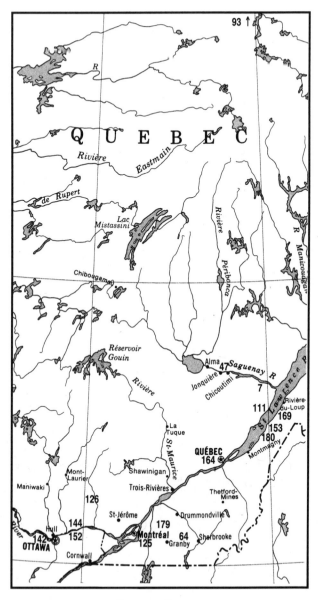

CENTRAL QUEBEC

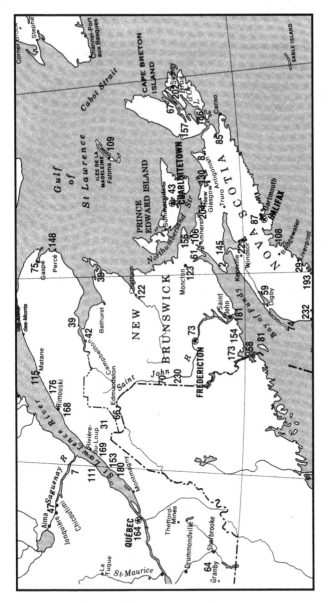

EASTERN QUEBEC & THE MARITIMES

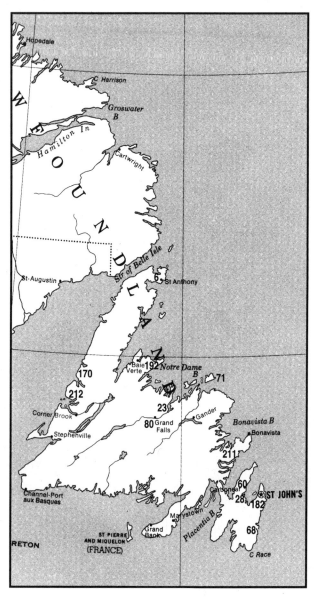

NEWFOUNDLAND & LABRADOR

30.00 a head (39.99 on jazz nights). The cheeseboard is ambitious and well maintained. Manon is in charge of the sweets, and the wine-list is always full of good things. *Open Tuesday to Saturday 11.30 am to 3 pm, 5.30 pm to 10 pm. Closed on Sunday and Monday. Licensed. Amex, Master Card, Visa. No smoking.* &

WHITEHORSE, Yukon   MAP 225

We don't know of any really good restaurants in Whitehorse, but there are several places that you should know about. The Sanchez Cantina at 211 Hanson Street (telephone (867) 668-5858) claims to have the only authentic Mexican cooking in the Yukon. Otelina Sanchez knows how to cook and she makes a lot of things from scratch, among them guacamole, enchiladas, adobos, chilli rellenos and mole poblanos. Don't expect big helpings and don't order the chicken or any of the daily specials. The Cantina is open for lunch and dinner every day but Sunday, has a licence and takes Master Card and Visa. The Burnt Toast Café at 2112 2 Avenue (telephone (867) 393-2605) is very popular in spite of its name, which is almost as bad as that of a café we know of called Cold Coffee. It's a quirky little place with quite good cooking. There are tapas nights and several vegetarian dishes. The current owners are young and very much into fresh regional cuisine. They're open every day but Monday for lunch and every day but Sunday and Monday for dinner. They have a licence and take Amex, Master Card and Visa. One of the hottest spots in town right now is a bakery called Baked at 100 Main Street (telephone (867) 633-6291). It's a terrific place for breakfast, and at noon they have big, healthy sandwiches. Baked is open every day for lunch, has a licence and takes Master Card and Visa.

WHITE LAKE, Ontario   MAP 226
CASTLEGARTH   ☆
90 Burnstown Road   **$150**
(613) 623-3472

Matthew and Jennifer Brearley make the best of their unlikely location—Castlegarth is an hour's drive from Ottawa, the nearest city. But the two chefs (both graduates of the Stratford Chefs School) have stayed true to their belief that everything should come straight from the garden to the table. (The family farm down the road makes it possible to serve tomatoes on the vine and just-picked beans.) The house, which is right in the middle of the village, has no frills, but it seats 30 people in comfort. The menu changes frequently, and during the year there are some special occasions. Not long ago, Robbie Burns Day brought a salad of brussels sprouts with haggis and rabbit sausage with pickled rutabaga. At other times they offer things like seared quail with butter-braised cabbage, wild-rice pancakes and onions with hawthorn honey. The coffee is marvellous.

Open Wednesday to Sunday 5.30 pm to 10 pm. Closed on Monday and Tuesday. Licensed. Master Card, Visa. No smoking. &

WINDSOR, Ontario   MAP 227
TOSCANA
3891 Dougall Avenue   **$100**
(519) 972-5699

Gino Parco keeps appearing and disappearing from the Windsor restaurant scene. Luckily, the last time this happened he left behind Jonathan Reaume, an old partner, at Toscana. Smoked salmon on a potato pancake is still always on the menu, as well as a number of daily specials. Reaume likes to say that his cuisine is contemporary Italian with Asian grace notes. Certainly, he never overcooks his fish or any of his pasta. The soup of the day is usually a better buy than either the carpaccio or the portobello mushrooms. There's a sushi menu as well, but it's basically just a list of ceviches. The wine-list has a number of upscale wines, among them a Caymus Conundrum, which costs only 58.00 a bottle. Toasted Head chardonnay is also sold quite cheaply by the glass.

Open Monday to Friday 11 am to 2 pm, 5 pm to 10 pm, Saturday 5 pm to 10 pm. Closed on Sunday. Licensed. Amex, Master Card, Visa. No smoking. &

WINNIPEG, Manitoba   **MAP 228**
BISTRO DANSK   ☞
63 Sherbrook Street   **$90**
(204) 775-5662

Josef Vocadlo started the Bistro Dansk many years ago;
nowadays the place is run by Josef's son, Paul. The restaurant hasn't changed much since it opened, and it still has
its Danish menu, with a few Czech dishes to give it variety. Start with the herring and go on to the frikadeller,
the kylling (half roasted chicken stuffed with apricots and
walnuts), the veal tenderloin stuffed with ham and
cheese, the pan-fried rainbow trout or the pork tenderloin sautéed in garlic with sweet-and-sour cabbage. With
your dinner, ask for a bottle of Mondavi Woodbridge,
which costs almost nothing. Indeed, everything at Bistro
Dansk is spectacularly cheap.
Open Tuesday to Saturday 11 am to 2.30 pm, 5 pm to 9 pm.
Closed on Sunday and Monday. Licensed. All cards. No smok-
ing. Book ahead.

WINNIPEG   **MAP 228**
EAST INDIA COMPANY   ☆
349 York Avenue   **$75**
(204) 947-3097

This is one Indian restaurant where nobody has to apologize for the décor or, for that matter, for anything else.
The dining-room is bright and cheerful. It has a big buffet
table that starts with salads and yogurts, goes on to tandoori chicken and such things as mussels, shrimps and
whole fish. There are vindaloos on order and a variety of
vegetarian dishes. The dessert table has a number of custards, of which we think the mango is the best. There are
a few wines on offer and a couple of Indian beers. When
it comes to value for money, no restaurant in the city can
compare with the East India Company.
Open Monday to Friday 11 am to 2 pm, 5 pm to 10 pm, Satur-
day 5 pm to 10 pm, Sunday noon to 8 pm. Licensed. Amex,
Master Card, Visa. No smoking. Book ahead if you can. ♿

WINNIPEG   **MAP 228**
THE LOBBY
295 York Avenue   **$160**
(204) 896-7275

Dale and Barb Yuell are no longer at the Lobby. Shan
Shuwera is in charge now. Prices are still quite high and
the rib steak now costs 55.00. It's a big steak, however,
and if you have an appetite to match perhaps it's worth
it. The chocolate torte is still as good as ever and so is the
wine-list. The Lobby is basically an upscale steak house,
with plenty of the best wines, all the right cocktails and
first-class service. One thing it doesn't have, however, is
off-street parking, so you just have to take your chances.
*Open Tuesday to Saturday 5 pm to 10 pm. Closed on Sunday
and Monday. Licensed. All cards. No smoking. Book ahead.* ♿

WINNIPEG   **MAP 228**
NORTH GARDEN
33 University Crescent: Unit 6   **$60**
(204) 275-2591

The North Garden is actually in south Winnipeg and it
has no garden. But it's popular with Chinese students and
faculty from the nearby University of Manitoba, and
rightly so because they have a great variety of authentic
szechuan and cantonese dishes. Dim sum is offered in
steamer baskets every day until 3.30 pm. This is by far
the best dim sum to be had in Winnipeg. They also have
lobster and crab at market prices, and the place is crowded
every evening during the school year. After about 9 o'-
clock, however, things become quieter and the service
improves.
*Open Monday to Thursday 10 am to midnight, Friday and Sat-
urday 9 am to 1 am, Sunday 10 am to midnight. Licensed. All
cards. No smoking. Book ahead if you can.* ♿

We accept no advertisements. We accept no payment for
listings. We depend entirely on you. Recommend the
book to your friends.

WINNIPEG   **MAP 228**
THE PALM ROOM   ☆
Fort Garry Hotel   **$125**
222 Broadway Avenue
(204) 942-8251

The Fort Garry Hotel was built in 1913. Later taken over
by the C.N.R., it was eventually allowed to fall into dis-
repair. A few years ago, it was restored by Richard Bel
and Ida Albo and turned into a grand hotel with a period
dining-room. The menu at the Palm Room, as it's called,
is that of a road-house, presented in high style. In the
evening you dine on gravlax, roast chicken and pecan pie,
all to the gentle music of a string quartet. On Sunday
they put on a magnificent buffet costing 50.00 (40.00 for
seniors and children under twelve). There's a massive
array of eggs, pancakes, roasts, pastries, tarts and tortes,
as well as a fine selection of whiskies. If you want to recover from all this excess, the hotel operates a Turkish-
style spa.
Open Monday to Thursday 11 am to midnight, Friday and Sat-
urday 11 am to 1 am, Sunday 9 am to 2 pm (brunch), 3 pm to
11 pm. Licensed. All cards. No smoking. Book ahead for Sunday
brunch. ♿

WINNIPEG   **MAP 228**
PEASANT COOKERY   ☞
283 Bannatyne Avenue: Unit 100   **$90**
(204) 989-7700

Oui has now been renamed Peasant Cookery. Oui, in
turn, was a cheaper version of the extravagant 529 steak
house. The name raises some important questions. It
could be intended to suggest either a rural truck-stop or
a minimalist, perhaps also an inexpensive, restaurant. Or
it could be just an up-market joke. As it happens, there
are some wonderful things to be had here as well as things
to avoid. The dining-room is large and the tables generously spaced. The service is efficient and in summer you
can dine *al fresco* and listen to the bands playing in the park

across the street. Everything at the Peasant Cookery is surprisingly cheap. A huge slice of tourtière, for instance, costs less than 20.00. There's a charcuterie platter, which is available all day for 15.00. Poutine is on every day at lunchtime, mussels at dinnertime. If you want to go really downmarket, there's bangers and mash and (wonderful) short-ribs. But be sure to avoid the french fries.
Open Monday to Saturday 11.30 am to 10 pm, Sunday 5 pm to 9 pm. Licensed. All cards. No smoking. ♿

WINNIPEG   **MAP 228**
RAE & JERRY'S
1405 Portage Avenue   **$100**
(204) 783-6155

Rae & Jerry's takes you back more than 50 years to 1957, the year the place opened. Very little has changed since then. They still have thick red carpets on the floor and deeply cushioned booths. The bar still treats martinis as if they were a fashionable cocktail. The kitchen still caters to people—of all ages and incomes—who want roast beef or beefsteak. The steaks are all good—surprisingly good. There's a fine pecan pie, as well as a coconut-cream pie and bread pudding. They have some good cabernets from Australia and several good malbecs from Argentina. The wines are all fairly priced and so is the food.
Open Monday to Saturday 11 am to 11 pm, Sunday 11 am to 8.30 pm. Licensed. Amex, Master Card, Visa. No smoking. Book ahead if you can. ♿

WINNIPEG   **MAP 228**
LA SCALA
725 Corydon Avenue   **$125**
(204) 474-2750

Perry Scaletta has run La Scala for twenty years and more. It's always had an Italian menu with touches here and there of fusion cuisine. But to enjoy the place to the full you have to know what to order. That means dumplings, which are Chinese in concept but ethereal on your plate.

It means seafood linguine and penne with spicy sausage. Best of all, it means penne with garlic and tomatoes, chillies and red and green peppers. Main dishes run from osso buco and cioppino to veal scaloppine and rib steak with black beans. The wine-list is large and features cabernets from Italy and Australia. The service is competent, the prices reasonable.

Open Monday to Friday 11.30 am to 1.30 pm, 5 pm to 11 pm, Saturday and Sunday 5 pm to 10 pm from 1 May until 31 August, Monday to Saturday 5 pm to 10 pm from 1 September until 30 April. Closed on Sunday in winter. Licensed. All cards. No smoking.

WINNIPEG   **MAP 228**
SYDNEY'S AT THE FORKS   ☆☆
1 Forks Market Road   **$175**
(204) 942-6075

There's no more elegant restaurant in Winnipeg than Sydney's at the Forks. True, to get there you have to make your way through the schmaltz that the Forks Market has become. But it's worth it—Sydney's is an island of calm and good taste. The menu is at once imaginative and clever, the service perfect. Dinner costs 55.00 a head, plus wine, tip and taxes. For that they give you a lovely soup, an appetizer (cured salmon, say), followed by masterly versions of chicken confit or pork chops with apple, ending with crème brûlée or pumpkin pudding. The wine-list offers everything from an old barolo to a Pétrus priced at only 342.00, which (believe it or not) is cheap for what it is. Lunch is much the same, though cheaper, featuring linguine with scallops and prawns, which at 19.00 is actually a very good buy. Sydney's treats everybody as a somebody and, in spite of its high prices, always offers fair value for money. In other words, it's expensive but worth it.

Open Monday 5 pm to 9 pm, Tuesday to Friday 11.30 am to 2 pm, 5 pm to 9 pm, Saturday 5 pm to 9 pm. Closed on Sunday. Licensed. All cards. No smoking. Book ahead. ♿

TRE VISI
173 McDermot Avenue   **$110**
(204) 949-9032

The original Tre Visi is in a shabby district, but inside everything is warm and comfortable. The creation of the chef-owner, Giacomo Appice, it has the best Italian kitchen in Winnipeg. They have a variety of cured meats and marinated vegetables. They have some amazing pastas—just try the capellini with roasted red peppers and saffron cream. They do a fine piccata of veal in white wine as well, and their saltimbocca of pork has few equals. If you don't feel like another zabaglione marsala, ask for the chocolate ganache instead. Recently, Tre Visi has opened a second restaurant at 926 Grosvenor Avenue (telephone (204) 475-4447). It has a similar but smaller menu that emphasizes pasta, but they don't take reservations.

Open Monday to Friday 11,30 am to 2.30 pm, 5 pm to 9 pm, Saturday 5 pm to 10 pm. Closed on Sunday. Licensed. All cards. No smoking. Book ahead. ♿

BLOMIDON INN   ★★
195 Main Street   **$150 ($325)**
(800) 565-2291

The Blomidon Inn has a number of handsome bedrooms and a dining-room of mid-Victorian splendour. The place is run by two of Jim and Donna Laceby's sons. Sean is in charge of the kitchen; his brother, Michael, is the *sommelier*. At the moment, Michael has the advantage, because he has several Benjamin Bridge wines on offer. Best of all, he has a few bottles of the Benjamin Bridge sparkling wine, which is much the best of its kind ever produced in Nova Scotia. It's a celebrated wine and hard to find elsewhere, even at the going price of 125.00 or more a bottle. Sean's menu is conservative—lobster tails, grilled lamb, filet mignon—but everything is prepared exactly as it should be. Some things—the maple-cured salmon is one—are brilliant. Laceby has his own smoke-house, where he smokes his own chicken, his own bacon and his own salmon. The service is formal but relaxed, and the prices are surprisingly low. The maple-cured salmon costs only 9.95, and it's worth twice that.

Open Monday to Friday 11.30 am to 2 pm, 5 pm to 9.30 pm, Saturday and Sunday 10 am to 3 pm (brunch), 5 pm to 9.30 pm. Licensed. Master Card, Visa. No smoking.

WOLFVILLE   MAP 229
CELLAR DOOR
Luckett Vineyards   **$50**
1293 Grand Pré Road
(902) 542-2600

Pete Luckett made an instant success of his grocery stores, which he calls Pete's Frootiques. He then opened a vine-yard called Luckett's. That was in 2010 and the Luckett Vineyards were rated the top tourist attraction in Wolfville just two years later. The wines are still young, of course, but the restaurant offers spectacular views of Minas Basin and Cape Blomidon. The Cellar Door itself is reserved for private parties, but the outside patio has seating for ordinary travellers. Here you can have a soup, a sandwich (Italian ham with figs, say) and a salad (patty-pan squash with chanterelles, perhaps). They also have cheese-and-charcuterie platters, as well as one or two excellent sweets. The German tasting varietal, Ortega, is the best of the wines on offer, though it's often sold out. Good news—they have a red telephone booth from which you can call anyone in North America free of charge.

Open daily 10 am to 5 pm from 1 June until 31 October. Licensed. Amex, Master Card, Visa. No smoking. Book ahead if you can.

Every restaurant in this guide has been personally tested. Our reporters are not allowed to identify themselves or to accept free meals.

WOLFVILLE   **MAP 229**
FRONT & CENTRAL
117 Front Street   **$130**
(866) 542-0588

Michael Howell was a leading proponent, perhaps the
leading proponent, of the slow-food movement in Nova
Scotia. And located as he was in Wolfville, he was able to
say (with truth) that most of what he served came from
the Annapolis Valley. Illness, however, has forced him to
sell Tempest to his chef de cuisine, Dave Smart. Smart
has renamed the restaurant Front & Central. He has a
good reputation, but the new menu was not available
when this edition went to press. Further reports needed.
Open Tuesday and Wednesday 5 pm to 9 pm, Thursday to Sun-
day 11.30 am to 2.30 pm, 5 pm to 9 pm. Closed on Monday.
Licensed. All cards. No smoking. &

WOLFVILLE
See also GRAND PRE.

WOODSTOCK, N.B.   **MAP 230**
HEINO'S   ☞
John Gyles Motor Inn   **$75**
Highway 165
(866) 381-8800

To get to Heino's, which is no longer right on the Trans
Canada Highway, take Exit 200 a few miles south of
Woodstock, turn left at two stop signs and proceed a few
hundred yards to the north. The John Gyles is at the top
of a hill on the west side of the road. Heino Toedler
cooks in the German style, which means sauerbraten,
schnitzels and several kinds of sausage—bratwurst,
debreziner, knackwurst and weisswurst. He also makes
such things as butterfly shrimps and deep-fried scallops,
but it's usually best to stick to a schnitzel or one of the
sausages. (Actually, our favourite dish is the potato pancake.) There's only one (indifferent) German wine by the
glass, and it's a good idea to ask for a beer instead. Heino's

is trim and neat inside and out and always very well
served. Everybody seems to like the place.
*Open Monday to Saturday 5 pm to 9 pm, Sunday 5 pm to 8 pm.
Licensed. Amex, Master Card, Visa. No smoking.* ⚕

WOODY POINT, Newfoundland   (MAP 170)
THE OLD LOFT
Water Street   **$75**
(709) 453-2294

The Old Loft is a success because they took the trouble
to find the best suppliers of local fresh produce. Another
reason for their success is, of course, that Clarice Bursey
is a good cook and a keen baker, turning out multi-grain
bread, bake-apple cheesecake and all kinds of fresh berry
pies. When it comes to the cooking, she turns out a lot
of traditional Newfoundland dishes. Clam chowder is always on the menu, as are salmon, halibut and capelin. All
the fish is pan-fried and nothing is ever overcooked. The
vegetables are steamed and the french-fried potatoes are
made right on the premises. Woody Point is on the south
arm of Bonne Bay in Gros Morne National Park. The
town was settled more than a hundred years ago and the
big old houses with their lovely gardens have been cared
for lovingly ever since. The Old Loft occupies one of
these and it's been completely restored. To get here, leave
Highway 431 on the road to Trout River. The Old Loft
is right on the highway.
*Open daily 11.30 am to 9 pm from Victoria Day until Thanks-
giving. Licensed for beer and wine only. Amex, Master Card,
Visa. No smoking.*

YARMOUTH, N.S.   MAP 232
OLD WORLD BAKERY   ☞
232 Main Street   **$40**
(902) 742-2181

In spite of the recent cancellation of ferry sailings between Yarmouth and Bar Harbour, Tony and Nova Papadogiorgakis are carrying on at the bakery as if nothing

had happened. Their breads and pastries are as good as ever. Their huge muffins are good enough to take home. (They come with cheese, cranberry, lemon, blueberry, bran, cinnamon, dates, apples and oranges.) They make rye, whole-grain, sourdough and sweet-potato bread. There's also a homemade soup every day and big, filling sandwiches, of which our favourite is the smoked lamb. (The lamb, like the turkey and the sausages, is smoked on the premises.) The coffee is fairly traded and it's always great.

Open Tuesday to Friday 7 am to 6 pm, Saturday 7 am to 5 pm. Closed on Sunday and Monday. No liquor, no cards. No smoking. &

YARMOUTH
See also MIDDLE WEST PUBNICO.

YELLOWKNIFE, N.W.T.   MAP 233
BULLOCK'S BISTRO   ☆
3534 Weaver Drive   **$130**
(867) 873-3474

Everybody likes Bullock's. It used to be a working fish shack, and it's always been here—small, crowded, noisy and expensive. The chairs are rickety, the tables carved with old initials, the service easy-come, easy-go. But the fish is about as fresh as it gets. Most of it comes from Great Slave Lake—whitefish, cod, pickerel and trout are always on the menu. Renata serves all the fish grilled, pan-fried, poached, blackened Cajun-style or deep-fried in a beer batter. Meals all come with warm sourdough bread and a slab of butter. If you want something to drink, help yourself from the cooler—there's always plenty of beer and a couple of wines in there.

Open Monday to Saturday 11.30 am to 9 pm. Closed on Sunday. Licensed. Master Card, Visa. No smoking. Book ahead if you can.

If you use an out-of-date edition and find it inaccurate, don't blame us. Buy a new edition.

YELLOWKNIFE
FROLIC
5019 49 Street
(867) 669-9852

MAP 233
★★★
$220

The recession of 2008-09 wiped out Pierre LePage's dream of a grand restaurant in Yellowknife. He shouldered his loss and promptly turned Frolic into an elegant restaurant operating on two floors. Downstairs they offer fondues and on Wednesday mussels and beer as well. Upstairs the menu is much more ambitious, the wine-list astonishing. Pierre LePage is a culinary gold medallist who's travelled the world, studying the food and wine of many countries. Wild game and fresh fish are his specialties, but he adds his signature to every dish, whether it's halibut or char, bison or caribou. Every evening he offers two main dishes. One might be halibut poached with vermouth, another might be Barren Lands caribou with maple, cranberry and port wine. Appetizers include pâté, snow crab, Malpèque oysters and prawns en croûte. Sweets don't much interest him, but he always has a fresh-fruit tart on his menu. Pierre LePage also holds the lease on the Wildcat Café in the old town. But they're working on the foundations there and the Wildcat won't be open until next year.

Open Monday to Saturday 3 pm to 1 am. Closed on Sunday. Licensed. All cards. No smoking. Book ahead if you can.

We will soon be preparing the next edition of this guide. To do that, we need the help of our readers, many of whom routinely send us information and comments on restaurants that interest them, whether or not they are already in the guide. Please address us by mail at 145 Spruce Street: Suite 205, Ottawa, Ontario K1R 6P1, by fax at (613) 238-3275 or by e-mail at oberon@sympatico.ca

We acknowledge the support of the Government of Canada through the Canada Book Fund for our publishing activities.

First published July 1971. Reprinted September 1971, November 1971, January 1972. Second edition published June 1972. Reprinted July 1972. Third edition published June 1973. Reprinted July 1973. Fourth edition published June 1974. Fifth edition published June 1975. Book-of-the-Month Club edition published July 1975. Sixth edition published June 1976. Seventh edition published June 1977. Eighth edition published June 1978. Ninth edition published June 1979. Tenth edition published June 1980. Eleventh edition published June 1981. Twelfth edition published June 1982. Thirteenth edition published June 1983. Fourteenth edition published June 1984. Fifteenth edition published June 1985. Sixteenth edition published June 1986. Seventeenth edition published June 1987. Eighteenth edition published June 1988. Nineteenth edition published June 1989. Twentieth edition published June 1990. Twenty-first edition published June 1991. Twenty-second edition published June 1992. Twenty-third edition published June 1993. Twenty-fourth edition published June 1994. Twenty-fifth edition published June 1995. Twenty-sixth edition published June 1996. Twenty-seventh edition published June 1997. Twenty-eighth edition published June 1998. Twenty-ninth edition published June 1999. Thirtieth edition published June 2000. Thirty-first edition published June 2001. Thirty-second edition published June 2002. Thirty-third edition published June 2003. Thirty-fourth edition published June 2004. Thirty-fifth edition published June 2005. Thirty-sixth edition published June 2006. Thirty-seventh edition published June 2007. Thirty-eighth edition published June 2008. Thirty-ninth edition published June 2009. Fortieth edition published June 2010. Forty-first edition published June 2011. Forty-second edition published June 2012. Forty-third edition published June 2013.

INDEX TO MAPS

MANITOBA

26 Brandon
48 Churchill
188 St. Pierre-Jolys
228 Winnipeg

NORTHWESTERN ONTARIO

9 Atikokan
191 Sault Ste. Marie
206 Thunder Bay

SOUTHERN ONTARIO

3 Algonquin Park
4 Amos
12 Barrie
13 Bayfield
19 Belleville
(19) Brighton
33 Cambridge
40 Cayuga
51 Cobourg
52 Collingwood
78 Goderich
83 Gravenhurst
(83) Bala
(83) Bracebridge
(83) Rosseau
84 Guelph
(84) Morriston
88 Hamilton
(88) Ancaster
(88) Burlington
(88) Dundas

98 Kingston
(98) Ivy Lea
100 Kitchener
(100) Waterloo
105 London
112 Manitoulin Island
114 Massey
116 Mattawa
119 Midland
(119) Penetang
131 Niagara-on-the-Lake
139 Orangeville
140 Orillia
141 Oshawa
142 Ottawa
(142) Chelsea
143 Owen Sound
146 Pembroke
149 Peterborough
150 Picton
(150) Bloomfield
(150) Wellington
158 Port Stanley
172 Rouyn
174 St. Catharines
(174) Beamsville
195 Singhampton
199 Stratford
(199) St. Marys
201 Sundridge
207 Tobermory
209 Toronto
(209) Nobleton
(209) Port Credit
(209) Whitby
215 Val d'Or
226 White Lake
227 Windsor

111 La Malbaie
(111) Cap à l'Aigle
115 Matane
122 Miramichi
123 Moncton
130 New Glasgow
(130) Pictou
(130) Stellarton
(130) Trenton
145 Parrsboro
148 Percé
(148) St.-Georges de Malbaie
153 La Pocatière
154 Pocologan
156 Port Elgin
157 Port Hood
(157) Glenville
(157) Northeast Margaree
164 Quebec
(164) Ile d'Orléans
(164) St.-Georges-de-Beauce
168 Rimouski
(168) Le Bic
169 Rivière du Loup
173 St. Andrews
176 Ste.-Flavie
180 St.-Jean-Port-Joli
181 Saint John
186 St. Peter's

193 Shelburne
(193) Clark's Harbour
202 Sydney
204 Tatamagouche
229 Wolfville
(229) Grand Pré
230 Woodstock
232 Yarmouth
(232) Middle West Pubnico

NEWFOUNDLAND & LABRADOR

6 l'Anse-aux-Meadows
(6) Cape Onion
(6) St.-Lunaire-Griquet
23 Botwood
28 Brigus
60 Dildo
68 Ferryland
71 Fogo Island
80 Grand Falls
170 Rocky Harbour
(170) Norris Point
(170) Woody Point
182 St. John's
(182) Portugal Cove
192 La Scie
211 Trinity
212 Trout River

ABBOTSFORD, B.C.

MAP 1

CLAYBURN VILLAGE STORE
34810 Clayburn Road **$50**
Clayburn
(604) 853-4020

The Clayburn Village Store is closed for the months of January, May and September. That's when Bryan Haber takes off, perhaps to a food festival in California, perhaps to Betty's Tea-Shop in York, where he buys Tippy Assam tea for the Village Store back home. (His is the only cream tea with clotted cream to be had anywhere this side of Victoria.) He makes all his own chutneys, pickles, cheese scones and sticky-toffee puddings. Every year he brings home new soup recipes, and his recipe for carrot-and-coconut soup has been published in *Bon Appetit*. We also like his caramelized onion soup with garlic and parmesan cheese, though many of the customers seem to prefer the Thai coconut-and-squash soup. Bryan Haber is also keen on British ales, which he buys from Samuel Smith's Yorkshire Brewery in Tadcaster. There's Imperial Stout, Nut Brown and Teddy Porter, and he now has an organic ale and an organic cider as well. There's always an assortment of British candies on the candy counter, all sold from big glass jars, just the way they used to be in the nineteen-thirties. They didn't have a frozen-yogurt machine then though; he does.

Open Tuesday to Saturday 10 am to 5 pm. Closed on Sunday and Monday. Licensed. Master Card, Visa. No smoking. ⅃

ADVOCATE HARBOUR, N.S.

MAP 2

WILD CARAWAY ★★★
3721 Highway 209 **$95 ($175)**
(902) 392-2889

Who would have expected to find one of the best restaurants this side of Halifax in a village of 200 souls like this? But the fact is that a young couple, Andrew Aitken and Sarah Griebel, have restored a mid-Victorian house overlooking Cape d'Or, and opened two charming guest-rooms. There's a huge garden behind the house that supplies most of the herbs and vegetables the restaurant needs. When you get there, look for the crisp-fried local squid, the terrine of chicken and wild mushrooms, the pan-fried fillet of char, the pan-roasted fillet of halibut with aged cheddar and buttered cucumber, the seared local scallops with cauliflower and white truffles. The sweets are equally amazing and they make their own rhubarb lemonade and their own ginger beer. They smoke their own seafood and cut their own fries. They start every meal with fresh dulse and caraway buns. Every Sunday there's a fabulous brunch, but the menu is always a surprise.

Open Monday and Wednesday to Saturday 11 am to 8 pm, Sunday 9 am to noon (brunch), 5 pm to 9 pm. Closed on Tuesday. Shorter hours in winter. Licensed. Master Card, Visa. No smoking. &

ALGONQUIN PARK, Ontario   MAP 3
AROWHON PINES   ☆
Highway 60   **$190 ($550)**
(866) 633-5661

All the recipes at Arowhon Pines were worked out over the years, then put onto a computer in such detail that no hired chef could put a foot wrong. And so it has worked out. Meals are planned a week in advance, which means that nobody ever gets the same meal twice. As you enter the great hexagonal dining-room, you're confronted by a large buffet table, where there are several pâtés and terrines, smoked mousse of lake trout, honey-garlic chicken wings and a wild-rice salad. You can eat as much of any of these as you like. When you sit down at your table—don't try to book a window table, because it's first come first seated—there's a choice of four entrées, one of which will be fish, another a vegetarian dish. The sweets are all famous, so try to save room for one. There's a huge assortment of pies, tarts and cakes, at least one of which will be hot. The coffee is excellent, but you have to bring your own bottle—there's no corkage fee.

Lunch is also served buffet-style on weekends only. The price in parentheses above covers three meals a day, plus all the recreational facilities on offer.

Open daily 12.30 pm to 2 pm, 6.30 pm to 9 pm from 25 May until 7 October. Bring your own bottle. Master Card, Visa. No smoking. Book ahead. &

ALGONQUIN PARK   MAP 3
BARTLETT LODGE   ☆
Highway 60   **$175 ($425)**
(705) 633-5543

People write to us about the hospitality of the people at Bartlett Lodge. The Lodge is on Cache Lake, which is about fifteen miles from the West Gate. Drive to the far end of the car park, where you'll find a free telephone to the Lodge. A boat will come to pick you up in about two minutes. In fine weather they'll come in a custom-built Giesler; if it's raining they'll come in a covered pontoon boat. On the far side you'll be offered an elaborate dinner for 59.00 a head. There's a new chef this year, Jakob Lutes; he comes from the Atelier in Ottawa. His meal begins with a pumpkin soup, or sometimes with a tomato or red-pepper soup, followed by a hazelnut gnudi with lancaster cheese or a chicken-pistachio terrine with a reduction of rhubarb. Next comes pan-roasted pickerel, rack of lamb with a purée of celery root, or perhaps beef tenderloin. Finish off with a baked apple. Coffee is on the house.

Open daily 6 pm to 8 pm from 11 May until 12 October. Bring your own bottle. Master Card, Visa. No smoking. You must book ahead.

AMHERST, N.S.
See LORNEVILLE.

Where an entry is printed in italics this indicates that the restaurant has been listed only because it serves the best food in its area or because it hasn't yet been adequately tested.

AMOS, Quebec **MAP 4**
LE MOULIN ☆☆
100 1 Avenue O **$140**
(819) 732-8271

Le Moulin has one of the best kitchens in northern Quebec, and it's doing well in spite of its remote location. (It's 50 miles west of Val d'Or and 75 miles northeast of Noranda.) Jean-Victor Flingou is an excellent cook who enjoys his work, but after more than twenty years he's turned the evening meal over to his son, Maxim. He and his son still bring in all their seafood from Montreal, and there's always a surprising variety on the menu: Atlantic salmon, mackerel, grouper, halibut, scallops, mussels and occasionally red tuna. But Flingou cooks what he feels like cooking. It may be lamb (sometimes from Ontario, sometimes from Alberta), veal, sweetbreads, or duck. He's never much liked pork and these days he doesn't serve it at all. He forages himself for mushrooms to go with his provimi veal; when he can't find enough mushrooms he'll just make a blanquette de veau. He's doing more with shrimps nowadays, because there's always a demand for them. Bison is a new favourite. Chicken is often on the menu, because he needs the bones for his stock. Every day there's a menu *du jour* for 20.00 at lunch and 35.00 at dinner. It starts with soup or snails, goes on to duck or salmon and ends with a crème pâtissière with local strawberries.
Open Monday to Friday 11 am to 2 pm, 5 pm to 9 pm, Saturday 5 pm to 9 pm. Closed on Sunday. Licensed. Amex, Master Card, Visa. No smoking. Book ahead. ♿

ANCASTER, Ontario **(MAP 88)**
THE OLD MILL
548 Old Dundas Road **$125**
(905) 648-1828

The Old Mill has always been known for weddings and corporate functions. But there's more to the place than that. Jeff Crump got into slow cooking and organic produce before most chefs in the area, and he still has an earth-to-table paragraph in all his menus that offers farm-fresh eggs, local greens, wild mushrooms and charcuterie from nearby farms. Meals start simply enough with wild-mushroom soup or calamari with spinach. Lamb will follow, cooked two ways (loin stuffed with fennel and shoulder cooked *sous vide*). There's also beef with béarnaise sauce (an old standby) and roasted organic chicken with pickled red cabbage.

Open Tuesday to Saturday 11.30 am to 10 pm, Sunday 9.30 am to 2.30 pm (brunch), 5 pm to 9 pm. Closed on Monday. Licensed. Master Card, Visa. No smoking. &

L'ANSE-AUX-MEADOWS,   MAP 6
Newfoundland
THE NORSEMAN   ☆
(877) 623-2018   **$130**

Bella Hodge played around the Viking Settlement as a child, and when she grew up she opened the Valhalla Lodge. That was in 1986. In the years since then, Bella's daughter, Gina, and her husband, Adrian Nordhoff, have made the Norseman, as they called it, into one of the best places to eat in Newfoundland. They started off with seafood, but have since added things like saddle of rabbit and caribou tenderloin. The caribou graze on the local lichen, which is what gives the meat its special flavour. Gina keeps lobster, which she buys across the street, on the menu until the middle of August, when it's at its best. She buys crab, shrimps, scallops and cod locally. Mussels she gets from a fish farm in Gunner's Cove. She makes all her own multi-grain bread, all her own partridge-berry pies and all her own chocolate and bake-apple tarts. Bella Hodge still runs the Valhalla next door, which is equipped with state-of-the-art kitchens and flat-screen television.

Open daily 11.30 am to 9 pm from late May until late September. Licensed. Diners, Master Card, Visa. No smoking. Book ahead if you can. &

25

L'ANSE-AUX-MEADOWS
See also CAPE ONION, ST.-LUNAIRE-GRUQUET.

L'ANSE-SAINT-JEAN, Quebec   MAP 7
AUBERGE DES CEVENNES   ☆
294 rue St.-Jean-Baptiste   **$110**
(877) 272-3180

L'Anse-Saint-Jean is one of the prettiest villages in the province and it's only four hours from Quebec City. The Auberge des Cevennes has a superb setting, just a few minutes from the starting point of Saguenay cruises. Enid Bertrand has energy, charm and a good command of English. She also likes to cook. Local people usually ask for one of the handful of dishes they've enjoyed for the last twenty years. Outsiders are apt to be more venturesome. Mme Bertrand has a big garden where she makes good use of the early springs and late winters in these parts. Her soups are full of garden-fresh vegetables, her cakes and pastries full of fresh raspberries and strawberries. Caribou have almost vanished from this area, but there are still roe deer that show up in her salads. There's usually quite a lot of seafood—salmon, scallops and lobster. She makes a beautiful white-mountain cake, which is a génoise filled with apples and maple syrup and served with fresh cream.
Open daily 6 pm to 9 pm from the beginning of June until the end of October, Saturday and Sunday 6 pm to 9 pm from the beginning of November until the end of May. Closed Monday to Friday in winter. Licensed. Master Card, Visa. No smoking. You must book ahead. ⅊

ANTIGONISH, N.S.   MAP 8
GABRIEAU'S BISTRO   ☆
350 Main Street   **$135**
(902) 863-1925

Gabrieau's has always been the place to eat in Antigonish, but that has never been truer than it is today. Gabrieau has continued to expand and enrich his wine-list, which now offers such glorious things as a couple of tignanellos, three sassicaias and several barolos, to say nothing of the many pauillacs and a number of the best wines from California. Many of these are too expensive for most people (ourselves included), but there are two mid-range St.-Emilions, one of which, a Château Cantena, costs only 89.00. If you choose this wine, be sure to order it early to give it plenty of time to breathe. (Fresh from the cork, it's quite disappointing.) The menu is sophisticated, always offering its seafood chowder, for instance, en croûte. There's Atlantic salmon, fishcakes and local lamb, but we haven't yet tried the lamb. Meanwhile, the dinner will end magnificently, with a fine chocolate soufflé.

Open Monday to Thursday 11 am to 9 pm, Friday 11 am to 9.30 pm, Saturday 4 pm to 9.30 pm. Closed on Sunday. Licensed. All cards. No smoking. &

ATIKOKAN, Ontario   MAP 9
TOWN & COUNTRY
(807) 597-2533   **$95**

There may be days when Stephanie Torbiak gets tired of running this place, but she's not ready to give it up yet. Business has been slow in recent years, but Stephanie took the opportunity to install en suite bathrooms throughout the house. Recent work at the nearby generating station means business for the Town & Country, and so does the Ukrainian Christmas. But she knows her market. People want steak, baked beans and frozen seafood, period. All these are cooked to order and she makes all the soups and all the pasta. She makes a good quiche too and a very good salad, which comes with a poppyseed dressing. People like her cooking and that makes everything worthwhile for her.

Open Monday to Saturday 8 am to 9 pm (sometimes later). Closed on Sunday. Licensed. Master Card, Visa. No smoking.

This is a guide to Canadian restaurants from coast to coast—the first ever published and the only one of its kind on the market today.

BALA, Ontario   **(MAP 83)**
MOON RIVER LOOKOUT
1002 Bala Falls Road   **$140**
(705) 762-2393

People find the Moon River Lookout captivating, partly
(we think) because of the freight trains that come in one
window and leave by another every few minutes. As for
the food, it's about as good as you can expect anywhere
in Muskoka. They no longer have their great tapas menu.
Instead they concentrate on substantial, conservative
dishes like breast of chicken and rack of lamb. Not that
they don't do some nice things. Their chicken comes to
the table with mushrooms and calvados, their salmon
with mango and pineapple, their pickerel with local ale.
They have mussels and fishcakes and short-ribs cooked
Korean-style. Their wine-list isn't large, but it's not expensive either. Leaping Horse, for instance, costs less than
30.00 a bottle, which makes it a great buy. The pinot noir
from Kim Crawford costs only 48.00. There's a new chef
this year, so further reports are needed.
Open Monday and Tuesday, Thursday and Friday 5 pm to 9
pm, Saturday and Sunday 11.30 am to 2.30 pm, 5 pm to 9 pm
from Victoria Day until Thanksgiving. Closed on Wednesday.
Licensed. Amex, Master Card, Visa. No smoking. Book ahead
if you can.

BANFF, Alberta   MAP 11

Banff has a number of surprisingly good inexpensive restaurants.
Bumpers at 603 Banff Avenue (telephone (403) 762-2622)
even encourages children. It's at the far end of town and doesn't
look much from the outside. But inside it's a different story. They
have swift, cheerful service and an all-you-can-eat salad bar.
They specialize in well hung Alberta beef, and they sell a lot of
triple-A prime rib. The Balkan at 120 Banff Avenue (telephone
(403) 762-3454) was opened in 1982 by a Greek couple who
had a lot of old family recipes. The cooking has always been com-
pletely authentic and the prices are as low as ever. The thing to
have here is the so-called arni-psito, which is a version of lamb

Greek-style, and it's a stunning dish. A few years ago, they decided to try something new, so they brought in a belly-dancer, and every Tuesday and Thursday invited customers to throw their plates on the floor. Some people love this sort of thing and the place is always crowded. The St. James Gate at 207 Wolf Street (telephone (403) 762-9355) is an Irish-style pub where they have 24 beers on tap and 30 single malts. Everybody admires the choice of beers and nearly everybody likes their barley soup, their meatloaf and their spicy shepherd's pie. The cooking is good, the helpings big and the prices fair. Finally, there's Nourish, a vegetarian bistro and tea-house located upstairs at 215 Banff Avenue (telephone (403) 760-3933). People seem to like almost everything on the menu, from the tapas and the daily specials to the sweets. There's plenty to drink—fully-blended teas, organic wines and real ale. The Balkan and the St. James are open all day every day, Bumpers every evening from 5 pm to 10 pm. Nourish is open on weeknights after 4.30 pm, on weekends from noon to 3 pm and 5 pm to 9 pm. They all have a licence and take most cards.

BANFF	**MAP 11**
LE BEAUJOLAIS	☆☆☆
212 Buffalo Street	**$250/$100**
(403) 762-2712	

Thomas Moser has been in charge of the kitchen at the Beaujolais for a year and a half now and he's every inch— or almost every inch—an outstanding performer. His fish may sometimes be overcooked (avoid the Manitoba pickerel), but his foie gras is always perfect, his salmon trio a delight, his Alberta tenderloin magnificent, his vegetables impeccable. The veal zurichoise is a newcomer to the menu and it's an impressive dish. If you remember to order a soufflé when you sit down, it'll be brought to you without delay at the end of the meal, pierced and filled with strawberries. The machiato is like no other and you shouldn't miss it. The wine-list is amazing. Last winter Albert Moser (no relation to the chef) offered us a bottle of white beaujolais (we paid) that put most of the grander vintages to shame. The Beaujolais is expensive, but everything on the menu at the adjacent Café de Paris (telephone (403) 762-5365) is prepared in the same kitchen and sold a lot more cheaply.

Open Monday to Friday 5.30 pm to 10.30 pm, Saturday and Sunday 11.30 am to 2.30 pm, 5.30 pm to 10.30 pm from mid-April until mid-October, Tuesday to Friday 5.30 pm to 10.30 pm, Saturday 11.30 am to 2.30 pm, 5.30 pm to 10.30 pm from mid-October until mid-April. Closed on Sunday and Monday in winter. Licensed. Master Card, Visa. No smoking. Book ahead.

BANFF

EDEN
Rimrock Resort Hotel
300 Mountain Avenue
(403) 762-3356

MAP 11
★★★
$275

The Rimrock is built right into the side of a mountain, which gives it spectacular views in every direction. There are people who complain about this or that at Eden, but they all agree that the views are stunning. As for the menu, it's wonderfully innovative. The tartar of Arctic char, for instance, tastes of lemon, bourbon, blue spruce and orange-blossom gelée. High-country bison is flavoured with elderflowers, juniper berries and saskatoons. Gilt-head sea-bream is grilled over Douglas fir and served with foie gras in vanilla consommé. Everything is beautifully presented and impeccably served. There are people who want more for their money. They should just settle for the multiple-course tasting menu at 124.00 a head, or go elsewhere. For those who don't want to do that, there's a seven-course tasting menu of foie gras. The wine-list is as extraordinary as everything else, and has 70,000 bottles from all over the world. Eden is the only triple-diamond restaurant, not just in Banff, but in the whole province of Alberta.

Open Wednesday to Sunday 6 pm to 9.30 pm. Closed on Monday and Tuesday. Licensed. Amex, Master Card, Visa. No smoking. Book ahead if you can. &

BARRIE, Ontario　　　　　　　　　　**MAP 12**
THE CRAZY FOX
135 Bayfield Street　　　　　　　　　　　**$150**
(705) 737-5000

Coos Uylenbroek came here with his wife Lawna in 1986
and later moved up-market to the present location. His
prices aren't low, but he cooks well and he has an impressive wine-list. The two-storey dining-room is dramatic
and so is the kitchen, behind its wall of glass. The menu
may not be particularly ambitious, but the ingredients
are all the best that money can buy. The steaks, for instance are always tender, the vegetables (even the asparagus) correctly cooked and carefully seasoned. The
wholewheat ravioli stuffed with spinach and butternut
squash is a fine vegetarian dish. There are always some
fresh berries at the end of the meal, and there's no sugar
at all in the blood-orange sorbet. Lunch is a big, important meal and many of the evening dishes are also available at noon. Uylenbroek still does most of the cooking
himself and it shows.
Open Tuesday to Thursday 11.30 am to 2.30 pm, 5 pm to 9.30
pm, Friday 11 am to 2.30 pm, 5 pm to 10 pm, Saturday 5 pm
to 10.30 pm. Closed on Sunday and Monday. Licensed. Amex,
Master Card, Visa. No smoking. Free parking.

BARRIE　　　　　　　　　　　　　　**MAP 12**
OSCAR'S　　　　　　　　　　　　　　　☆
52B Bayfield Street　　　　　　　　　　**$130**
(705) 737-0522

Oscar's is owned by Randy Feltis, who is also the chef.
Randy's father operates Feltis Farms and supplies his son's
restaurant with the fine fresh produce, for which Oscar's
has always been known. Over the years the interior of
the place has been fixed up, and this year they have at last
earned their first star. They have a three-course tasting
menu for 33.00 and a four-course menu for 44.00. These
low prices also apply to the à la carte, which starts with
pan-seared scallops, grilled squid and smoked salmon

with maple syrup. Main courses begin with Pacific black cod in a shellfish broth and go on to rack of lamb with rosemary and Wagyu steak with garlic mash. Michael Sulberg chardonnays and cabernet sauvignons are available by the glass and the bottle for a modest price. *Note:* as this edition went to press, we received reports that Randy Feltis had decided to relocate the restaurant to 268 Bradford Street under the name The Farmhouse, with a cheaper and simpler menu.

Open Monday to Friday 11 am to 3 pm, 5 pm to 9 pm, Saturday and Sunday 5 pm to 9 pm. Licensed. Amex, Master Card, Visa. No smoking. ♿

BAYFIELD, Ontario   **MAP 13**
THE BLACK DOG   ☆
5 Main Street S   **$160**
(519) 565-2326

For years the Little Inn and the Red Pump were thought to be the two best restaurants in Bayfield. You won't go wrong with either of them, but in our opinion the Black Dog now takes first place. Like the other two, it's in an historic building that was built in 1850 and is now the oldest commercial building on the street. It's always been known for its twenty draft beers and its many single-malt whiskies. But it's the kitchen we're interested in at the moment. They make a fine mushroom soup with fresh herbs and stilton cheese. They offer snails simmered in white wine with focaccia. Their chicken-liver pâté is big enough and good enough to share. They make their shepherd's pie with lamb and serve their Atlantic salmon with buttermilk mash, their black-angus beef with hand-cut fries.

Open Wednesday to Sunday 11.30 am to 5 pm (lunch), 5 pm to 9 pm (dinner). Closed on Monday and Tuesday. Licensed. Amex, Master Card, Visa. No smoking. Book ahead if you can. ♿

Nobody can buy his way into this guide and nobody can buy his way out.modest wine, tax and tip.

BAY FORTUNE, P.E.I.   (MAP 43)
THE INN AT BAY FORTUNE
Highway 310   **$200 ($450)**
(902) 687-3745

The kitchen at the Inn at Bay Fortune is famous, if only as the first home of Michael Smith, who has become a star television chef. Several chefs have been in charge of the kitchen since Michael Smith left. Warren Barr was here for six years until he was forced to return to British Columbia last year. His place has been taken by Domenic Serio, who came with degrees in culinary and pastry arts from the Culinary Institute in Charlottetown. He has the resources of the Farmer's Market to draw on, as well as the Inn's own huge vegetable garden. Nearby suppliers bring him everything from local oysters and mussels to local beef and lamb. Serio is back and he'll be at Bay Fortune again this summer. David Wilmer believes in sticking with what he knows, and it's true, Serio is improving. His menu is still quite short, beginning with house-cured bresaola, pork terrine and mussels from St. Peters Bay and going on to salmon from New Brunswick, local pork and flank steak, now a rather fashionable dish. The specialty of the house is North Lake bluefin tuna, served both hot and cold, but since bluefin tuna is an endangered species we've always hesitated to mention it. This kitchen, however, is usually at its best with its sweets, the best of which (we think) is the chocolate pâté, beautifully served with house-made ice cream. The pâté goes particularly well with a glass of apple wine from Rossignol, which is the local winery.
Open daily 5.30 pm to 8.30 pm from 1 June until 30 September. Licensed. Amex, Master Card, Visa. No smoking. Book ahead.

BEAMSVILLE, Ontario   (MAP 174)
AUGUST   🖝
5204 King Street   **$95**
(905) 563-0200

Beth Ashton and Marc McKerracher, who opened August in Beamsville a couple of years ago, are serious about regional cuisine. They grow most of their own vegetables and forage locally for whatever they don't grow themselves. Their menu is small and simple. There are always one or two homemade soups, and they make their own pasta—a different one every day of the week. They smoke their own fish and cure their own beef; they bake their own bread and make all their own sweets. Outwardly, August is plain and straightforward, with hard chairs and bare tables. But for lunch you can expect an omelette, a quiche, a burger, a club sandwich or a beef ragoût. On Tuesday, Wednesday and Thursday evenings they put on an extensive tapas menu for next to nothing a plate. There's blackened shrimp with lemon aioli, southern-fried squid, chipotle chicken and curried lamb meatballs, all for 5.00 or less. Everything is the best that money can buy. The quiche, for instance, will be stuffed with fresh lobster or lashings of spinach. There may be only a handful of wines, but the grapes are all grown on or near the Beamsville bench. They also have several local beers, which go well with everything on the menu.

Open Tuesday to Saturday 11.30 am to 3 pm, 5 pm to 9 pm, Sunday 9 am to 3 pm (brunch). Closed on Monday. Licensed. Master Card, Visa. No smoking. &

BEAVER CREEK, Yukon   MAP 16
BUCKSHOT BETTY'S
Highway 1   **$60**
(867) 862-7111

Betty's is open all year, which makes it a good place to look for a good meal out of season. Not that there's a lot of choice. Beaver Creek is really just a place to stop after the magnificent but scary drive from Whitehorse. It's 2500 feet above sea-level and quite close to the border with Alaska. Betty does a lot of baking, making all her own blueberry and lemon-meringue pies, her own cinnamon buns and her own pizzas. People often write to us about the cinnamon buns. Buckshot Betty's is just a small diner with a few sleeping-cabins, but they serve

good sandwiches and very good hamburgers.
Open daily 7 am to 9 pm (shorter hours in winter). Licensed.
Master Card, Visa. No smoking.

BEDEQUE, P.E.I. (MAP 43)
MAPLETHORPE CAFE ☆
2123 Highway 112 **$65**
(866) 770-2909

Maplethorpe is hidden by a magnificent row of giant lin-
den trees. The old blue farmhouse behind has a first-class
cook, who happens to be a graduate of the Charlottetown Culinary Institute. She makes a fairly good lobster
roll, but it's probably better to ask for a fishcake or the
Acadian meat pie, which will remind you of the traditional rappie pie. She also has a first-class quiche and
sometimes a lamb curry. If you're in a hurry, there are
always plenty of sandwiches, all made with home-baked
bread. The soups are great—just try the apricot soup
with red lentils and fresh ginger. There are a number of
beers from cottage breweries and a fine shiraz from Peller.
But don't skip the caramelized bread pudding—it will
amaze you. In the evening she offers a lovely seafood pie,
served in puff pastry. Dinner costs only 24.95 for three
courses, which is a great buy.
Open Tuesday to Thursday 11 am to 3 pm, Friday 11 am to 3
pm, 5 pm to 9 pm, Saturday 5 pm to 9 pm. Closed on Sunday
and Monday. Licensed for beer and wine only. Master Card,
Visa. No smoking.

BELFAST, P.E.I. (MAP 43)
BELFAST MINI-MILLS 🖎
1820 Garfield Road **$40**
Eldon
(902) 659-2202

Eldon is a small village next door to Belfast, which is
where Linda Nobles and her family have set up a mill to
manufacture small machines for export to a number of
countries around the world. (One of these is Libya, where

the machines are used for milling camel hair.) They arrange free tours of the plant as well as classes in felting, knitting and weaving. Several years ago they opened a tearoom, where they serve soups, quiches, tourtières and pot-pies. They have one great sandwich, which is made with smoked turkey on house-baked bread. There's also a toffee-cream pie with lots of real whipped cream. Helpings are big, prices very low.

Open daily 10 am to 5 pm from early May until late October. No liquor. All cards. No smoking. &

BELLEVILLE, Ontario   MAP 19
L'AUBERGE DE FRANCE
304 Front Street   **$125**
(613) 966-2433

We had high hopes for this place when it opened early in 2008 and, in fact, lunch has turned out to be a very reliable meal. The suppliers are all local and organic, and every Saturday morning they make hundreds of warm, buttery chocolate croissants—come early before they run out. They also make a fine quiche and a number of sandwiches. But the service is rough, even at noon, and the kitchen itself is very erratic in the evening. Your dinner may be a memorable meal or it may not. We suggest you come for lunch or to shop in the gourmet grocery store next door. If, however, you find yourself at a table set for dinner, try the veal osso buco with fresh homemade pasta. Most of the wines come from Prince Edward County or from France, and they're all fairly priced.

Open Monday 10 am to 5 pm, Tuesday to Friday 10 am to 5 pm, 5 pm to 10 pm, Saturday 5 pm to 10 pm. Closed on Sunday. Licensed. Master Card, Visa. No smoking. &

BELLEVILLE
See also BRIGHTON.

Every restaurant in this guide has been personally tested. Our reporters are not allowed to identify themselves or to accept free meals.

LE BIC, Quebec (MAP 168)
CHEZ SAINT-PIERRE ☆☆
129 Mont St.-Louis **$215**
(418) 736-5051

Colombe Saint-Pierre had a second child this year, but
that hasn't kept her away from the kitchen that's become
her passion. Le Bic is only ten miles west of Rimouski,
but Chez Saint-Pierre isn't that easy to find. It's on a back
street facing a car park and you'll probably have to ask
your way. In these simple surroundings, Colombe is
cooking as well as anyone in Quebec. Most of her ingredients come from neighbouring farms. She gets her pork
from St.-Gabriel. She forages for mushrooms, for mountain spinach and salsify des prés. Sorrel grows wild on the
shoulders of local roads. Colombe likes to begin her
meals with something like ravioli of chanterelles or scallops marinated in Chinata paprika and finished with
lemon and sundried tomatoes—a compelling and dramatic dish. She'll continue, perhaps, with fillet of bison
or gravlax of Arctic char. She'll end with a chocolate
financier, a biscuit bavarois or a plate of local cheeses. The
choice of French and Italian wines matches the menu in
quality and finesse. Chez Saint-Pierre is a restaurant you
must discover for yourself. Be sure to book ahead.
Open daily 5 pm to 9 pm from 1 June until 31 December,
Wednesday to Sunday 5 pm to 9 pm from 1 January until 31
May. Closed on Monday and Tuesday in winter. Licensed. Mas-
ter Card, Visa. No smoking. Book ahead.

BLAIRMORE, Alberta MAP 21
STONE'S THROW CAFE ☞▯
13019 20 Avenue **$40**
(403) 562-2230

Steve and Jessica are starting their tenth year in this unlikely location, and so far they're making a success of it.
They left Jasper because it had too many tourists; here
they close at 5 o'clock because they want to have some
time for their children. Everything in the place is cheap;

nothing matches and everyone is Green. Steve and Jessica make everything themselves, and that means the bread, the scones, the wraps and the focaccia. Rhubarb squares are the best thing they do and they're worth the trip to Blairmore. But readers are pretty high also on their all-day breakfast. Right up to closing time, they'll make you an omelette or two eggs any style with bacon, potato pancakes and wholewheat toast. For lunch they have all the usual soups, salads and sandwiches, as well as several wraps and pitas. Blairmore is about twelve miles from the B.C. border on the way from the Crow's Nest Pass.

Open Monday to Saturday 7 am to 5 pm, Sunday 10 am to 4 pm. No liquor, no cards. No smoking. &

BLOOMFIELD, Ontario   (MAP 150)
ANGELINE'S
433 Main Street   **$120**
(613) 393-3301

Last year the old Angeline's was closed and replaced with a bistro serving a *prix-fixe* menu from early spring to late fall. It costs 35.00 for three courses. Regular visitors will recognize many of the dishes, including blackened red snapper with potatoes, beets and chorizo and roasted pumpkin risotto with pistachios and truffle oil. Among the mains, we like the lamb two ways, which is served with homemade gnocchi, though others may prefer the brined pork with barley and seasonal vegetables. There's a big list of Prince Edward County wines, as well as a number of single malts and many cocktails.

Open Thursday to Sunday 5.30 pm to 9.30 pm from mid-May until late November. Closed Monday to Wednesday. Licensed. All cards. No smoking. &

BLOOMFIELD   (MAP 150)
THE CARRIAGE HOUSE   ☆
260 Main Street   **$150**
(613) 393-1087

The Carriage House was already in business long before

Bloomfield became a destination for gourmets from Toronto. Nowadays it's probably the best restaurant in the area. It concentrates on local produce cooked in the Parisian style. Dinners usually begin with something like scallop-and-potato gnocchi or, perhaps, poached breast of pheasant served in a mushroom salad. That will be followed by wild salmon with creamed leeks or lamb-shank cannelloni with a ragoût of white beans. The sweet might be a triple-chocolate brownie or a selection of local cheeses. Lunch is a simpler meal and features soups, salads and quiches, as well as a variety of sandwiches. There's an extensive list of wines from Prince Edward County. Prices seem lower this year, so you should probably try a glass or two of sparking vidal, which is certainly more fun than a Duboeuf beaujolais.

Open daily 11.30 am to 2.30 pm, 5 pm to 9.30 pm from 1 July until 31 August. Licensed. All cards. No smoking.

BOTWOOD, Newfoundland   MAP 23
DOCKSIDE
243 Water Street   **$125**
(709) 257-3179

Forget the Beothuk Indians. That was a long time ago. Botwood is in the middle of beautiful country in central Newfoundland. It's only twenty minutes by car from the Trans Canada on Highway 350. There's really only one place to eat in town and that's been true for many years. Jim Stuckless taught himself to cook when he took over this old warehouse. He cooks the sort of plain food he himself likes to eat, and that means fresh greens in summer and root vegetables in winter. His beef is all reserve Angus from Alberta. This summer he plans to expand into pork and lamb as well. Every week in season he sells at least 50 pounds of mussels, as well as a lot of salmon. He makes all his own sweets, including the Bavarian apple torte and the partridge-berry kuchen. Every Sunday he puts on a roast-beef dinner with carrots, turnips and cabbage, all for just 12.00.

Open daily noon to 2 pm, 4.30 pm to 8 pm. Licensed. All cards. No smoking. ♿

BRACEBRIDGE, Ontario (MAP 83)
ONE FIFTY-FIVE
155 Manitoba Street **$130**
(705) 645-1935

One Fifty-Five occupies an old cottage on the main street. Inside it's all white, with crisp, fresh table-cloths and comfortable armchairs. The chef came here from the Inn at the Falls and he's good. His menu is large, perhaps too large. It starts with a number of salads (caprese, octopus, Caesar) and goes on to pickerel, free-range chicken, Alberta beef, rack of lamb and pork tenderloin. But that's only half the story. The pickerel is crusted with panko; the beef is served with oyster mushrooms and caramelized shallots, the pork with apple and calvados, the lamb with fresh mint and dijon mustard. The pasta is all made in-house and there's Swedish gravlax, Alberta beef carpaccio and Digby scallops. There's a first-class lemon tart to follow, as well as a couple of good buys on the wine-list, among them a Leaping Horse merlot for 36.00 and a Cattail Creek pinot noir for 39.00. Both are pretty hard to beat.
Open Tuesday to Sunday 11.30 am to 2.30 pm, 5 pm to 9.30 pm. Closed on Monday. Licensed. Amex, Master Card, Visa. No smoking. Book ahead if you can. &

BRACKLEY BEACH, P.E.I. (MAP 43)
THE DUNES ☆☆
Highway 15 **$145**
(902) 672-1883

There isn't much point in advising people to go to the Dunes, because they're all headed that way as soon as they get to the Island. It's a spectacular place, with four stories of artwork and ceramics. The café on the ground floor overlooks a lush garden filled with ornamental grasses and flowering shrubs. Emily Wells came here in 2003, first as a chef and later as a chef-owner. She's an excellent cook. We know of one traveller who comes to the Dunes every year. He thinks her fish chowder is an amazing dish, filled as it is with lobster, scallops, mussels, salmon and halibut. At noon, which is cheaper, there's tomato pie, crab-cakes and a Thai chicken curry. In the evening they add pork tenderloin, roast beef and a wonderful rack of lamb. In season, there are fresh-berry pies. There aren't a lot of wines on the list, but they've been very carefully chosen.

Open daily 11.30 am to 4 pm, 5.30 pm to 10 pm from 15 June until 30 September. Licensed. Amex, Master Card, Visa. No smoking. Book ahead. &

BRANDON, Manitoba   MAP 26
BLUE HILLS BAKERY
1229 Richmond Avenue   **$40**
(204) 571-6762

Nothing ever changes at the Blue Hills, not even the frozen fruit pies. But Kelly and Becky, who run the place, have found a formula that works, no easy thing in a town like Brandon. They both come from a Hutterite background and both are passionate believers in fresh organic produce. They buy their vegetables and grains from nearby organic farms. They make their own granola and their own bread and serve them for breakfast until 11 o'clock on weekdays and 2 o'clock on Saturdays. At noon they offer old-fashioned soups—on Friday and Saturday it's always borscht. Every day there are sandwiches, salads and a special, which might be shepherd's pie or perhaps a quiche. After that there's a wide choice of cookies, muffins, squares and cinnamon buns. The pies are still frozen, but the coffee comes in fresh from Salt Spring Island.

Open Monday to Saturday 7 am to 5 pm. No liquor. Master Card, Visa. No smoking. &

BRIER ISLAND, N.S.
See FREEPORT.

Our website is at www.oberonpress.ca. Readers wishing to use e-mail should address us at oberon@sympatico.ca.

BRIGHTON, Ontario (MAP 19)
THE GABLES ☆
14 Division Street N **$160**
(613) 475-5565

We've always been grateful to Dieter Ernst for the fine
dinners he gave us at the Sherwood Inn, which came at
the end of the long drive to Port Carling and beyond.
The Gables, like the Sherwood Inn, is a reminder of an
older and gentler day. There are still white table-cloths
on the tables, attractive art on the walls, excellent service
and a warmly comfortable atmosphere. The menu isn't
large or particularly adventurous, but it's pleasant to find
wienerschnitzel back on the card, after so many years
when veal was unpopular in these parts. Actually, the
wienerschnitzel is probably the best dish they make, that
and the roasted half-duck, which at the moment is served
with red cabbage and cherries. There's an excellent Caesar
salad too and first-class pan-seared scallops. The sweets
are as good as everything else, whether you ask for the
old-fashioned apple strudel or the black-pepper ice cream
with scotch.
Open Tuesday to Friday 11.30 am to 2 pm, 5.30 pm to 9 pm,
Saturday 5.30 pm to 9 pm. Closed on Sunday and Monday. Li-
censed. Master Card, Visa. No smoking. Book ahead if you can.
&

BRIGUS, Newfoundland MAP 28
NORTH STREET CAFE 🖝
29 North Street **$55**
(709) 528-1350

Debbie O'Flaherty is keeping her original menu because
it works. She was born and brought up in these parts and
she knows everyone in the village and what they want to
eat. Her sandwich board offers ham and tuna sandwiches,
though she knows very well that most people will ask for
the egg salad, which is made to order on the spot. She
also offers things like codfish cakes and beans and toutons
with blackstrap molasses, as well as split-pea soup and

42

macaroni and cheese. She has several sweets, among them blueberry ginger-cake with warm caramel, carrot cake and homemade scones with clotted cream. Helpings are big and the service is prompt. The café may open late or close early, especially in the spring and fall, but if you call ahead Debbie will be there when you arrive.

Open daily 11 am to 7 pm from mid-May until mid-October. Licensed for beer and wine only, Master Card, Visa. No smoking. &

BROAD COVE. N.S.   MAP 29
BEST COAST COFFEE GALLERY   ☆
7070 Highway 331   **$60**
(902) 935-2031

The Coffee Gallery is a great place to stop for a meal after a day at one of the local beaches (Cherry Hill, Beach Meadows, Green Bay, Rissers and Crescent are all nearby.) Lunch features imaginative creations like fish-cakes with rhubarb chutney, grilled vegetable paninis and baked-ham sandwiches with wonderful homemade mustard. On Friday they serve a three-course *prix-fixe* dinner by appointment only. The menu changes every week and is always full of surprises. For sweet, try a root-beer float. You've never had one before.

Open daily 9.30 am to 4 pm (7 pm on Friday) from mid-June until Thanksgiving. Licensed. No cards. No smoking.

BROAD COVE
See also MILL VILLAGE, SUMMERVILLE BEACH.

BURLINGTON, Ontario   (MAP 88)
BLACKTREE   ☆☆
Roseland Plaza   **$160**
3029 New Street
(905) 681-2882

Matteo Paonessa has had a distinguished career, having worked with the likes of Marc Thuet, Susur Lee and Michael Stadtländer. Blacktree is the realization of his dream of providing the best of Italian nouvelle cuisine in Burlington. His restaurant is located down an alley in a quiet corner of Roseland Plaza. There he'll start you off with an *amuse-bouche* of calamari on a slice of taro root or a baby clam on a wafer with pomegranate syrup and lime aioli. Next comes foie gras, a composed salad or a disc o' pig with apricot and sage. To make this extraordinary dish, a pig's head is roasted for twelve hours. The meat is then removed and shaped into a ring, sliced, coated with cornmeal and fried. Then there's octopus tentacles, say, or pork belly with kumquats or black cod with pineapple and bok choy. Paonessa is not supposed to be interested in sweets, but none the less there are some remarkable things on his list, among them a delightful chocolate-orange tiramisu with eggplant.

Open Wednesday to Saturday 6 pm to 10 pm. Closed Sunday to Tuesday. Licensed. Master Card, Visa. No smoking. Book ahead if you can. &

BURLINGTON (MAP 88)
PANE FRESCO
414 Locust Street **$45**
(905) 333-3388

Pane Fresco is a bakery and café located close to the lakeshore in downtown Burlington. They sell a lot of artisanal bread, which is handmade and contains no artificial preservatives. Apart from the bread, the menu has always been very limited. In the last year or so, however, it's been much enlarged. They now always serve two soups, one of which is usually black bean. This year, the black-bean has been disappointing, and we now prefer something like roasted red pepper with crumbled goat-cheese. Some of the specials, like homemade meatballs in a fresh tomato sauce with provolone cheese, are available only on certain days of the week. Others are offered every day, and the best of these is probably the crab cakes with cabbage and mango relish in a lime-and-ginger vinaigrette. There used to be just two salads offered every day; now there are six. For dessert there are countless brownies, croissants, cannolis and handmade biscottis. In the summer they make some excellent ice creams as well. *Open Monday to Thursday 8 am to 6 pm, Friday and Saturday 8 am to 7 pm, Sunday 8 am to 4 pm. No liquor, no cards. No smoking.* &

BURLINGTON (MAP 88)
SPENCER'S ☆
1340 Lakeshore Road **$115**
(905) 633-7494

Spencer's on the Waterfront is a little less formal than its sister restaurant, the old Mill in Ancaster. The appetizers here are usually the most exciting part of the meal. You can start with raw oysters, albacore tuna, calamari piri-piri, red-fife-and-ricotta gnocchi, charcuterie or foie gras—an unusual list of choices. Actually, there are more—we ourselves like to start with lobster dumplings in a bamboo steamer. The best of the main courses is probably the Alaska black cod, though there's also first-class Arctic char with chorizo, cauliflower and brown butter. This is almost as good as the Arctic char they served last year with quinoa and fresh lobster. There's also a nice rack of lamb with harissa and Jerusalem artichokes. At noon they have elk burgers with oyster mushrooms and blue cheese and beef burgers with black-truffle mayonnaise and brie. The sweet list has recently been done over and now features a chocolate-chestnut mousse-cake and a pear tart with ricotta and honey in an almond crust. *Open Monday to Saturday 11.30 am to 4.30 pm (lunch), 4.30 pm to 9.30 pm (dinner), Sunday 9.30 am to 3.30 pm (brunch), 5.15 pm to 9 pm. Licensed. Master Card, Visa. No smoking. Free parking.* &

CABANO, Quebec MAP 31
AUBERGE DU CHEMIN FAISANT ☆☆
12 rue Vieux Chemin **$150**
(877) 954-9342

This place is described in all the guides as an historic

house. That's because for Cabano history began in 1950, when a disastrous fire burned most of the town. The Auberge is built in nineteen-fifties style and overlooks Lake Temiscouata. The restaurant is run by Hughes Massey and Liette Fortin. Massey comes from the Magdalen Islands and plays the piano almost as well as he cooks. The dining-room has only 21 seats, but the kitchen goes through 35 gallons of maple syrup every year. It's famous for such dishes as trout in maple syrup, which happens to be the chef's favourite. Every evening there are five seafood dishes and three meats. Cod comes with shiitaki mushrooms and old cheddar, venison with red cabbage, mashed potatoes and mustard. They also have an eight-course *menu de dégustation* priced at 50.00 a head. On the à la carte the meal ends with a chocolate ganache and a crème brûlée with caramelized bananas. There are 200 labels on the wine-list and 1500 bottles in the cellar.

Open daily 6 pm to 8 pm from 1 June until Labour Day, Sunday 6 pm to 8 pm from Labour Day until 31 May. Closed Monday to Saturday in winter. Licensed. All cards. No smoking. ♿

CABANO
See also NOTRE-DAME DU LAC.

CALGARY, Alberta	**MAP 32**
BELVEDERE	☆☆
107 8 Avenue SW	**$220**
(403) 265-9595	

Belvedere is darkly handsome, well served and very expensive. They have, however, a great wine-list with many of the best pauillacs and super-Tuscans and at least one outstanding open wine, the Heitz chardonnay from the Napa Valley. The cooking is plainer than it used to be, and at noon the kitchen stoops to such things as shepherd's pie and basil ravioli. But the staples of the menu are still triple-A beef tartar, rack of lamb, Pacific oysters and sturgeon caviar. A new chef took charge of the kitchen last year, but so far he doesn't seem to have made many important changes.

Open Monday to Friday 11.30 am to 2 pm, 5 pm to 11 pm, Saturday 5 pm to 11 pm. Closed on Sunday. Licensed. Amex, Master Card, Visa. No smoking. Book ahead. ♿

CALGARY   MAP 32
BLINK   ☆☆
111 8 Avenue SW   **$145**
(403) 263-5330

At first glance Blink appears to be faux-smart, with a ridiculous name and a super-trendy menu. But look again. The cooking is both skilful and well informed. Dinners begin with a twice-baked soufflé or perhaps with squash soup with crème fraîche. But you'll usually do better if you ask for the golden bull's-eye beets or the Quebec foie gras with grilled bread. Tuna can be had with ponzu sauce or, better still, as a main course with daikon, spinach and dashi broth. Most of the wines are expensive, but the cheeses are not. Take a pass on the grizzly gouda from Sylvan Lake in Alberta and go instead for one of the soft cheeses from Salt Spring Island.

Open Monday to Friday 11 am to 2 pm, 5 pm to 10 pm, Saturday 5 pm to 11 pm. Closed on Sunday. Licensed. All cards. No smoking. Book ahead if you can. ♿

CALGARY   MAP 32
BOXWOOD CAFE
340 13 Avenue SW   **$130**
(403) 265-4006

The Boxwood Café opened to a flood of praise, as one would expect of a restaurant owned by the River Café. The setting is spectacular. The interior is beautiful and the patio overlooks Central Memorial Park. At noon you pay in advance, cafeteria-style, but at night there's good table service. Most of the vegetables come from the River Café, but the rotisserie meats are the best thing they do, especially the pork and the lamb. Both come with intriguing garnishes, but there are no vegetables on the

plate, so it's a good idea to ask for a side-salad of quinoa
or arugula. They have only four entrées and no reservations, so things often run out. But there are excellent fruit
tarts to follow and some unusual wines from Australia,
like Engine-Room shiraz, which is better than it sounds.
*Open daily 11 am to 10 pm. Licensed. Amex, Master Card,
Visa. No smoking. No reservations.*

CALGARY   MAP 32
BRAVA
723 17 Avenue SW   **$150**
(403) 228-1854

Brava is a friendly, unpretentious neighbourhood bistro
conveniently located on 17 Avenue at 7 Street. As we've
said before, people come here for the gingerbread soaked
in whisky. It's a wonderful dish, but there are other good
things on the menu too, notably the shrimp-and-avocado
salad with beautiful ripe cherry tomatoes and the mussels
with white wine and leeks. The salmon is usually overcooked, but the Alberta beef tenderloin is a fine dish,
with its boursin mash and garlic mushrooms. The wine-
list features wines from California and Australia, but it's
weak on wines from the Okanagan. However that may
be, there aren't many restaurants in Calgary that we enjoy
as much as Brava.
*Open Monday to Wednesday 11.30 am to 3 pm, 5 pm to 10 pm,
Thursday to Saturday 11.30 am to 3 pm, 5 pm to midnight,
Sunday 5 pm to 10 pm. Licensed. All cards. No smoking. Book
ahead.* &

CALGARY   MAP 32
DIVINO   ☆
113 8 Avenue SW   **$170**
(403) 410-5555

Divino started out as a wine-and-cheese bistro, and in a
sense it still is. Its wine-list begins with Blue Mountain
and goes on from there to some of the best wines from

Napa and the Okanagan. It has a large list of cheeses from all over the world—from Alberta, Quebec, Leicestershire, Italy, France and Switzerland. Which is the best of these is a matter of opinion, but one thing is for sure, it's not the grizzly gouda from Alberta. Maybe it's the ciel de charlevoix, the leafy tête de moine or the stilton from Leicestershire. You can have three of these for 17.00 or five for 25.00. There's a long list of single malts, all of which go well with cheese. One of the best and one of the cheapest—and several cost more than 35.00 a glass—is Berry's Own bowmore.

Open Monday to Friday 11 am to 4 pm, 5 pm to 10 pm, Saturday 5 pm to 11 pm. Closed on Sunday. Licensed. All cards. No smoking. ♿

CALGARY   MAP 32
MODEL MILK
308 17 Avenue SW   **$125**
(403) 265-7343

Model Milk occupies the old Model Milk Dairy factory, which makes for an intriguing interior. The menu is unusual, but take care: some of the tapas dishes are better than others. The foie gras parfait in a blackberry crust, for instance, is delightful, the octopus with bone marrow is merely tough; the medley of chanterelles is a charming dish, the fricassee of squid with edamame dull, dull, dull. But Model Milk is fun. The wine-list is quite small, but it has some interesting drinking. The Joie Farm dry muscat, for example, is a surprising wine, as is the Angel's Gate late-harvest riesling, which goes well with the trifle. (They don't call it trifle, but that's what it is.)

Open Monday to Saturday 5 pm to 1 am, Sunday 5 pm to 10 pm. Licensed. Amex, Master Card, Visa. No smoking. Book ahead if you can. ♿

Where an entry is printed in italics this indicates that the restaurant has been listed only because it serves the best food in its area or because it hasn't yet been adequately tested.

CALGARY   **MAP 32**
NOTABLE   ☆
4611 Bowness Road NW   **$150**
(403) 288-4372

Notable answers the telephone with the message,
"Happy chicken to go." Not a good sign, but let it go.
The place looks like a big, upscale burger joint, but it has
Michael Noble in the kitchen and that makes all the difference. First of all, the menu is large and quite unfamiliar, offering salmon with pickled daikon, saltspring
mussels, baked garganelle pasta, panko-crusted tuna and
Moroccan lamb sausages. The salmon with pickled
daikon is a wonderful dish and so is the panko-crusted
tuna. The St. Clair Pioneer Block sauvignon blanc from
Marlborough is a lovely drink and so, in a different way,
is the Spire cabernet sauvignon from Paso Robles. (Both
are available by the glass as well as the bottle.) They also
have bottles from Joie Farm, Cakebread and Laughing
Stock, as well as Sarpa di Poli grappa by the glass. They
don't have an espresso machine, but their filter coffee is
very good indeed. The service is perfect.
Open Tuesday to Friday 11.30 am to 11 pm, Saturday 11 am
to 11 pm, Sunday 11 am to 9 pm. Closed on Monday. Licensed.
Amex, Master Card, Visa. No smoking. Book ahead if you can.
&

CALGARY   **MAP 32**
OX & ANGELA   ☆
528 17 Avenue SW   **$130**
(403) 457-1432

Ox & Angela has a stylish interior and a central location
in midtown Calgary. Ox is the chef; Angela is the hostess
and she's the kind of person who puts on a winter coat
and feeds your meter for you. Their menu features a variety of tapas dishes at prices that start at 5.00 for salt-
cod with potato croquettes and rise to 27.00 for a
charcuterie platter. They have a classic treatment of
patatas bravas and it's worth its weight in gold. Their scal-

lops come with peas and cherry tomatoes, their prawns with garlic, chilli and sherry, their serrano ham with harissa and mint. You can drink Canadian with a Quail's Gate dry riesling or a Dancing Coyote verdilho. Or you can drink Spanish with a rioja from Ramon Bilbao. We generally ask for the rioja.

Open daily 11.30 am to 11 pm (later on weekends). Licensed. Amex, Master Card, Visa. No smoking. ♿

CALGARY   **MAP 32**
RAW BAR   ☆
Arts Hotel   **$145**
119 12 Avenue SW
(403) 266-4611

Don't come here expecting a tartar, a carpaccio or a ceviche, because the Raw Bar, despite its name, serves no raw meat or fish except oysters on the half-shell and the occasional piece of tuna or crab. But when it comes to lobster bisque, wild salmon, breast of chicken or Alberta beef, they do a very good job indeed. Their Alaska black cod is a masterpiece, and so are their beef satays and their wild salmon. Their cellar is full of the best Okanagan wines, to say nothing of their two sakes, which are both lovely. There's a long list of sweets, the best of which is the cheese plate. The Raw Bar is spacious and stylish, with great, friendly service. Prices are quite modest.

Open daily 6.30 pm to 10.30 pm. Licensed. Amex, Master Card, Visa. No smoking. Book ahead if you can.

CALGARY   **MAP 32**
RIVER CAFE   ☆☆
Prince's Island Park   **$180**
(403) 261-7670

Andrew Winfield has an unusual menu that makes the most of local organic produce. He starts with carrot soup with preserved lemon and Holliewood oysters on the half-shell and goes on to rabbit pot-pie and albacore tuna with corn fritters. Winfield's cooking is good, but his wine-list is absolutely stunning. He has three great wines from Quilceda Creek in the State of Washington, five from Spottswoode in the Napa Valley, an ornellaia and a Mouton-Rothschild, both surprisingly good buys at 485.00 a bottle. If you're looking for a *really* good buy, ask for the gewurztraminer from Dirty Laundry, which costs just 52.00. The River Cafe is well worth the walk, even in winter—maybe not if the wind is blowing.

Open Monday to Friday 11.30 am to 2.30 pm, 5.30 pm to 10 pm, Saturday and Sunday 10 am to 3 pm (brunch), 5.30 pm to 10 pm. Licensed. Amex, Master Card, Visa. No smoking. Book ahead if you can. &

CALGARY   MAP 32
RUSH   ☆
207 9 Avenue SW   **$160**
(403) 271-7894

Rush still has its stunning interior. It still has superb service. Trouble arrives with the suppliers. The kitchen used to be known for its beautiful regional produce. The lamb, once local, is now imported from New Zealand. The oysters come in from New Brunswick, though wonderful Kusshi oysters are close at hand. The sparkling water is no longer supplied by San Pellegrino. There are, of course, still good things to be had here, among them the minted pea soup, the cured salmon belly, the pork cooked *sous vide*, the dry-aged beef. As for the wine-list, it's big and handsome, though the choice of wines from the Okanagan, apart from the white wines from Joie Farm, is rather disappointing. Nothing, however, is ever overpriced.

Open Monday to Friday 11 am to 4 pm, 5 pm to 11 pm, Saturday 5 pm to 11 pm. Closed on Sunday. Licensed. All cards. No smoking. Free valet parking after 6 pm. &

If you wish to improve the guide send us information about restaurants we have missed. Our mailing address is Oberon Press, 145 Spruce Street: Suite 205, Ottawa, Ontario K1R 6P1.

CALGARY   MAP 32
TEATRO   ☆☆
200 8 Avenue SE   **$235**
(403) 290-1012

Teatro occupies an old bank building on 8 Avenue SE.
It's very well appointed, very well served and very expensive. You start with Pacific oysters on the half-shell
or bison tartar. Follow that with seared scallops, which
are usually better than the albacore tuna or the T-bone
steak, which, it has to be admitted, is pretty rough.
Teatro's place in the sun really depends on its marvellous
wine-list, with its stupendous selection of pauillacs and
super-Tuscans from Bolgheri. (They also offer a number
of Niagara wines, an unusual amenity in the West.)
Teatro is open late, which makes it the place to go after a
play at the performing arts centre or a concert by the Calgary Philharmonic. Both are quite nearby.
Open Monday to Thursday 11.30 am to 2.30 pm, 5 pm to 11
pm, Friday 11.30 am to 2.30 pm, 5 pm to 11.30 pm, Saturday
5 pm to 11.30 pm, Sunday 5 pm to 10 pm. Licensed. All cards.
No smoking. Book ahead. ♿

CALGARY
See also CANMORE.

CAMBRIDGE, Ontario   MAP 33
LANGDON HALL   ☆☆
1 Langdon Drive   **$275 ($510)**
(800) 268-1898

Langdon Hall has been a member of the order of Relais
& Châteaux for some years, but they don't wear their
honours lightly. They ask guests to wear a dinner jacket
in the evening, something few restaurants would pre-
sume to do. But if you have 275.00 in your pocket, they
let you into the dining-room without. The Hall was built
in 1898 in the Federal style and restored as a restaurant a
century or so later. The chef is Jonathan Gushue. Last
winter he disappeared for some weeks, but the kitchen

53

staff carried on without him and not a single guest complained. He's back on the job now and his dinners usually begin with a lovely scallop soup. Medallions of lamb follow, though guests generally order the lobster, which is gorgeous. Most of the vegetables are organic. The pick of the sweets is the honey soufflé with crème anglaise. The cellar has a thousand labels on offer, but take note that there's nothing by the glass that costs less than 15.00. Every day they put on splendid afternoon teas at 2 and 4 o'clock, but be prepared to pay 64.00 for two. The service is impeccable, but all the prices surpass belief.

Open daily noon to 2.30 pm, 5.30 pm to 9.30 pm. Licensed. All cards. No smoking. Book ahead.

CAMPOBELLO ISLAND, N.B.   *(MAP 81)*
FAMILY FISHERIES
1977 County Road 774   *$45*
Wilson's Beach
(506) 752-2470

This is the only restaurant on Campobello Island and it has a carry-out window where they serve the same food as at the tables inside. While we don't admire their pre-cut french fries, their fish is certainly very fresh. You won't get better scallops or shrimps anywhere on this shore. As for the lobster, which is caught daily, it's astonishing, and the lobster stew is almost as good. Start with smoked salmon and end with one of the homemade pies. Raspberries for the raspberry pies are picked in their own garden and served with real whipped cream, which is uncommon in this country. Family Fisheries is open daily noon to 3 pm, 6 pm to 11 pm. There's no liquor, but they take Master Card and Visa. No smoking.

CANMORE, Alberta   (MAP 32)
THE CRAZY WEED
1600 Railway Avenue   **$150**
(403) 609-2530

The Crazy Weed is a successful upscale restaurant, but the truth is that it deteriorates with every year that passes.

Meanwhile, prices have been rising. You now have to pay 38.00 for a rib-eye of beef and 10.00 for a butterscotch pudding. Prices are lower at noon, when they serve pork meatballs, confit of duck and jerk-pork flatbread for 10.00 or 15.00. The wine-list has expanded, though there are still only five Canadian whites and one Canadian red. The service can be hurried and it's hard to keep your table long enough to eat your meal in comfort.

Open Monday to Friday 11.30 am to 3 pm, 5.30 pm to 8.30 pm, Saturday and Sunday 5.30 pm to 8.30 pm. Licensed. Master Card, Visa. No smoking. Book ahead if you can. &

CANMORE (MAP 32)
THE TROUGH ☆
725 9 Street **$200**
(403) 678-2820

Cheryl and Richard Fuller, mother and son, run the kitchen at the Trough; a daughter, Rebecca, runs the front of the house. They have only ten tables, but they always buy the best available produce, use nothing but Riedel glasses for their wine and employ experienced servers. Inevitably, the prices are high, but you can count on a menu that's full of new ideas and novel effects. For example, there's a bruschetta made with organic chèvre and a ceviche made with coconut milk, cilantro and crisp won-tons. Next, perhaps, an East Indian organic chicken with raita and red onions or jerk-spiced Alberta baby back ribs with a pineapple salsa. After that there's a date pudding with warm toffee and a wild-berry cobbler. There are no Canadian wines on the wine-list, but they do have some of the best grappas on the market today.

Open Tuesday to Sunday 5.30 pm to 10 pm. Closed on Monday. Licensed. Master Card, Visa. No smoking.

☞ This symbol means that the restaurant is rated a good buy. This & means that there is wheelchair access to both the tables and the washrooms. *Smoking only* means that the restaurant has no area for non-smokers.

CAP A L'AIGLE, Quebec   (MAP 111)
AUBERGE DES PEUPLIERS   ☆
381 rue St.-Raphael   **$175 ($375)**
(888) 282-3743

Patrice Desrosiers is now in charge of the kitchen at the Auberge des Peupliers. Like his predecessor, he's passionate about local produce, especially his gravlax of salmon and his ravioli stuffed with salt-marsh lamb. He's still in his first year here, so it's hard to say how well he'll perform over the whole menu, which covers a lot of ground—from carpaccio and foie gras to cannelloni, fillet of veal and confit of duck. But we can say that dinner is a stylish meal and so is breakfast. The bedrooms up the hill are comfortable and well appointed. The wine-list is a little disappointing, but there's good drinking from Smoking Loon, which offers an attractive sauvignon blanc for 48.00 a bottle.
Open daily 7.30 am to 10.30 am, 6 pm to 9 pm. Licensed. All cards. No smoking. Book ahead. ♻

CAPE ONION, Newfoundland   (MAP 6)
TICKLE INN   ☞
Highway 437   **$90 ($165)**
(709) 452-4321

David and Barbara Adams and their cousin, Sophie Bessie, will still be in charge at the Tickle Inn this summer. Guests will still be seated around the big table in the kitchen, trading stories and listening to David talk about old Newfoundland. Cape Onion is at the far end of the Viking Trail, overlooking a bright blue sea studded with tiny islands, the surrounding hills thick with wildflowers. Captain William Adams settled here in this small frame house four generations ago. His descendants have since restored the house and turned it into a celebrated bed-and-breakfast. The owners have their own suppliers and their own pickers, because fresh produce isn't easy to get in these parts. Dinner starts with a soup, followed perhaps by a triple-fish casserole in puff pastry. Sundays are special. You can expect Arctic char or chicken wellington with screech. Upstairs there are several comfortable bedrooms. If you decide to spend a night or two, you'll find that there are good walking trails as well as the village of Anse-aux-Meadows, where you can visit the remains of the original Viking settlement, now almost a thousand years old.

Open daily at 7.30 pm by appointment only from 1 June until 30 September. Licensed. Master Card, Visa. No smoking. You must book ahead. ♿

CARAQUET, N.B.   MAP 38

If you want to spend the night in Caraquet, go to the Hôtel Paulin at 143 boulevard St. Pierre (telephone (866) 727-9981). Three generations of the Paulin family have made this one of the oldest family-run hotels in the country. Built in 1891, it's a prime example of Acadian architecture. It was completely redecorated inside when Gérard Paulin, who had run the place alone since 1974, married Karen Mersereau, who happened to be an experienced chef. She changes her menu twice a day, but seating for non-residents is in short supply. If you call ahead and get a table for dinner, chances are you'll feel like a third wheel on a bicycle. They have a license and take Master Card and Visa. Mitchan Sushi is just along the street at No. 114 (telephone (506) 726-1103). Mitchan probably has the best food in town and certainly the cheapest. He's equally accomplished with teriyaki, tempura and Japanese noodle dishes, but he's open by appointment only from Wednesday to Sunday 5 pm to 9 pm. He takes Master Card and Visa and has a licence. The Café Phare at No. 186 (telephone (506) 727-9469) has a very good lunch. It's a small French bistro with a talented chef, Robert Landry, who bought the house in 1996 with a view to offering a three-course prix-fixe every evening. But the demand wasn't there, so instead he offers a substantial breakfast and lunch. Look for things like homemade soup, croque monsieur and a choice sweet. He's open every day but Saturday, has a licence and takes Master Card and Visa.

If you use an out-of-date edition and find it inaccurate, don't blame us. Buy a new edition.

CARLETON-SUR-MER, Quebec   MAP 39
LE MARIN D'EAU DOUCE
215 route du Quai   **$130**
(418) 364-7602

Mustapha Ben Amidou bought this old house ten or twelve years ago. It was built in 1820 to overlook the beach and the sea. There's a jetty at the back and a bright dining-room serving a variety of fish and shellfish. The menu is very straightforward and you'll do just as well on the table d'hôte, which for about 37.00 a head offers marinated herring with apple, scallops on a bed of lentils, ris de veau with wild mushrooms, lamb tagine and rabbit with mustard. Most of the wines come from France and Italy, Argentina and Chile, with only two or three from Niagara or the Okanagan. We still advise readers to avoid the local caviar.
Open daily 5 pm to 9 pm. Licensed. All cards. No smoking.

CAYUGA, Ontario   MAP 40
THE TWISTED LEMON   ☆
3 Norton Street W   **$135**
(905) 772-6636

The Twisted Lemon opened in the summer of 2009, but it promises soon to become a star attraction in the village of Cayuga. Chef Dan Megna and his wife, Laurie Lilliman, have brought many years of experience to their dream. At the Twisted Lemon they offer wine-tasting nights as well as cooking classes, in an effort to build a market for their restaurant. Already Dan Megna knows all the best local suppliers and in summer almost all of his ingredients come from Haldimand County. Before he settled in Cayuga, he worked for four years at North 44° under Mark McEwan, who taught him a lot. He makes a variety of sandwiches at noon and serves either Yukon Gold or sweet potatoes with them. Every Thursday there's a three-course *prix-fixe* dinner for just 35.00. The regular menu offers rack of Cumbrae lamb and tenderloin of kangaroo with a reduction of blackberries. We ourselves have tried several of the sweets, among them a chocolate pâté and a custard made with whole vanilla beans. The wine-list has been greatly expanded and now offers an ambitious selection of wines from both the Old World and the New.

Open Tuesday and Wednesday 4.30 pm to 9.30 pm, Thursday and Friday 11 am to 2 pm, 4.30 pm to 9.30 pm, Saturday 4.30 pm to 9.30 pm. Closed on Sunday and Monday. Licensed. Master Card, Visa. No smoking.

CEDAR, B.C. (MAP 128)
THE MAHLE HOUSE ☆☆
2104 Hemer Road **$145**
(250) 722-3621

The big news at the Mahle House this year is that Maureen Loucks and Delbert Horrocks have sold the place to Maureen's daughter, Tara Wilson, and her husband, Stephen. So far no really important changes are planned. Naida Hobbs, who worked with Maureen for several years, will still be in charge of the kitchen. Stephen Wilson will continue to sell his wines at rock-bottom prices, as Delbert Horrocks always did, to encourage customers to buy more and better wines. Lunch is being served for the first time this year and will feature a homemade soup and a mixed-green salad. Dinner will begin with porcupine prawns and a so-called seafood tower, which is a take on dungeness crab-cake, as well as osso buco and Arctic char, free-range chicken and New York steak. The meal will end with peanut-butter pie and sticky-toffee pudding. The wine-list majors, as it always did, in the better wines from the Okanagan, California and Australia, and they've recently added an outstanding cabernet sauvignon from Burrowing Owl, priced at 80.00. You need a big appetite for all this, but you won't do better this side of Sidney.

Open Wednesday and Thursday 5 pm to 9.30 pm, Friday to Sunday 11.30 am to 2 pm, 5 pm to 9.30 pm. Closed on Monday and Tuesday. Licensed. Amex, Master Card, Visa. No smoking. Book ahead if you can. ♿

CHARLO, N.B.   MAP 42
LE MOULIN A CAFE
210 Chaleur Street   **$40**
(506) 684-9898

This tiny place on the Baie des Chaleurs has few tables
and a big reputation. We've tried the seafood chowder,
the bread-rolls and the fabulous pies, and heard good
things of the corn chowder. The daily specials sometimes
include fresh local fish, and Acadian dishes often appear
on public holidays. The proprietor likes his coconut pie
and his strawberry-rhubarb pie; our favourite is the
cherry pie. The prices are all very modest and there are
fine views from every window.

Open Tuesday to Sunday 10 am to 8 pm. Closed on Monday.
Bring your own bottle. Master Card, Visa. No smoking. Book
ahead if you can.

CHARLOTTETOWN, P.E.I.   *MAP 43*

We always urge visitors to the Island to go to the Farmer's Mar-
ket, which is held every Saturday morning. Most of the produce
is organic, and you can snack on Kim Dormaar's smoked salmon
or some of the best sausages you've ever tasted. Not far away, on
a short stretch of University Avenue, there are three attractive
restaurants. The newest, Leonhard's Café and Bakery at 42
University Avenue (telephone (902) 367-3621), has some of
the best coffee in town. The young German owner also makes
fine homemade bread and pastries, glorious Florentines, home-
made stews and big, substantial sandwiches. This is a perfect place
for lunch, but they aren't open for dinner and are closed on Sun-
day. Beanz at 38 University Avenue (telephone (902) 892-
8797) is an espresso bar, but they also have soups, sandwiches
and salads, and their squares, cookies and cheesecakes are all won-
derful. They're open all day every day and take Master Card and
Visa, but there's no liquor. Along the street from Beanz, at 44
University Avenue (telephone (902) 368-8886), is Shaddy's,
a nice, comfortable Lebanese restaurant that has the only upright
broiler in Charlottetown. The best thing they do is the shawarma
with tabouleh. As for the falafel in a pita, one visitor thought it

the best in the world. We ourselves admire the lamb kebabs and the kofta. The pastries all come from Montreal, where the chef spent ten years before coming here. Shaddy's is open all day Monday to Friday and all afternoon Saturday and Sunday, has a licence and takes Master Card and Visa. Off Broadway at 125 Sydney Street (telephone (902) 566-4620) has performed erratically for several years. This year it's become the Daniel Brenan Brickhouse. They've got rid of the old booths and developed a style of cooking that's sometimes excellent. The best things on the menu are the fishcakes and the lamb rogan gosht. The service may be slow, but the Brickhouse has great potential. They still have Off Broadway's awkward hours. They're open Monday to Thursday 11 am to 10 pm, Friday and Saturday 11 am to 11 pm, Sunday 11 am to 10 pm from Victoria Day until Thanksgiving, Monday to Thursday 11 am to 2 pm, 4.30 pm to 9 pm, Friday and Saturday 11 am to 2 pm, 4.30 pm to 10 pm, Sunday 5 pm to 9 pm from Thanksgiving until Victoria Day. They have a licence and take Amex, Master Card and Visa. The Pilot House at 70 Grafton Street (telephone (902) 894-4800) is a heritage property specializing in seafood, draft beer and scotch whisky. It's a great place for a quick lunch. They have a fine lobster sandwich and perfect fish and chips. They're open all day every day but Sunday, have a licence and take all cards. Finally there's the Terre Rouge at 72 Queen Street (telephone (902) 892-4032). It opened in 2012 and quickly became the place to go in downtown Charlottetown. The cooking is good and everything is elegantly plated. Out in front there's a deli where you can get a pastry, local cheeses, prosciutto, homemade gelatos—or a whole barbecued chicken. Terre Rouge is open all day every day, has a license for beer and wine only and takes all cards.

CHARLOTTETOWN   MAP 43
LOT 30   ☆☆
151 Kent Street   **$150**
(902) 629-3030

Lot 30, so-called because the property had that number on the original survey, is the work of Gordon Bailey, who cooked at Seasons in Thyme, Dayboat and the Inn at Bay Fortune before coming here in 2008. Every day he serves oysters, either raw on the half-shell or grilled with garlic. If you don't want oysters, he'll make you beautiful seared scallops in a coulis of carrot butter. There's also lovely barbecued pork with udon noodles and spring onions. The wine-list is expensive but well chosen. The service is knowledgeable, and if you want a piece of ice-cream cake, just ask for it; it costs only 8.00. *Open Tuesday to Sunday 5 pm to 9 pm. Closed on Monday. Licensed. Master Card, Visa. No smoking.* &

CHARLOTTETOWN
See also BAY FORTUNE, BEDEQUE, BELFAST, BRACKLEY BEACH, GEORGETOWN, MONTAGUE, NORTH RUSTICO, ST. PETERS BAY, SOURIS, TYNE VALLEY, VICTORIA-BY-THE-SEA.

CHELSEA, Quebec (MAP 142)
L'OREE DU BOIS ☆
15 chemin Kingsmere **$135**
(819) 827-0332

The Orée du Bois has a pronounced *après-ski* feeling, though of course it's open also in summer. Dinner costs 38.00 a head, but for that you get several very good things—among them chilled green-pea soup, shrimps with tiny slices of tomato and fish soup with quenelles of pike and oil of tarragon. The kitchen is at its best with pastry and one of its finest dishes is the feuilleté of mushrooms from Le Coprin. But there are many other pleasures to be had here: white shrimps with local asparagus, breast of chicken from Saveurs des Monts, cervelle de veau with capers and green peppercorns and medallions of venison from Boileau with red-wine and black peppercorns. The thing to drink is the half-bottle of ornellaia (a rare find in Canada). As we went to press, they had only two left.
Open Tuesday to Saturday 5 pm to 10 pm. Closed on Sunday and Monday. Licensed. Amex, Master Card, Visa. No smoking. Book ahead if you can.

CHEMAINUS, B.C.   (MAP 62)
ODIKA ☆
2976 Mill Street   **$125**
(250)324-3303

Odika is the seed-kernel of the African wild mango, and when cooked and crushed it's used in soups and stews. The chef, Murray Kereliuk, likes to cook West African dishes, perhaps because his wife, Marina, comes from Ghana. He thickens his soups with odika; his gnocchi is made with baked polenta, stuffed with mozzarella and topped with wild mushrooms. His fish and chips are made with cod and crusted with a pakora batter that's a lot less greasy than the traditional English batter. His panaeng curries are all made with bok choy served on a bed of basmati rice; his lamb shanks come in a curry inspired by West African recipes. The best of the sweets, unless you like crème brûlée with grand marnier, is the mango sorbet. When the restaurant is busy, the service can seem hurried.

Open Sunday to Thursday 11 am to 9 pm, Friday and Saturday 11 am to 10 pm. Licensed. All cards. No smoking. ♧

CHESTER, N.S.   (MAP 87)
CHESTER GOLF CLUB
227 Golf Course Road   **$85**
(902) 275-4543

The Chester Golf Club has breathtaking views of the open sea and the islands that lie offshore. The building used to be a traditional farmhouse; today the plain white-frame structure is surrounded by an open deck where you can take your meal if you like. The menu is large and full of seafood. Don't bother with the salads or perhaps even the lobster sandwich. Ask instead for one of the so-called club favourites (scallops with fries and fish and chips). The pastries and breads all come from the kitchen, and though they're proud of their carrot cake, you'll probably do even better with the chocolate-lava cake or one of the fruit crisps.

Open daily 11 am to 7 pm from 1 May until 15 October. Licensed. All cards. No smoking. ♿

CHESTER (MAP 87)
NICKI'S
28 Pleasant Street **$100**
(902) 275-4342

Nicki's is an attractive place, with floor-to-ceiling windows and an abundance of fresh flowers. The menu is seasonal, but the Sunday-night carvery has become a local institution. There's roast beef, lamb, pork and chicken, with Yorkshire pudding and roasted vegetables, all served from 5 o'clock until 8.30. On weeknights they offer a variety of small plates. There may be Village Bay oysters, beet salad with greens and a goat-cheese fritter. They also have some larger plates: steak-and-kidney pie with mashed potatoes, planked salmon and lamb shanks braised in red wine. Every night there are several lavish (and very filling) sweets. They have an impressive wine-list and very good coffee, which is served by the carafe.
Open Wednesday to Sunday 5 pm to 8 pm from 1 May until 15 October, Thursday to Sunday from 16 October until 30 April. Closed on Monday and Tuesday in summer, Monday to Wednesday in winter. Licensed. All cards. No smoking. Book ahead if you can.

CHICOUTIMI, Quebec **MAP 47**
LA VOIE MALTEE
777 boulevard Talbot **$75**
(418) 549-4144

Saguenay cruises start at L'Anse-Saint-Jean and the Auberge des Cevennes (see above). La Voie Maltée is light-years away from both. The Cevennes is an exercise in nostalgia, the Voie Maltée is very much now—the current rage among young local people, crowded and very noisy. A second Voie Maltée has been opened in Jonquière at 2509 rue St,-Dominique (telephone (418) 542-4373) and a third is planned for Quebec City. They all offer ten micro-brews, ranging from a dark stout to a blond pilsner, made on site from local ingredients. There are also a number of dishes based on beer. The food is good and very cheap. Start with a plate of spiced northern shrimps and go on to a salmon salad, followed by fish and chips, a pork chop or a steak. After that everyone seems to like the biramisu, which is a tiramisu made with beer.

Open Monday to Friday 11.30 am to 3 am, Saturday and Sunday noon to 3 am. Licensed. All cards. No smoking. No reservations.

CHURCHILL, Manitoba   MAP 48
GYPSY'S
253 Kelsey Boulevard   **$115**
(204) 675-2322

People still come to Churchill to see polar bears and beluga whales. The bears have to wait until the end of November before the sea-ice gets thick enough to support their weight. Visitors who want to keep warm usually go to Gypsy's for a meal. The place seats a hundred, but it's often full. It's a good idea to book ahead, because the food is good and the wine-list excellent. Tony De Silva likes to close up at the beginning of December, because he wants to keep warm too. He came to Churchill from Montreal almost 30 years ago and for a time he kept Gypsy's open all year. He's an expert on French pastry and Portuguese wine and his kitchen has always been known for the consistency of its cooking. They usually have Arctic char, Manitoba pickerel and local caribou, but if you want to have caribou you should let them know the day before. The menu never changes. If you can't get what you want this year, try again next year.

Open Monday to Saturday 7 am to 9 pm from 1 March until 30 November. Closed on Sunday. Licensed. All cards. No smoking.

The map number assigned to each city, town or village gives the location of the centre on one or more of the maps at the start of the book.

CLARK'S HARBOUR, N.S.   (MAP 193)
WEST HEAD TAKEOUT   🖾
81 Boundary Road   **$40**
(902) 745-1322

About 800 people live in Clark's Harbour, which is the only settlement on Cape Sable Island. Everybody enjoys the drive in and everybody admires the white-sand beaches, but you may have to ask your way to the West Head Takeout. It's a tiny building at the end of the town wharf, with a fish-processing plant on either side. The place looks like nothing from the outside and there's little to indicate what goes on inside. Still, the Takeout is busy from morning till night. It used to be called the Seaview, but if the name has changed the menu hasn't. Nor has the fish. It's easy to recommend the lobster roll, which is as good as any we've tasted. They also have a scallop burger for 4.25 and very fresh fish and chips for 8.95. Anyone who finds himself within 25 miles of this place and doesn't come in for a meal is making a big mistake.
Open daily 10.30 am to 8 pm from late March until late September. No liquor, no cards. No smoking. &

COBBLE HILL, B.C.   (MAP 62)
BISTRO AT MERRIDALE   ☆
1230 Merridale Road   **$75**
(250) 743-4293

This place used to be called La Pommeraie and, like La Pommeraie, it's located right in the middle of a working apple farm producing organic cider. The restaurant offers cider pairings with many of its dishes, which are inspired by produce raised in nearby Cowichan Valley farms. In fair weather meals are served outside on a covered patio overlooking the apple orchards. Kim and Ian Blom, both of whom have had experience with Georg Szasz at Stage in Victoria, now do most of the cooking. Start with a brick-oven pizza prepared by Alain Boisseau, go on to a lamb tagine with figs and apricots and finish with a piece of apple pie, made with apples raised here on the farm.

There's nothing else quite like it.
Open Monday to Thursday noon to 3 pm, Friday and Saturday noon to 3 pm, 5 pm to 9 pm, Sunday 10.30 am to 3 pm (brunch). Licensed. Master Card, Visa. No smoking. &

COBOURG, Ontario   MAP 51
FRENCHIE'S   ☆
246 Division Street   **$70**
(905) 372-7200

The ebullient owner of Frenchie's suffered a serious concussion early in 2012 and had to cut down on her hours for a year. Come summer, however, she'll be running full steam again. Her menu is seasonal and everything is made on the premises—the bread, the pastries, the chutneys and the mayonnaise. Everybody likes her smoked-meat sandwich. It's piled high with smoked meat cut straight from the brisket and served with homemade coleslaw and dill pickles. Of course, there are other good things too. There are ham crêpes, seafood crêpes and a tourtière. With Steam Whistle beer on tap, you've got yourself a meal. There's a different sweet every day and right now Lawrence is planning an amaretto-espresso mousse. Not that she's resting on her laurels. She's bought three of the adjoining stores and before long there'll be a sweet shop, a deli and a bistro with a small bar. We plan to come back soon for an old-fashioned milkshake or perhaps a soda.
Open Monday to Wednesday 10.30 am to 5 pm, Thursday and Friday 10.30 am to 8 pm, Saturday 8.30 am to 8 pm. Closed on Sunday. Licensed. Master Card, Visa. No smoking. Book ahead if you can.

COBOURG   MAP 51
WOODLAWN INN
420 Division Street   **$125 ($295)**
(800) 573-5003

Cobourg is a lovely old town, with a magnificent beach and splendid views of Lake Ontario. We need a good place to stay there and fortunately that's not hard to find.

The Woodlawn Inn dates from 1835 and since 1988 has been kept up by the Della Casa family. To start with, they have a remarkable wine-list that offers five vintages from the Napa Valley, five from the Maipo Valley in Chile and many more from Italy, among them three from ornellaia. There's a formal dining-room where they serve such classic Italian dishes as boar ravioli and wild boar with caramelized sweet onions. Lamb chops are imported fresh from Australia and served with mission figs and rye whisky. The Dover sole is all frozen, but they can get seabass fresh. We start with Northumberland County carpaccio of beef and go on from there to the lamb or the sea-bass. There's a substantial buffet lunch and a magnificent brunch on Sunday.

Open Monday to Saturday 11.30 am to 2 pm, 5.30 pm to 9 pm, Sunday 11 am to 2 pm (brunch), 5.30 pm to 8 pm. Licensed. All cards. No smoking. &

COLLINGWOOD, Ontario   **MAP 52**
AZZURRA
100 Pine Street   **$110**
(705) 445-7771

There are several good Italian restaurants in Collingwood, but Azzurra is the best of the lot. They shave their own parmesan and use nothing but wholewheat flour in their pasta. There's sea-salt on every table. Lately they've started offering what they call pranzo dinners, which are supposed to remind you of what would be served in a typical Italian home. There are two pranzo menus, one that costs 39.00 for four courses; the other costs 59.00 for six courses. Guests sit around a common table and reach for what they want from a parade of platters. There's also an à la carte menu, of course. It includes all the pranzo dishes as well as confit of duck with white beans, Italian sausage, osso buco and a great seafood stew. The wine-list offers many of the most important Italian wines, but the house wines come from Lailey in Niagara and aren't Italian at all.

Open Tuesday to Friday 11 am to 3 pm, 5 pm to 10 pm, Satur-

day 5 pm to 10 pm, Sunday 5 pm to 9 pm. Closed on Monday. Licensed. Amex, Master Card, Visa. No smoking. &

COLLINGWOOD   MAP 52
CHARTREUSE
70 Hurontario Street   **$85**
(705) 444-0099

Most readers find Chartreuse one of the best buys in town. It's a relaxed and informal place, with a big sofa filled with children's toys. You order your meal at the counter and it comes to your table in a moment. Patrick Bourachot, the chef, trained in France and worked at Montebello before settling down in Collingwood with his wife, Ruth, who manages the restaurant. Others do much of the cooking nowadays, especially Zacharie, the pastry chef, whose creations, among them a double-chocolate mousse-cake with fresh strawberries, are fabulous. At lunchtime there are several imaginative soups (potato-and-leek), several interesting salads (apple and beets in a raspberry vinaigrette) and three or four sandwiches. The service is friendly and helpful.

Open Monday and Wednesday to Saturday 2 pm to 5 pm, Sunday 11.30 am to 4 pm. Closed on Tuesday. Licensed. Master Card, Visa. No smoking. &

COLLINGWOOD   MAP 52
DUNCAN'S
60 Hurontario Street   **$110**
(705) 444-5749

Duncan was a cat that had nothing whatever to do with the restaurant of today. The menu is enormous and never changes. Popular dishes, like the potato soup with leeks and stilton cheese, remain on the list for years. The salad-dressings are all made in the kitchen and the mango salad with jerk chicken is a knockout. People come here for the chicken club sandwich, the quesadillas, the baked brie in phyllo and the wild-mushroom ravioli. Prices are higher in the evening, when you can have a fine 10-ounce striploin with blue cheese or a fillet of Atlantic salmon in puff pastry. (The chicken stuffed with goat-cheese is big enough to keep two people full for a week.) The kitchen isn't much interested in sweets, but there's a big wine-list. *Open Monday to Thursday 9 am to 8 pm, Friday and Saturday 9 am to 10 pm, Sunday 9 am to 4 pm. Licensed. Master Card, Visa. No smoking.* &

COLLINGWOOD   **MAP 52**
HURON CLUB
94 Pine Street   **$130**
(705) 293-6677

We're not sure why the Huron House came to be known as the Huron Club. Perhaps it's because they have live music from Wednesday to Saturday and a jazz-and-blues brunch on Sunday. But anyway, there's no membership fee. (The musicians are all local and they still have a way to go.) The cooking is familiar. Every night there's a blue-plate special—roast beef on Sunday, meat-loaf on Monday, schnitzel on Tuesday and so on. If you come between 5 and 7 o'clock, they'll give you a glass of wine or a bottle of draft beer for 5.00, plus an appetizer for 7.00. Meals are served inside or out—it's your choice. *Open daily 11 am to midnight. Licensed. Master Card, Visa. No smoking.* &

COLLINGWOOD   **MAP 52**
THE SIAMESE GEKKO
14 Balsam Street   **$50**
(705) 446-2167

The Siamese Gekko has moved back to Balsam Street, where they started out. Their smart new quarters on the main street have gone, but the menu hasn't changed. Narry Dopp comes from Bangkok, and her recipes are all completely authentic. She starts her meals with Tom Yum soup, which is a mixture of mushrooms, lime, lemon grass and chicken, beef, shrimps or tofu. Curries come next—red, yellow, orange and green. People who should know really admire her pad ho ra pa, with its hot chillies and Thai basil. We ourselves prefer the pad kee mow, with lime and lemon grass. If you insist on meat, ask for the gang penang, a red curry with beef, lamb or chicken and no vegetables at all. They have Thai beer to drink and several wines, but we usually go for a pot of jasmine tea.

Open Monday 5 pm to 9 pm, Tuesday to Saturday 11.30 am to 3 pm, 5 pm to 9 pm. Closed on Sunday. Licensed. Master Card, Visa. No smoking. &

COLLINGWOOD

MAP 52

THE STUFFED PEASANT ☆☆
206 Hurontario Street **$125**
(705) 445-6957

Scott Carter believes in service. He has an attentive staff and a chef who takes the time to chat with the customers. He has a three-course *prix-fixe* menu—three courses for 33,00. Some things never leave it, things like the mushroom pâté, the provimi liver, the cassoulet of lamb. Last Christmas he tried sweetbreads, sautéed in a reduction of port with spinach and potatoes. He also got in two cases of Alberta lamb. Both sold well. Nearby there's an organic fish hatchery, the only one in Canada. They supply him with rainbow trout and speckled trout, and he grills them and serves them with chopped chives. The steaks are always first-rate and so is the duck with pomegranates. The best of the sweets is usually the sticky-toffee pudding. The wine-list is small but useful.

Open Tuesday to Saturday 5 pm to 10 pm. Closed on Sunday and Monday. Licensed. Amex, Master Card, Visa. No smoking.

COOMBS, B.C.

(MAP 163)

THE CUCKOO
2310 Alberni Highway **$120**
(250) 248-6280

At the Cuckoo, which describes itself as a trattoria and pizzeria, they aim to give you an authentic Italian dining experience.—and they do. The place is almost always crowded, in spite of its location at the back of the Coombs market area on the road from Parksville to the west coast. They have the best thin-crust pizzas on Vancouver Island as well as the linguine pescatore, which is crammed with shellfish of all sorts. If you come as a party of four you can share a huge platter of pizzas and pasta, which is fun. There are also a number of fresh salads with goat-cheese, cranberries and caramelized pecans. After that there's a really good tiramisu, if you have room for it. Most of the wines are from Italy or the Pacific Northwest.

Open Tuesday to Sunday 11 am to 9 pm. Closed on Monday. Licensed. All cards. No smoking. ⅃

COWICHAN BAY, B.C. (MAP 62)
THE MASTHEAD ☆
1705 Cowichan Bay Road **$120**
(250) 748-3714

At the Masthead they have a magnificent old house, great views, professional service and good food, all prepared by Martin Harrison. We still like to start with Cortes Island clams and mussels in a broth of tomato and white wine seasoned with garlic. Sometimes we start with weathervane scallops in a truffled wild-mushroom risotto. The house chowder is rich and thick with house-smoked salmon and fresh vegetables. The simple salad is anything but simple, mixing as it does organic greens with smoked sockeye salmon and goat-cheese in an apple-cider vinaigrette. The Caesar is prepared at your table by the owner himself, and it's a good one. The best of the fish is either the halibut or the seared tuna with lemon and capers, the best of the meats either the grilled lamb or the grilled bison, which comes with sautéed cabbage and sundried cranberries. The list of Cowichan Valley wines is exceptional and you won't go wrong with any of them.

Open daily 5 pm to 10 pm. Licensed. All cards. No smoking. Book ahead if you can. ⅃

COWICHAN LAKE, B.C.   (MAP 62)
STONE SOUP INN   ☆☆
6755 Cowichan Lake Road   **$215**
(250) 749-3848

The Stone Soup Inn is a charming bed-and-breakfast nestled in the heart of the Cowichan Valley. Brock Windsor, the chef, spent some time at the Sooke Harbour House and the Bearfoot Bistro before opening his own restaurant. The Stone Soup is open only three nights a week, but everything is made from scratch and served with the best local wines. He has a small farm where he raises pigs. He forages for wild mushrooms and is famous for his local chanterelles. At Stone Soup there's no written menu. Instead, Windsor offers a five-course tasting menu for 65.00. It usually starts with stinging-nettle soup or marinated black cod with warm cucumber and celery-root slaw and goes on to side-striped shrimps or house-smoked picnic ham braised with fresh oregano. The sweets are all inviting, especially the rhubarb soufflé with sour cream ice cream. If you stay the night, the breakfast will usually feature house-smoked bacon and farm-fresh eggs.
Open Thursday to Saturday 5 pm to 10 pm. Closed Sunday to Wednesday. Licensed. Master Card, Visa. No smoking.

CRANBROOK, B.C.   MAP 56
CANCUN   🖘
303 Cranbrook Street N   **$65**
(250) 426-7525

Mira and Arturo Iguenza do everything here themselves. Some people call this slow service; others (rightly) think it means that everything is cooked to order. Arturo is reluctant to change his menu, his recipes—or his prices. If you come in at noon, when there's no menu at all, Arturo will make you just about anything you fancy. In the evening he offers most of the classic Mexican dishes. Don't think of it as Tex-Mex or Cal-Mex, because it isn't. It's the real thing. The dishes are all fresh, the spicing is light. Most people ask for the plato combinato, because it has a lot of different flavours. Apart from that, we suggest the quesadillas, the chicken burritos or the chilli rellenos, which still cost less than 10.00. Everything is made right here, everything is perfectly fresh and the helpings are enormous. There aren't many wines, but they have some lovely fresh-fruit drinks, as well as Mexican beer and really good margaritas. Cancun has lasted in this unlikely location because it's cheap and cheerful.

Open Monday to Saturday 11 am to 2.30 pm, 4.30 pm to 9 pm. Closed on Sunday. Licensed. No cards. No smoking. &

DAWSON CITY, Yukon   MAP 57
LA TABLE ON FIFTH   ☆
Aurora Inn   **$125**
5 Avenue at Harper Street
(867) 993-6860

Dawson City still has plenty to offer the tourist. This is where the Klondike Gold Rush turned a hamlet into a town of 30,000. We suggest you take the time to explore the old wooden sidewalks, after which you should book a table at the Aurora Inn. The hotel was built in 1998 with spacious rooms and contemporary décor. Five years later they opened an elegant dining-room and called it La Table on Fifth. This may not be the Paris of the North (as they like to call it), but Carolyn Wong and Bruce Irniger always aimed high. People write to us about what they call their "fantastic find." Bruce has now retired, but Carolyn is still offering cooking you'd be lucky to find in the south. The wienerschnitzel and jaegerschnitzel are both outstanding and the triple-A Alberta beef is just that. The vegetables are all fresh and properly cooked. The wine-list offers many good things and is cheaper than most in the north.

Open daily 5 pm to 9 pm from early May until late September. Licensed. All cards. No smoking. Book ahead if you can. &

If you use an out-of-date edition and find it inaccurate, don't blame us. Buy a new edition.

DEER ISLAND, N.B.   MAP 58
SPIRIT OF THE ISLAND   🖐
20 County Road 772   **$45**
Stewart Town
(506) 747-0101

It's a short ferry trip from Letete to Deer Island. The
ferry runs all day, departing every half-hour. Michel and
his wife, Michelle, came here from Quebec City and
liked it so much they never left, even in winter. Everything they serve in their tiny restaurant comes from the
kitchen or the kitchen garden. There are fresh flowers on
every table and edible flowers in the salads. Greens are
picked early every morning. If you order scallops, Michel
will ask you whether you want them well cooked or
good. The lobster rolls are as good as they get. The potatoes are peeled and sliced just before they're fried. The
sweets change every day. In season, there's always blueberry cake and a chocolate layer cake, which they call a
weir cake because Michel inserts chopsticks to hold
the cake together. The milkshakes are made in the old-
fashioned way and they're irresistible.
Open Tuesday to Sunday 11.30 am to 8 pm from mid-May until
Labour Day, Wednesday to Sunday from Labour Day until late
October. Closed on Monday in summer, Monday and Tuesday
in the fall. No liquor. Master Card, Visa. No smoking.

DIGBY, N.S.   MAP 59
BOARDWALK CAFE
40 Water Street   **$85**
(902) 245-5497

Esther Dunn will be back in the kitchen full-time this
summer. We may think her split-pea soup is too thick,
but there's certainly nothing wrong with her shrimp-
and-avocado salad. Come to that, she makes everything
herself: the quiches and the lasagne, of course, but also
the bread and the salad-dressings. The pies are all brilliant—try the apple-lattice and see for yourself. In the
evening you can expect fresh haddock, halibut, scallops

(from Digby Bay), lobster and salmon. The Boardwalk doesn't have any bottled wines, just one or two house wines served by the glass. Inside, the restaurant is pretty plain, but the big windows look out on the harbour and the scallop fleet. The servers are all friendly and everyone has a good time here, especially if they have one of Esther's pies.

Open Monday to Friday 11 am to 2 pm from the beginning of March until late June, Monday to Saturday 11 am to 2 pm, 5 pm to 8 pm from late June until the end of September, Monday to Friday 11 am to 2 pm from 1 October until 20 December. Closed on Saturday and Sunday in the spring and fall, on Sunday in the summer. Licensed. All cards. No smoking. &

DILDO, Newfoundland	**MAP 60**
INN BY THE BAY	☆
80 Front Road	**$130 ($240)**
(888) 339-7829	

Dildo is on the south arm of Trinity Bay, a little over an hour's drive from St. John's. The town's codfish hatchery used to be the biggest in the world. Nowadays the 1500 people in Dildo are dependent on the tourist trade. The Inn by the Bay and the nearby bed-and-breakfast are owned by Todd Warren and Dale Cameron, who have restored them both. Warren and Cameron are self-taught cooks and they're both committed to organically grown regional produce. There are still two fish plants in Dildo, and you can actually watch the crab boats coming in with fresh crab for your dinner. There are also plenty of steelhead trout in Trinity Bay and occasionally tilapia as well. The menu here changes daily, depending on what's fresh and in season. The homemade soups are all first-class, especially the roasted red pepper and the lobster bisque. The salads are all made with local organic lettuce. Broccoli and leeks come from an organic farm at nearby Heart's Content. Every day Todd makes at least one of his celebrated blueberry butter-cakes and serves it with hot screech. If you don't want a stiff drink with your cake, ask for the bread pudding with partridge-berries or the lemon pound-cake with homemade ice cream. The wine-list has grown over the years to 50 vintages, 12 of them sold by the glass as well as the bottle.

Open daily noon to 2 pm, 6 pm to 8 pm from early May until late November. Licensed. All cards. No smoking. Book ahead.

DORCHESTER, N.B.   MAP 61
THE BELL INN   ☞
3515 Cape Road   **$55**
(506) 379-2580

David McAllister and Wayne Jones are soldiering on here after 26 good years on the job. The Bell Inn is said to be the oldest stone building in New Brunswick. It was once a stop-over for stage-coaches, but in time it fell into dis-repair. Eventually it was restored as a restaurant and filled with comfortable Victoriana. True, Jones and McAllister serve frozen lobster and sole as a matter of course, but that hardly seems to matter. They have a first-class home-made soup every day. They have fresh greens in their garden salad. They make fine sandwiches (turkey, tuna, egg-salad and cheese). There are also three or four hot dishes—scrambled eggs or an omelette, lasagne or liver and onions. They make all their own sweets, the best of which is probably the apple crisp. There's no liquor, not even a glass of Moosehead. Fortunately, they make very good coffee.

Open Wednesday to Sunday 11 am to 7 pm from 1 April until 15 November. Closed on Monday and Tuesday. No liquor. All cards. No smoking. Free parking.

DUNCAN, B.C.   MAP 62
BISTRO 161
161 Kenneth Street   **$95**
(250) 746-6466

Fatima da Silva, who is running both Bistro 161 and Vinoteca (see below), was born and grew up in Mozam-bique. Her background has Portuguese, Indian, Arabic, Spanish and Chinese elements, all of which show up in her cooking. Chris Szilagyi, the chef de cuisine, also has a multicultural background, stemming from Chinese, African, Portuguese and Irish ancestors. We like almost everything they do: the yam-and-ginger soup with garlic, the penne with sundried tomatoes and artichokes, the mussels steamed in wine with chorizo, the ceviche of scallops with orange and star anise, the duck biryani and even the pork and beans with its ten secret spices. The service, however, is uneven at best, poor at worst.

Open Monday to Saturday 11 am to 3 pm, 5 pm to 10 pm. Closed on Sunday. Licensed. Amex, Master Card, Visa. No smoking. &

DUNCAN   MAP 62
CRAIG STREET BREW PUB
25 Craig Street   **$100**
(250) 737-2337

They have Cajun-style catfish for lunch here. It comes with a fruit salsa and sweet-potato fries. There are a couple of beers (Shawnigan Irish and Arbutus pale ale) that are made right on the premises. Steaks come on at 4.30 pm and they're said to be good, but we haven't tried them. The tuna with wasabi and the pan-seared wild salmon with blackberries are, however, both outstanding. When you're ready, ask for the triple-chocolate cake, or any of the house-baked pies for that matter. If you want something quieter and more intimate, go next door to Just Jake's, which is also owned by Lance Stewart.

Open Monday to Wednesday 11 am to 11 pm, Thursday to Saturday 11 am to midnight, Sunday 11 am to 10 pm. Licensed. Master Card, Visa. No smoking. &

DUNCAN   MAP 62
RIVERWALK
200 Cowichan Way   **$90**
(250) 746-8119

Beverly Antoine has left Riverwalk, which, however, still makes it its business to marry First Nations traditions with West Coast styles of cooking. If you want to sample a recent menu, ask for the pulled bison slow-roasted in a fireweed-peppercorn sauce, topped with sautéed peppers and onions. That or the farmed venison with fresh tomatoes, aged cheddar cheese, sour cream and avocado. There's also a Salish seafood platter that features wild Pacific salmon, cod and prawns garnished with sea asparagus.

Open Monday to Saturday 11 am to 4 pm from 15 June until 15 September. Closed on Sunday. Licensed. Master Card, Visa. No smoking. Book ahead if you can. &

DUNCAN   **MAP 62**
VINOTECA
Zanatta Winery   **$100**
5039 Marshall Road
(250) 709-2279

Vinoteca is located in an old farmhouse near the Zanatta winery. It was recommended in *Where to Eat in Canada* from 2000 until 2005, when it was run by Fatima da Silva. When she left, the restaurant ran quickly downhill and was taken out of the guide. All that has changed now that Fatima is once again in charge. She has created a new menu based on produce grown on or close to the Zanatta farm. Further reports needed.

Open Wednesday to Sunday 11.30 am to 2.30 pm from mid-May until mid-October. Closed on Monday and Tuesday. Licensed. Master Card, Visa. No smoking.

DUNCAN
See also CHEMAINUS, COBBLE HILL, COWICHAN BAY, COWICHAN LAKE, MILL BAY.

DUNDAS, Ontario   **(MAP 88)**
QUATREFOIL   ☆
16 Sydenham Street   **$120**
(905) 628-7800

Quatrefoil is a fairly new restaurant. It's run by Fraser

Macfarlane and Georgina Mitropoulos, who met when they were both working at Scaramouche in Toronto. The cooking is a mixture of classic and modern French, and the chef has a vigorous interest in fresh, organic local produce. He starts with sea scallops in a clementine vinaigrette, white asparagus with the yolk of an egg, tagliatelle of braised rabbit and a textbook-perfect smoked salmon with red-onion pickles. The best of the main courses is the beef tenderloin from Cumbrae, served with a purée of smoked potatoes and cheek cromesquis, a dish so good that it reminded one diner of one of his mother's Easter dinners. The vanilla crème brûlée delighted the same diner, when he broke the crust and smelled the hot vanilla inside.

Open Tuesday to Saturday noon to 2.30 pm, 5 pm to 9.30 pm. Closed on Sunday and Monday. Licensed. Amex, Master Card, Visa. No smoking.

EASTMAN, Quebec　　　　　　　　　　**MAP 64**
LE PETIT EASTMAN
424 rue Principale　　　　　　　　　　　　**$85**
450 297-0433

This small café 30 miles from Sherbrooke was originally built as a private house; later it served as the town's only grocery store. Since 2005 Philippe Nock and his wife have run the place as a restaurant, which is now one of the best in the Eastern Townships The menu for the evening is posted every afternoon on a blackboard. Everything there is made on the premises. The meal will begin with a homemade soup (usually gazpacho in summer), followed by a fresh green salad and pasta, then mussels, say, or salt-cod. The salt-cod always sells out early on, but there's also a veal burger and maybe a bavette of beef with hand-cut fries. Sweets cost extra, but they're worth it, especially the ravishing tarte tatin. On weekends you can get a brunch of smoked salmon or eggs benedict from noon to 3 o'clock. If you order a week in advance, the chef will make you a tarte flambée with apples and calvados, served in the traditional manner with a glass or two of wine.

Open Tuesday to Friday 5 pm to 10 pm, Saturday and Sunday noon to 10 pm from late May until Labour Day, Thursday and Friday 5 pm to 10 pm, Saturday and Sunday noon to 10 pm from early April until late May and from Labour Day until the middle of November. Closed on Monday in summer, Monday to Wednesday in the spring and fall. Licensed. No cards. No smoking. ♿

EDMONTON, Alberta   **MAP 65**
BLUE PEAR   ☆
10643 123 Street   **$195**
(780) 482-7178

Blue Pear is a small restaurant northwest of downtown Edmonton. It has a short, expensive menu, but the cooking is good and the service has improved. The soup changes daily, but there's an excellent butternut squash that costs almost as much as the curried cauliflower with pakoras and cheese. The beef tartar and the snails are both eccentric dishes. The tartar of beef is seared and served with cream cheese, the snails with poached crabmeat. The veal that follows is milkfed, a rarity west of Montreal, and the Arctic char goes well with its lentils and stuffed cabbage. The wine-list, unlike the menu, is large, offering such good things as a Barbi brunello, an Antinori tignanello and, perhaps best of all, a lovely shiraz from Burrowing Owl. There are also two surprise menus and two wine pairings, but it's cheaper (and better) to choose your own meal from the à la carte.

Open Wednesday to Sunday 5 pm to 9 pm. Closed on Monday and Tuesday. Licensed. Amex, Master Card, Visa. No smoking. Book ahead.

EDMONTON   **MAP 65**
CHARACTERS
10257 105 Street   **$175**
(780) 421-4100

What a difference a year can make! When we first came

to Characters, we gave it a single star. This year we are more cautious. It's true that they still have a first-class wine-list that offers a generous selection of wines from the Okanagan and a splendid list of Italian reds, from chiantis and valpolicellas to solaias and ornellaias. But the cooking has lost much of its old excitement. Gravlax is now served with red grapefruit, which is way over the top, scallops with bacon, which never really works. Dover sole is on the menu, though Edmonton is 4000 miles from the English Channel. The only really great dish costs 60.00. It's an Iberican pork chop, which comes from the famous black-hoof pig and is privately imported from Spain. Every dinner begins with an *amuse-bouche* of potato chips with a wonderful dipping sauce of fermented black beans. If you have just that and the pork chop with a bottle of solaia, Characters is still a one-star restaurant. Of course, that will cost you a lot.

Open Monday 11.30 am to 2 pm, Tuesday to Friday 11.30 am to 2 pm, 5.30 pm to 10 pm, Saturday 5.30 pm to 10 pm. Closed on Sunday. Licensed. All cards. No smoking. Book ahead. &

EDMONTON	**MAP 65**
CORSO 32	☆☆
10345 Jasper Avenue	**$120**
(780) 421-4622	

Corso 32 is a newcomer to Edmonton. It's an Italian restaurant but it has no fish, no veal and no liver, most of which other Italian restaurants have in spades. What it does have is noise, deafening noise. Apart from noise, Corso 32 is all about local ingredients—milkfed veal, for instance, is almost unknown in Alberta and so it doesn't appear on the menu. Daniel Costa starts his list of antipasto with pear carpaccio and ends it with house-made goat ricotta. His pork-cheeks terrine isn't a terrine at all, not at least as we think of it. Terrine or not, it's a wonderful dish. If they don't have any, ask for the gnocchi of wild boar, which is out of the class of most other gnocchis on the market. Cornish game hen is rarely offered in Tuscany, or in Puglia for that matter, but this one is charming. The chocolate cake is made with salted hazel-nuts in the modern fashion, and it's good. They have a Batasiolo barolo by the glass and it's about as good as any we've had. The same is true of the machiato.

Open Wednesday to Saturday 5 pm to midnight. Closed Sunday to Tuesday. Licensed. Amex, Master Card, Visa. No smoking. You must book ahead. &

EDMONTON	**MAP 65**
MARC	
9940 106 Street	**$150**
(780) 429-2828	

Marc occupies the ground floor of a modern office block near the high-level bridge. Inside it's all white, with wide steel-and-glass windows. Scott Ards is no longer in charge of the kitchen, having been replaced by Bryan Cruz. At noon, Cruz serves salmon tartar, smoked breast of duck, fresh trout, braised open-faced lamb sandwiches and steak with (far too many) fried potatoes. In the evening he adds scallops, char and charcuterie. The wine-list offers a little of everything, from California to Portugal, all at reasonable prices. Marc may not be exciting, but it's a useful, convenient restaurant with capable cooking and first-rate service.

Open Monday to Friday 11.30 am to 2 pm, 5.30 pm to 9 pm, Saturday 5.30 pm to 9 pm. Closed on Sunday. Licensed. Amex, Master Card, Visa. No smoking. Book ahead. &

EDMONTON	**MAP 65**
NICHE	
11011 Jasper Avenue	**$130**
(780) 761-1011	

Niche is new and chic. The menu is small, especially at noon, when they have first-class ginger pork and a tomato tart with roasted peppers and tequila. In the evening they add onion soup with beer and a wild-mushroom risotto. Main courses are equally unusual, starting with short-rib stroganoff and rising to candied pork. The wine-list is small too, but there's a merlot and a chardonnay from Burrowing Owl, both of which offer excellent drinking. Best of all, there's a seductive salted-caramel brownie, laced with real whipped cream. The service is calm and elegant.

Open Monday to Thursday 11 am to midnight, Friday 11 am to 2 am, Saturday 4 pm to 2 am. Closed on Sunday. Licensed. Amex, Master Card, Visa. No smoking. Book ahead if you can.

EDMONTON   **MAP 65**
NUMCHOK WILAI
10623 124 Street   **$75**
(780) 483-7897

This is one of the best Thai restaurants in Edmonton and one of the cheapest. They have a liquor licence and offer Singha beer, which is the thing to drink. Lunch costs just 10.95, for which you get a small bowl of lemon-grass soup and red and green curries of beef and chicken, as well as panaeng chicken and beef, pad Thai and a variety of vegetarian dishes. In the evening they add several scallop, squid and mussel curries for only a few dollars more. Numchok Wilai is a streetfront restaurant with a comfortable arrangement of tables and chairs inside. The service is competent but rather impersonal.

Open daily 11.30 am to 2.30 pm, 4.30 pm to 9 pm (later on weekends). Licensed. Master Card, Visa. No smoking.

EDMONTON   **MAP 65**
THE RED OX INN
9420 91 Street   **$175**
(780) 465-5727

The Red Ox Inn is bare inside and out, but it's a sensible place with a short, straightforward menu and good cooking. The pork belly with sweet-and-sour marmalade is a good way to start—that or the beef tartar. Both are much better than the house-smoked salmon, which with its plain slice of corn bread is dry and rather tasteless. When it comes to the main course, the kitchen is at its best with its halibut with quinoa and scallions and its breast of duck, which is tender and quite piquant. Berkshire pork appears again as a main course and for only 38.00 you can have a good, substantial rack of lamb. Most of the real excitement, however, takes place on the wine-list. For almost nothing there's a good Amity pinot blanc and a Columbia Crest grand-estates merlot—two of the best and most important wines from Oregon. If you prefer to drink Canadian, there's a first-rate cabernet sauvignon from Poplar Grove for 49.00. The cabernet from Rodney Strong costs a bit more, as it should. The service is attentive and personal. They care.

Open Tuesday to Sunday 5 pm to 9 pm. Closed on Monday. Licensed. Amex, Master Card, Visa. No smoking. &

EDMONTON   **MAP 65**
THE UNHEARDOF   ☆
9602 82 Avenue   **$220**
(780) 432-0480

Lynn Heard has been in the kitchen here for many years and she's starting to look tired. Not that it shows in her cooking, which is always intelligent and well informed. Her seafood bisque may be a bit too thick, but her tomato soup spiked with gin is as good as ever. The vegetables are plain and mostly undercooked, but the lamb is deftly flavoured with mustard and chilli, and the same is true of the gin-rubbed beef tenderloin. The breast of chicken with apricots sometimes suffers from an excess of white sauce, but the bison is flattered by its cranberries and sage. Lynn Heard disapproves of Okanagan wines, which she thinks overpriced, and most of her wines come from California or Australia. This doesn't do justice to such a thing as the Noble Blend from Joie Farm on the Naramata Bench. The rice pudding, however, is a marvel, so settle for that.

Open Tuesday to Saturday 5.30 pm to 8.30 pm (earlier on Sunday). Closed on Monday. Licensed. Amex, Master Card, Visa. No smoking. Book ahead. &

EDMUNDSTON, N.B.   MAP 66
LOTUS BLEU   🍵
52 chemin Canada   **$55**
(506) 739-8259

Estelle and Louise run Lotus Bleu with so much passion
and dedication that it seems likely the place will last,
which in this town in something of a miracle. They claim
to have the best coffee west of Paris, which is probably
not true, good though the coffee may be. They also claim
to be the best place to stop for a meal between Toronto
and Halifax, which is certainly not true. What is true is
that they do wonderful things with fresh organic vegetables. Most travellers go for one of the salads, which are
all made with local greens. They also have some first-class
soups and they make a fine, light quiche. They buy their
bread from Première Moisson in Montreal, but they
themselves make very good muffins and dark-chocolate
biscuits. The sweets are all made in-house and their
choice of leaf teas is astonishing. The service is friendly
and very quick.
Open Monday to Wednesday 7.30 am to 6 pm, Thursday and
Friday 7.30 am to 7 pm, Saturday 9.30 am to 5 pm. Closed on
Sunday. No liquor. Master Card, Visa. No smoking. ⅃

ENGLISHTOWN, N.S.   MAP 67
THE CLUCKING HEN   🍵
45073 Cabot Trail   **$40**
(902) 929-2501

Look for the Clucking Hen ten miles north of the Eng-
lishtown ferry. Melody Dauphney offers plain, simple
home-cooking seven days a week in season. You line up
to place your order and pay the bill, then carry your tray
to a table. She makes a good soup (turkey or fish chowder) and a number of sandwiches, as well as lobster stew,
which everyone seems to like. There's a lot of baking here
too and there are always cinnamon rolls and butter tarts
as well as oat-cakes, which are a specialty of the house.
The Clucking Hen is a good place to stop for breakfast,

lunch or dinner before you set out on the Cabot Trail.
Open daily 7 am to 8 pm from 1 July until 31 August (shorter hours in the spring and fall). Licensed for beer and wine only. Master Card, Visa. No smoking. ♿

FERRYLAND, Newfoundland   **MAP 68**
LIGHTHOUSE PICNICS
Highway 10   **$55**
(709) 363-7456

Jill Curran will have another baby to look after when the Lighthouse reopens this summer. But at least she'll have a staff of thirteen to help her, many of whom have been with her since opening day. The Lighthouse was built in 1869 and there isn't much left of it now. The site, how-ever, is glorious. There's a rocky headland where waves break, whales surface and the fog rolls in and out again. Mind you, the lighthouse is a stiff half-hour by foot from the nearest road and an hour's drive from St. John's. The picnics, which cost between 20.00 and 25.00, consist of a salad, a sandwich on homemade bread, a sweet and lemonade. The salad might be cold spaghetti with garlic, chillies and feta cheese or perhaps with green peppers, orzo and parmesan cheese. The sandwiches are made with molasses-and-oatmeal bread and come with smoked salmon and cold-water shrimp or with goat-cheese, sun-dried tomatoes and beansprouts. For sweet, most people ask for gingerbread with a warm vanilla sauce. If you want to make a day of it, there are a couple of interesting museums in the area.
Open Wednesday to Sunday 11.30 am to 5 pm from 1 June until 30 September. Closed on Monday and Tuesday. No liquor. Mas-ter Card, Visa. No smoking.

Every restaurant in this guide has been personally tested. Our reporters are not allowed to identify themselves to the management or to accept free meals. We accept no advertisements. We accept no payment for listings. We depend entirely on you. Recommend the book to your friends.

FIELD, B.C.   **(MAP 102)**
TRUFFLE PIGS   ☆
Kicking Horse Lodge   **$110**
318 Stephen Avenue
(250) 343-6303

We started coming to Truffle Pigs when it was in a general store on Centre Street. Then, in the spring of 2008,
they bought the fourteen-room Kicking Horse Lodge,
with the help of a number of local people. That changed
everything. They found themselves with ten tables and
a modern kitchen. The chef, Sean Cunningham, is young
and ambitious. He has a number of sous-chefs and a wife,
Jen Coffman, who makes the sweets. To find cooking like
this in a town like Field is more than surprising, but so it
is. Breakfast is designed for bikers and skiers. There are
omega-3 eggs, Hutterite smoked sausages with bacon and
organic maple syrup. At lunch they have a truffled-
tomato tarte tatin with brie, black truffle-oil and wild
greens. Fish and chips are made with wild lingcod in beer
batter with hand-cut fries and homemade tartare sauce.
In the evening there are coffee-crusted steaks and blue
mussels with Dijon mustard. The wine-list is full of the
best Okanagan wines.
Open daily 7 am to 10.30 am, 11 am to 3.30 pm, 5 pm to 9 pm
(shorter hours in winter). Licensed. Amex, Master Card, Visa.
No smoking. No reservations. ⅃

FLORENCEVILLE, N.B.   **MAP 70**
FRESH   ☆☆
9189 Main Street   **$175**
(506) 392-6000

The idea behind Fresh came from a group of history buffs
in Bristol. Bristol, however, has since been absorbed by
Florenceville, the home of McCain's frozen foods.
There's certainly nothing frozen at Fresh, which occupies
a restored dining-car on the site. Everything that leaves
the kitchen is prepared by Jeff MacLean; every drink is
made by Sara Gaines. MacLean makes everything on the

menu from scratch, and that means sea-bass grilled in a green-coconut curry, beef won-tons poached in won-ton skins and served in a reduction of plums and wasabi and pork tenderloin braised in apple cider. The chocolate-lover's plate is one dish that survives every menu change. The wine-list is ambitious, but the prices are mostly quite modest: the Wolf Blass Red Label cabernet merlot sells for only about 42.00.

Open Monday to Saturday 5.30 pm to 10 pm. Closed on Sunday. Licensed. Master Card, Visa. No smoking. Book ahead.

FOGO ISLAND, Newfoundland   MAP 71
NICOLE'S   ☆
Joe Batt's Arm   **$125**
(705) 658-3663

It's possible to get to Fogo Island, spend a few hours there and get back to Twillingate the same day, but that would be a pity. Fogo Island deserves a longer visit. It's just off the northeast shore of Newfoundland. It's windswept and wet and very beautiful. Caribou graze on the uplands in summer, humpback whales migrate past its shores in winter. Zita Cobb, a woman of enormous energy and substantial means, is determined to preserve the island through tourism. Early in 2013, a multi-million-dollar hotel, the Fogo Island Inn, opened on Joe Batt's Arm. It has only 29 rooms and each costs a thousand dollars a day, all of which will go back to the community. Not five minutes away, Nicole has opened a café right on the edge of the sea. The kitchen is manned by local people and so far we've received no complaints. Every day they have a cod chowder with shrimps as well as a crab panini with green-onion mayonnaise. They get their cod from cod-pots. The cod are caught in pots instead of nets, and they're kept alive until they're ready to be used. The vegetables are all organic and grown on nearby farms. For sweet there's a bake-apple crème brûlée, partridge-berry jam-and-molasses tarts and sorbets made from ice chipped off ancient icebergs. Nicole hopes to stay open all year now that the Fogo Island Inn is up and running.

Open Monday to Saturday 10 am to 2 pm, 5 pm to 8.30 pm. Closed on Sunday. Licensed. All cards. No smoking. &

FORT MACLEOD, Alberta — MAP 72
RAHN'S
228 24 Street — **$40**
(403) 553-3200

If you're anywhere near, Rahn's is a nice place for a quick lunch. It's part bakery, part café. The soups are so so, but the sandwiches are quite good. The pastries, however, are the real thing. They're all fresh and they're all first-rate. They also sell homemade ice cream. Rahn's is open for breakfast and lunch every day of the week. No liquor, no cards. No smoking. &

FREDERICTON, N.B. — MAP 73
DIMITRI'S
349 King Street — **$75**
(506) 452-8882

One diner remembers her meal here on a hot night last summer as the highlight of her year. "The cooking was great, the service was perfect and there was a cool breeze all evening." Dimitri is Greek and he cooks Greek. His cooking is as authentic as most of its kind. The village salad, for instance, may not be completely authentic, but it tastes good and is big enough for three. Dimitri grills his goat-cheese until it's soft. Then he flames it at the table and serves it as sagenaki. He has the best lamb in town and his avgolemono soup is second to none. What's more, you won't find him closed when you knock on the door after a long day on the road.

Open Monday to Saturday 11 am to 11 pm (later on weekends). Closed on Sunday. Licensed. Master Card, Visa. No smoking.

This is a guide to Canadian restaurants from coast to coast—the first ever published and the only one of its kind on the market today. We accept no advertisements. Nobody can buy his way into this guide and nobody can buy his way out.

FREDERICTON   MAP 73
THE PALATE   ☆
462 Queen Street   **$100**
(506) 450-7911

When the Palate opened in 2001 we didn't use italics for
its entry. We knew right away that it was a serious restaurant and, unlike most new restaurants in Fredericton, it's
still in business ten years later. Lunch is certainly a big
success. They're at their best with their soups, and the
seafood chowder costs only 7.00. The chocolate-lava cake
costs even less. The poached halibut, nicely served in lobster broth, the local lamb, the osso buco and the salmon
with lemon are all remarkably good. All the main courses
come with either a sweet potato or roasted-garlic mash.
There's a decent wine-list with many wines by the glass
or half-bottle.
Open Monday 11 am to 3 pm, Tuesday to Friday 11 am to 3
pm, 5 pm to 9 pm, Saturday 10 am to 3 pm (brunch), 5 pm to 9
pm. Closed on Sunday. Licensed. All cards. No smoking. Book
ahead.

FREDERICTON   MAP 73
WOLLASTOQ WHARF   ☆
527 Union Street $110
(506) 449-0100

In the past the St. Mary's First Nation has had a number
of remarkable commercial successes. Now they're trying
a restaurant, and already the Wollastoq Wharf has estab-
lished itself as the best place in town. The dining area has
a built-in waterfall and (in the evening) candles and linen
table-cloths. The service is quick and attentive. The
menu changes four times a year. You can have a steak if
you like, but most people seem to prefer the seafood. We
like the shrimp spring-rolls, but the oysters all come from
New Brunswick, which means that they're the best.
There's a good seafood risotto, which is full of lobster,
shrimps and scallops, and a very good seafood chowder.
The most popular dish is the salmon two ways—maple-

smoked and tequila-cured.

Open Monday and Tuesday 11 am to 4 pm (lunch), 4 pm to 8 pm (dinner), Wednesday to Friday 11 am to 4 pm (lunch), 4 pm to 10 pm (dinner), Saturday 9.30 am to 2 pm, 4 pm to 10 pm, Sunday 9.30 am to 2 pm, 4 pm to 8 pm. Licensed. All cards. No smoking.

FREEPORT, N.S.   **MAP 74**
LAVENA'S CATCH   ☆
15 Highway 217 W   **$70**
Long Island
(902) 839-2517

If you want to take a whale-and-seabird tour, you'll have an arduous journey from Digby to Long Island, which is the last stop before Brier Island. Freeport is a five-minute ferry trip from the tip of Digby Neck. It was settled by Loyalists in 1784 and many of the original buildings are still standing. St. Mary's Bay and its warm waters are on your left; Fundy's cold, rocky coast is on your right. Overhead, in the spring and fall, migrating birds travel the Atlantic Flyway in their thousands. On the Fundy side you may see, if you're lucky, minke or humpback whales. You can buy tour tickets at Lavena's Catch, which is run by the captain's sister and is the best place to eat anywhere near. Lavena makes everything from scratch. The service may be slow but the meal, when it comes, will be full of fresh seafood, served with mashed potatoes and a Caesar salad. The greens and the vegetables come straight from the garden. Don't overlook the chowder either, or the peanut-butter pie. The coffee is organic and it's very good.

Open Friday and Saturday 4 pm to 9 pm from 1 April until 31 May, daily 11.30 am to 8 pm from 1 June until 15 October, Friday and Saturday 4 pm to 9 pm from 16 October until 30 November. Closed Sunday to Thursday in the spring and fall. Licensed. All cards. No smoking.

FROBISHER BAY, Nunavut
See IQALUIT.

GANDER, Newfoundland
See BOTWOOD.

GASPE, Quebec   MAP 75
LA BRULERIE   ☜
101 rue de la Reine   **$70**
(418) 368-3366

It's always a treat to stop here. The place was built by the
C.N.R. as a telegraph office. Later it was used as the city
hall. It now makes a cozy restaurant that's open all year,
with the same chef, the same menu and enough English
for any anglophone. The fine fresh shrimps from Rivière-au-Renard appear in both the salads and the sandwiches. Home-smoked salmon comes by the plateful.
They make their own sausages, their own pizzas and their
own pasta. The helpings are generous, the prices low.
They roast their own coffee right here and offer everyone
endless refills. We couldn't find the Belgian-chocolate
truffle-cake this year, but we certainly liked the maple-
syrup cake.
*Open Monday to Friday 7 am to 10.30 pm, Saturday and Sun-
day 8 am to 10.30 pm. Licensed. Master Card, Visa. No smoking.*

GASPE   MAP 75
WILLIAM WAKEHAM   ☆
186 rue de la Reine   **$150**
(418) 368-5537

Desmond Ogden settled here because he fell in love with
the old houses on rue de la Reine. He runs the place as a
bed-and-breakfast (with an elaborate dinner) and uses the
earnings to restore the buildings. Ogden is a nimble chef,
but at the moment he's not doing a lot with fresh seafood.
He made his name with things like cods' tongues, cod
and maybe a shelling lobster or two, but nowadays he
seems to prefer to work with sweetbreads, terrine de foie
gras, Brome Lake duck, filet mignon and osso buco.
These are all good things, but you don't have to travel all

the way to Gaspé to get them. If you're in this neck of the woods, however, you won't do better than the William Wakeham. The wine-list is still ambitious, featuring burgundies, côtes du Rhône and Italian cabernet sauvignons, but there's no real choice of wine by the glass.

Open Monday and Tuesday 11.30 am to 2 pm, Wednesday to Friday 11.30 am to 2 pm, 5.30 pm to 10 pm, Saturday and Sunday 5.30 pm to 10 pm from 1 April until 30 June, Monday to Friday 11.30 am to 2 pm, 5.30 pm to 10 pm, Saturday and Sunday 5.30 pm to 10 pm from 1 July until 30 September, Monday and Tuesday 11.30 am to 2 pm, Wednesday to Friday 11.30 am to 2 pm, 5.30 pm to 10 pm, Saturday and Sunday 5.30 pm to 10 pm from 1 October until 31 December. Licensed. Master Card, Visa. No smoking. &

GEORGETOWN, P.E.I.   (MAP 43)
CLAMDIGGERS
7 West Street   **$110**
(902) 652-2466

This former railway station has a splendid location right on the shore of Cardigan Bay. It also has a big deck where you can dine al fresco in summer. They buy all their fish daily and fillet it by hand in the kitchen. The clams are served whole, battered and deep-fried only when you order them that way. Both steamer clams and regular clams are treated as an appetizer, much like mussels. The scallops, however, are deep-fried unless you ask for them with the Caesar salad, when they come to the table just lightly pan-fried. The fish chowder and the fish and chips are both outstanding, but that's not all. They also have lobster, crab, halibut, salmon and even a first-class steak. There's a nice salad of baby greens and the vegetables are all fresh, but the sweets are disappointing. Georgetown has one of the country's oldest live theatres, a three-acre memorial garden and a golf-course.

Open daily 11 am to 8.30 pm. Licensed. Amex, Master Card, Visa. No smoking. &

GLENVILLE, N.S. (MAP 157)
GLENORA DISTILLERY ☆
Highway 19 $145 ($350)
Cape Breton
(800) 839-0491

The dining-room is right next door to the distillery.
There's a ceilidh every evening and that's the main reason
for stopping here—that and the single-malt whisky.
(There are several vintages, the best of which is aged for
seventeen years.) There's also a big menu that offers such
things as scallops with (too little) whisky, lobster salad
with grapefruit (an interesting idea), pork tenderloin,
breast of chicken and rack of lamb with dark gravy. The
cooking is no longer what it used to be, but the ceilidhs
are and so are the bread pudding and the sticky-toffee
pudding. The wines are almost all from Jost. There are
also one or two from Gaspereau and they're the things to
ask for.
*Open daily noon to 3 pm (in the pub), 5 pm to 9 pm from mid-
May until mid-October. Licensed. Amex, Master Card, Visa.
No smoking.* &

GODERICH, Ontario **MAP 78**
THYME ON 21 ☆
80 Hamilton Street **$115**
(519) 524-4171

Peter and Catherine King and their chef, Terry Kennedy,
have stuck together for years, ever since this old Victorian
house was turned into a restaurant. Kennedy comes from
Toronto, but he has cultivated relationships with most
local suppliers and he has the priceless gift of cooking the
simplest dish as if it were foie gras. His grilled provimi
liver is the sort of dish that'll melt your heart. You can
order fresh pickerel and know that it'll be correctly
cooked. The pork tenderloin comes from Metzger and is
beautifully served in an orange sauce with cranberries.
The beef comes from Huron County and is always
cooked *à point*. If you start with panko-crusted crab-

cakes, you can if you like go on to fresh Atlantic salmon with lemon-dill butter. But you won't see Kennedy at his best unless you order his vegetable soufflé with goat-cheese and sundried tomatoes. It's surely a mistake, however, to offer (for a price) to add three garlic shrimps or a four-ounce lobster tail to your dish—any dish. How absurd!

Open Tuesday 5 pm to 8 pm, Wednesday to Sunday 11.30 am to 2 pm, 5 pm to 8 pm (later on weekends) from early May until late September, Tuesday to Friday 11.30 am to 2 pm, 5 pm to 8 pm, Saturday 5 pm to 8 pm, Sunday 11.30 am to 2 pm, 5 pm to 8 pm from early October until late April. Closed on Monday. Licensed. All cards. No smoking.

GOLDEN, B.C. MAP 79
THE CEDAR HOUSE
735 Hefti Road **$175**
(250) 290-0001

Darrin de Rosa and Tracy Amies have found it easier to market their chalets than their restaurant. Their predecessors began with the idea of offering nothing but local organic produce, but the chef announced that he couldn't afford such luxuries. The kitchen may cut corners to save money, but visitors still like the place and speak highly of the food. The salmon may be farmed, but the beef is triple-A from Alberta. They still have a big vegetable garden and they make full use of it. In the winter they do great things with root vegetables, and fresh bison is always on the menu, winter and summer. As for the wine-list, it may be small, but there are three Burrowing Owl wines on the list, one a pinot gris, one a syrah and one a cabernet sauvignon. Who else can match that? The Cedar House has a magnificent setting overlooking the Rocky Mountains. It's open Tuesday to Sunday 5 pm to 10 pm from 1 June until 30 September and from 1 December until 15 April. Closed on Monday. Licensed. Amex, Master Card, Visa. No smoking. &

We accept no advertisements. We accept no payment for listings. We depend entirely on you. Recommend the book to your friends.

GOLDEN MAP 79
ELEVEN 22 ☆
1122 10 Avenue S **$110**
(250) 344-2443

There are several good restaurants in Golden, but Konan Mars' little cottage charms everyone, young and old alike. The service is friendly and warm and so is the restaurant itself. The menu changes daily, but there's always a house cannelloni, made on the premises with local ingredients. There's always some fish and a Black Angus New York steak, perhaps with paprika butter or barbecue sauce laced with whisky. The kitchen makes all its own pasta. If you don't like the soup of the day, ask for the edamame with coarse salt or the roasted root-vegetable salad. The steak that follows will be unusually tender, the nasi goreng a winning version of a familiar dish. People seem to like all the sweets, especially the chocolate mousse-cake. The price of the three-course set dinner is very low. The wines are even cheaper and there are some very good buys on the wine-list. In summer you can sit outside, and many do.

Open daily 5 pm to 10 pm from mid-May until mid-October and from mid-November until mid-April. Licensed. Master Card, Visa. No smoking. ✿

GRAND FALLS, Newfoundland **MAP 80**
MOUNT PEYTON HOTEL
Trans Canada Highway **$85**
(709) 489-2251

Everyone knows about the steak house at the Mount Peyton, which is built over an abandoned swimming-pool. But the Mount Peyton also has quite a good all-purpose dining-room, which is open daily from 5 o'clock to 8.30. The steaks are all the well-hung Alberta product and they're all properly cooked. But the price of Alberta beef is rising and next year they may have to compromise on quality. Fresh cod is still available, as well as local greens and a number of wild berries. (Bake-apples are hard to get, but partridge-berries and wild blueberries are still plentiful.)

The steak house is open Monday to Saturday 5 pm to 10 pm, has a licence and takes all cards. No smoking. &

GRAND MANAN, N.B.   MAP 81
THE INN AT WHALE COVE   ☆☆
North Head $130 ($275)
(506) 662-3181

Last year they built a fast new car-ferry to Grand Manan that provided six round trips a day. But it keeps having mechanical problems and once had to return to dry dock. Inevitably, the Inn at Whale Cove had a disappointing season, though business got better late in the summer, partly because Laura Buckley's cooking has never been better. Visitors have been coming to this cluster of old buildings for more than a century. The main house was built in 1816, and Willa Cather once owned one of the cottages. The interior has recently been renovated and filled with old Shaker furniture. In the kitchen, Laura has been forced to improvise more and more as the groundfish that used to be the backbone of her cooking is gradually disappearing. There's a salmon-processing plant on the Island now, which means that salmon almost always appears on the menu, often in phyllo. There's plenty of lobster and sometimes there's pickerel as well. Scallops are getting scarce, but there's still local lamb, beef and pork, usually served with either rhubarb or sour cherries. Last year raspberries were hard to find, but blueberries and strawberries were plentiful, as, in the fall, were apples. The province has closed the liquor store on the Island, which makes it difficult for Laura to keep even a few wines in stock.

Open daily 6 pm to 8 pm from late June until mid-October. Licensed. Master Card, Visa. No smoking. Book ahead.

GRAND MANAN
See also CAMPOBELLO ISLAND.

If you use an out-of-date edition and find it inaccurate, don't blame us. Buy a new edition.

GRAND PRE, N.S.   (MAP 229)
LE CAVEAU   ☆
Highway 1   **$150**
(902) 542-7177

Le Caveau is designed to show off the best Acadie wines,
including the award-winning Tidal Bay. They also have
a longish list of imported wines, many of them from Australia. But, unless you want to drink Tidal Bay, it's best
to ask for a bottle of Vero from Benjamin Bridge. Nova
7 is a sparkling wine that sells for the same price, but most
drinkers will feel safer with the Vero. The brilliant tim-
bale of Arctic char with avocado and sticky rice is (we
think) the best thing on the menu, though the tasting
pâtés run it a close second. The main courses are rather
less interesting. Sea bream is aptly served with wilted
greens and quince and there's lobster risotto for 30.00 and
Moroccan chicken for 26.00. Le Caveau is a little hard to
find; look for it opposite the Evangeline (see below), two
or three miles east of Wolfville.
Open Tuesday to Saturday 5 pm to 9 pm from early April until
mid-May, 11.30 am to 2 pm, 5 pm to 9 pm from mid-May until
late October, 5 pm to 9 pm from late October until the end of
December. Closed on Sunday and Monday. Licensed. Amex,
Master Card, Visa. No smoking.

GRAND PRE   (MAP 229)
EVANGELINE   ☞
Highway 1   **$30**
(888) 542-2703

Marjorie Stirling ran the Evangeline, then called the
Evangeline Snack Bar, for almost 50 years until her death
in 1996. She left the place to her nephew, Ralph Stirling,
who sold it to his daughter, Sheila Carey, four years later.
Since then, the place has been completely redecorated inside and out and the lawns filled with flowers. For a time,
the cooking ran downhill, and the seafood chowder still
has too much potato and too little haddock. But the
homemade pies are now as good as ever. The blueberry

is now made, as it always used to be, without gelatine. The apple and the peach are everything they ought to be and the sour cherry is a rare wonder. As for breakfast, that still means pancakes with maple syrup or eggs with crisp bacon.

Open Monday to Saturday 8 am to 7 pm, Sunday 9 am to 7 pm from early May until late October. No liquor. Amex, Master Card, Visa. No smoking. &

GRAVENHURST, Ontario   MAP 83
BLUE WILLOW
900 Bay Street   **$90**
(705) 687-2597

This is a really delightful restaurant, right on Muskoka Wharf. They call themselves a tea-shop and indeed dinner does seem rather beyond them. But lunch is a choice meal. There's always a quiche (often quiche Lorraine), served with a mixed or Caesar salad (ask for the Caesar). The quiche too often runs out. If it has, check the blackboard for the daily specials—mini-quiche with a soup and salad, tourtière, meat-loaf and beef stew. There are a number of unusual sandwiches, such as bacon-and-brie and brie-and-cranberry, as well as a very satisfactory grilled cheddar. There's excellent gingerbread to follow, as well as lemon cake, caramel shortbread and, in season, fresh blueberry pie. High tea is served every day from 2 to 5 pm.

Open Monday, Tuesday, Thursday and Sunday 11 am to 5 pm, Wednesday, Friday and Saturday 11 am to 8 pm from 1 July until 31 August, Tuesday, Thursday and Sunday 11 am to 5 pm, Wednesday, Friday and Saturday 11 am to 8 pm from 1 September until 30 June. Closed on Monday in winter. Licensed. Amex, Master Card, Visa. No smoking. &

This is a guide to Canadian restaurants from coast to coast—the first ever published and the only one of its kind on the market today. We accept no advertisements. Nobody can buy his way into this guide and nobody can buy his way out.

GRAVENHURST
TABOO
Muskoka Beach Road
(705) 687-2233

MAP 83
☆☆
$345

The Culinary Theatre, as the top restaurant at Taboo is called, goes from strength to strength. In 2010, Ivan Loubier was the chef. In 2011, the chefs who replaced Loubier performed just as well as Loubier, perhaps better. We can't tell you who will be in charge this summer, but if there are no important changes there'll be an eight-course dinner from Tuesday to Sunday. There's just one sitting (at 7 o'clock) and it costs about 100.00 a head, 150.00 a head if you order the wine service as well (which you should). The menu changes frequently, but the meal usually starts with something like raw char with watermelon, followed by sea scallops in a coulis of lettuce and passion fruit. Next will come tomato and asparagus in white foam, then a ceviche of sea-bass with tender, young bok choy, then a fruit sorbet in chopped ice, then a morsel of filet mignon with parsnip and ginger. A cheval steak with barley, chopped onions and beetroot will follow, after which the meal will end with a chocolate confection of one sort or another. The Culinary Theatre is not a comfortable place to have dinner and most meals lack any genuine continuity. But there's a lot of excitement here and a lot of remarkable cooking.
Open Tuesday to Sunday at 7 pm by appointment only. Closed on Monday. Licensed. Amex, Master Card, Visa. No smoking. You must book ahead.

GRAVENHURST
See also BALA, BRACEBRIDGE, ROSSEAU.

GUELPH, Ontario
ARTISANALE CAFE
214 Woolwich Street
(519) 821-3359

MAP 84

$115

The Artisanale has recently moved to a new location in

downtown Guelph. Here they have a century-old stone building with white walls and linen table-cloths. The menu is quite small, but it changes with the seasons. Typically, they have a couple of appetizers and a couple of main courses. They also have a *prix-fixe* menu—four courses for the extraordinary price of 25.00. In January beef bourguignon comes, as it should, with carrots and basmati rice. Roasted chicken comes with root vegetables like turnips, carrots and sweet potatoes. There may also be rabbit on the menu and there's usually a steak. They have a big wine-list and a large number of wines from Niagara.

Open Tuesday to Saturday 11 am to 3 pm, 5 pm to 9 pm. Closed on Sunday and Monday. Licensed. Master Card, Visa. No smoking. Book ahead if you can. &

GUELPH
See also MORRISTON.

GUYSBOROUGH, N.S.   MAP 85
DESBARRES MANOR
90 Church Street   **$175 ($400)**
(902) 533-2099

Guysborough is in a patch of unspoilt country a few miles along Highway 16 from the Trans Canada. DesBarres is an old house that will remind you of Lunenburg, with its brightly painted houses and trim lawns. The DesBarres Manor was built in 1837 for W.F. DesBarres, who was a justice of the supreme court. It's been a restaurant for some years, serving a menu *surprise* by appointment only. There are two handsome bedrooms upstairs, and it's a good idea to ask for one when you book a table because Antigonish is 50 miles away by Highway 16 and 104. It isn't easy to say what the cooking will be like this summer and further reports are needed.

Open daily 6 pm to 7 pm by appointment only. Licensed. Master Card, Visa. No smoking. You must book ahead.

The village of Queen Charlotte is a mile or so east of the ferry terminal on Graham Island. There are two good places to eat in the village. One is the Purple Onion at 3207 Wharf Street (telephone (250) 559-4119). It's a straight-up deli serving soups, salads and sandwiches. Visitors ask the proprietor for the recipe for her corned-beef sandwich with avocado and brie, and she's actually won a prize for her carrot cake. Everything is made on the premises except the bread, which is supplied by a local baker. The other is Queen B's, which is at 3208 Wharf Street (telephone (250) 559-4463). It's a funky place with surprisingly good cooking. Long ago Bonnie turned over the reins to Dana, but they work together to show off Island produce like local vegetables and fish. They make a good prawn salad and cater to all sorts of special diets. The menu changes daily and in season they have blackberries, salmon-berries and huckleberries. The Purple Onion and Queen B's are both open from Monday to Saturday 9 am to 5 pm. Neither has a liquor licence. The Purple Onion takes Master Card and Visa; Queen B's takes all cards.

HAIDA GWAII   **MAP 86**
BRADY'S BISTRO
Sandspit Airport   **$45**
Moresby Island
(250) 637-2455

Some things you can count on, and one of these is Brady's. There's only one flight a day from Vancouver to Sandspit Airport, and the plane spends only about five minutes on the ground before taking off again for Vancouver. So Brady's has to depend on local people if they want to sell more than a quick cup or two of coffee. In fact, they sell a lot of sandwiches to people who have come to stay and want some lunch. There's always a pot of soup on a back burner, as well as a hot special like lasagne. Sometimes there's a fish chowder, made with fresh-caught fish, and if that's on offer be quick to ask for it. The kitchen also does a lot of baking—they make their own bread and all their own cinnamon buns, muffins and brownies. Their coffee is excellent.

Open Monday to Friday 11 am to 3 pm, Saturday and Sunday 7 am to 3 pm. No liquor. Master Card, Visa. No smoking. &

HAIDA GWAII   MAP 86
TROUT HOUSE
Tow Hill Road   **$65**
Masset
Graham Island
(250) 626-9330

Haida Gwaii is different from the rest of Canada. Hours are erratic. Credit cards are erratic. There are no addresses. Chefs come and go. But this year Trout House was sold to Mike Picher and Kaylene MacGregor. Picher is a certified chef. He and his partner plan to run a real, well-appointed restaurant here. Picher teaches from Monday to Friday, however, and so for the present their restaurant will be open only on Friday from 5 to 9 and on Saturday and Sunday for brunch from 10 to 2. Next summer they expect to be open all day from Wednesday to Sunday and have a full liquor licence as well. Meanwhile, brunch means eggs benedict, a number of omelettes and crêpes, corned beef hash and homemade chowders. For sweet there's Picher's specialty, chocolate mousse. Dinner on Friday might bring something like breast of chicken stuffed with cranberries and maybe lamb or duck or ostrich. Fresh fish is, however, less plentiful than you'd expect. North Beach is about a mile east of the Masset Causeway at the north end of the island. If you turn right there you'll come to Trout House. This ain't New York City.

HALIFAX, N.S.   MAP 87
BISTRO LE COQ   ☆
1584 Argyle Street   **$150**
(902) 407-4564

This is a new restaurant and it appears to be a winner. A lot of money has been spent on the interior, which has been made to look like an authentic Parisian bistro. (You're even greeted at the door in French.) The chef is Ashley Davis, who came here from Onyx. They have one big menu listing all the classic French bistro dishes. Disappointments are rare. The steak tartar, however, comes with a poached egg on top instead of a raw egg-yolk. The fries, which are cooked in duck fat, are soggy. But on the whole, the cooking is pretty reliable. Try the charcuterie, the mussels in white wine, the duck prosciutto, the Ahi tuna or even the steak. Meals certainly end well, with a chocolate soufflé in grand marnier.

Open Monday to Thursday noon to 10 pm, Friday noon to 1 am, Saturday 11.30 am to 1 am, Sunday 11.30 am to 10 pm. Licensed. All cards. No smoking. Book ahead if you can. &

HALIFAX   MAP 87
CHABAA THAI
1546 Queen Street   **$85**
(902) 406-3008

Win opened ChaBaa in 2009 and before long it was known as the best Thai restaurant in Halifax. If you like curry, this is the place for you. They offer red and green curries, masaman curry and duck curry. Our favourites are the green curry with eggplant, bamboo-shoots and red chillies and the masaman curry, which has sweet potatoes, onions and peanut sauce with coconut milk. But you won't go wrong with any of their curries. The fresh spring-roll (bean-sprouts with cucumber, carrots, coriander and basil) is lovely, but don't be tempted by the fried spring-rolls, which are not. Prices are low, but the service is poor, at its worst very poor. ChaBaa has a second location. It's in Dartmouth at 100 Isley Avenue (same telephone).

Open Monday to Friday 11.30 am to 2.30 pm, 5 pm to 10 pm, Saturday and Sunday 11.30 am to 3 pm, 5 pm to 10 pm. Licensed. Master Card, Visa. No smoking.

☞ This symbol means that the restaurant is rated a good buy. This & means that there is wheelchair access to both the tables and the washrooms. *Smoking only* means that the restaurant has no area for non-smokers.

105

CHEELIN   ☆
Brewery Market   **$95**
1496 Lower Water Street
(902) 422-2252

Cheelin is by far the best Chinese restaurant in Halifax;
in fact, in our opinion it's as good as any in New York.
Fanny Chen is back in the kitchen, her grip as firm as
ever. She's a master of seafood soup and tofu-and-garlic
sprouts with onions. She has two new dishes this year.
One is the twice-cooked pork (pork belly, green cap-
sicum, sweet tofu and chilli beans). The other is the spicy
chicken (breast of chicken, egg-yolk, garlic and hot chilli
peppers). Fanny will make almost anything to meet di-
etary requirements, and make it better than anyone
else—except maybe Jim Hanusiak over at Epicurious
Morsels.
Open Monday 11.30 am to 2.30 pm, Tuesday to Saturday
11.30 am to 2.30 pm, 5.30 pm to 10 pm, Sunday 5.30 pm to
10 pm. Licensed. All cards. No smoking. ♿

HALIFAX   **MAP 87**
CHEESE CURDS GOURMET BURGERS   ☞
380 Pleasant Street   **$25**
Dartmouth
(902) 444-3446

This place is located in a small strip mall a couple of
blocks from the Woodside ferry terminal. Bill Pratt is a
retired Navy chef. He opened Cheese Curds early in
2012 and it was an immediate success. The concept is
simple. You order a burger and then choose as many toppings from the list of 50 or more that are on offer. These
include sliced tomatoes, pickles, red onions, guacamole,
cilantro, banana peppers and lemon hummus. There are
long lineups at the door and Pratt plans to open a second
location in the Burnside Industrial Park before the end
of 2013.
Open Monday to Saturday 11 am to 10 pm, Sunday 11 am to

9 pm. No liquor. All cards. No smoking. No reservations. ♿

HALIFAX
MAP 87

CHIVES
★★

1537 Barrington Street
$150

(902) 420-9626

Craig Flinn continues to lead the eat-local movement in Halifax—Flinn along with Dennis Johnston of Fid. His menu is constantly changing, though several dishes carry forward from one season to the next. Dinner starts quite brilliantly with a double-baked goat-cheese soufflé, served with pickled beets, spiced walnuts, apple and buttermilk. Instead of the too-familiar smoked salmon, they offer salmon cured with spiced molasses and served with cucumber, red onions and a free-range hard-boiled egg. In season there's lobster gnocchi, which is an incredible dish. Of the main courses, the braised lamb shanks are as good as any in town, as are the sesame-crusted tuna and the sea trout with a potato cake, wilted greens and pickled beets. Finish up with the sugar-moon crème brûlée, which comes with locally-produced maple syrup.
Open daily 5.30 pm to 9.30 pm. Licensed. All cards. No smoking.

HALIFAX
MAP 87

COASTAL CAFE
☜

2731 Robie Street
$80

(902) 405-4022

Coastal Café costs 35.00 for breakfast, plus tip and tax, but everyone agrees that the cooking is good, some even say good enough to be worth the price. Mark Griffin opened the place in 2007 and he's still on the job. Breakfast, if you can afford it, means scrambled eggs with crushed tortillas, mole crema and salsa verde or perhaps fried eggs with maple sausages and butternut jam. Lunch brings duck-and-lamb Sloppy Joe and a shrimp-and-crab po'boy with a cajun-style lobster salad. The coffee is made with fair-trade organic beans supplied by the

Laughing Whale Coffee Roasters in Lunenburg.
Open Monday to Saturday 8 am to 3 pm, Sunday 10 am to 3 pm (brunch). No liquor. All cards. No smoking.

HALIFAX   MAP 87
ELEMENTS ON HOLLIS
Westin Hotel   **$110**
1181 Hollis Street
(902) 496-7960

The new chef at Elements, a man named Raj Gupta, has created quite a stir in recent months. The Farmers' Market is located right next door and Gupta gets most of his supplies from there. Two of his best dishes are currently his salt-cod cake and his brioche in a can (a take on a traditional Acadian dish). One visitor wrote of these to say that they were the best he'd ever eaten. All the seafood is very fresh and well prepared—you can't go wrong with anything. As for the wines, they're all sold at cost plus 5.00 a bottle, so most of us can afford everything on the list.
Open Monday to Friday 11.30 am to 2 pm, 5.30 pm to 10 pm, Saturday 5.30 pm to 10 pm, Sunday 11.30 am to 2 pm (brunch). Licensed. All cards. No smoking. ⅖

HALIFAX   MAP 87
EPICURIOUS MORSELS   ☆
5529 Young Street   **$110**
(902) 455-0955

Jim Hanusiak is shy and self-effacing. His restaurant has an out-of-the-way location. These factors make it easy to overlook him. That would be a mistake, because Epicurious Morsels is one of the best restaurants in town. Hanusiak is best known for his smoked salmon and his gravlax. He does all his own smoking and curing and his gravlax is as good as any we've had. There are always some new dishes on the menu. Recently there have been scallop-and-salmon cakes and a fine shrimp-and-avocado salad with mango, and there are always one or two new soups—curried parsnip or curried carrot, perhaps, with sweet-mango chutney. In the evening there's an excellent rack of lamb and roasted duck with honey and coriander. For brunch, keep an eye out for the French toast stuffed with banana and strawberries.

Open Tuesday to Friday 11.30 am to 3 pm, 5 pm to 8 pm, Saturday 10.30 am to 2.30 pm, 5 pm to 9 pm, Sunday 10.30 am to 2.30 pm, 5 pm to 8 pm. Closed on Monday. Licensed. All cards. No smoking. &

HALIFAX	**MAP 87**
FIASCO	☆☆
1463 Brenton Street	**$185**
(902) 429-3499	

Fiasco is probably the most underrated restaurant in Halifax. Michael Keyzlar, the chef and owner, lacks the ability to promote himself that people like Craig Flynn and Dennis Johnston have in spades, but he has the same passionate commitment to first-quality regional cooking. The menu changes frequently, depending on what the farmers' markets have to offer. So it's probably best to ask for the sampler menu, which will bring you flash-fried calamari with chilli and tomato, or spinach salad with smoked bacon and extra-virgin olive-oil. Or you can settle for tomato soup with cinnamon, a strange and exciting combination. Fiasco majors in meats and there aren't many fish courses on the menu, but the blackened halibut in red curry is a masterpiece. The wine-list is designed to flatter the food and it does just that.

Open Monday to Thursday 5 pm to 10 pm, Friday and Saturday 5 pm to 11 pm. Closed on Sunday. Licensed. All cards. No smoking. &

HALIFAX	**MAP 87**
FID	☆☆
1569 Dresden Row	**$130**
(902) 422-9162	

Dennis Johnston has always been a leader of the buy-local

movement in Halifax. People come here at lunchtime for the caramelized squash soup and a spicy beet salad. Steak frites come with the best fries in town, and the burgers put all others to shame. In the evening he puts on a remarkable hanger steak, which has been marinated for seven days. His pad Thai, that shop-worn dish, comes to the table tasting fresh and surprising, as if no-one had made it before—we don't know just how this is done. *Note:* as this edition went to press, we received reports that the restaurant might be planning to close. Call before you go.

Open Tuesday and Wednesday 11.30 am to 2 pm, 5 pm to 9 pm, Thursday and Friday 11.30 am to 2 pm, 5 pm to 9.30 pm, Saturday 11 am to 2 pm (brunch), 5 pm to 10 pm, Sunday 11 am to 2 pm (brunch), 5 pm to 9 pm. Closed on Monday. Licensed. All cards. No smoking. Book ahead. &

HALIFAX   **MAP 87**
DA MAURIZIO   ☆
Brewery Market   **$185**
1496 Lower Water Street
(902) 423-0859

Last year we talked about the service at Da Maurizio. This year we want to talk about the food. At its best, the cooking is brilliant. The squid, for instance, are spiked with garlic and tomatoes, and the result is amazing. There are other good things too, of course, like the zucchini stuffed with ricotta, lemon and basil, the carpaccio of lamb, the mussels sautéed with onions, garlic and white wine and, of course, the foie gras with honey, peaches and ginger. There's a nice scallop of veal to follow, as well as tenderloin of pork, pan-seared Atlantic halibut and, best of all, rack of lamb, tender and lean and naked on the plate. The sweets are indifferent, but the wine-list has improved. For the very rich there's now a sassicaia, a solaia and a tignanello, all of them well into three figures. For the rest of us, there's a very good chianti riserva from Grignano for 50.00.

Open Monday to Saturday 5.30 pm to 10 pm. Closed on Sunday. Licensed. All cards. No smoking. Book ahead if you can.
&

HALIFAX   MAP 87
MODA   ☆
1518 Dresden Row   **$170**
(902) 405-3480

Matthew Pridham is in charge here and he says his plan is to use local suppliers to make global cuisine. We think this means that he aims to use local produce to prepare dishes from all over, but we can't be sure. If you come here, it's probably a good idea to order the four-course tasting menu for 60.00. If, however, you prefer to order à la carte, there's usually a variety of local seafood (lobster, scallops and salmon), snails from France, risottos and pastas from Italy and curries from India. The kitchen does a surprisingly good job with this rather implausible menu. Their fishcakes and their beef tenderloin are equally accomplished. Lunch, of course, is a different story. The noon-hour menu features burgers and risottos (mushrooms stuffed with asiago cheese). Diners tell us that they can't recommend Moda highly enough.
Open Monday to Friday 11.30 am to 2.30 pm, 5 pm to 10 pm (later on Friday), Saturday 5 pm to 11 pm. Closed on Sunday. Licensed. All cards. No smoking.

HALIFAX   MAP 87
MORRIS EAST   ☆
5212 Morris Street   **$80**
(902) 444-7663

Jennie Dobbs is still making her wonderful wood-fired pizzas. Her oven was made in Naples and is fueled by applewood from the Annapolis Valley. The best of the pizzas, we think, are the lamb with apricots and the salmon with peaches. You can also have a wood-fired sandwich or even a charcuterie board. Korean tacos come with crisp pork belly, pickled garlic and kimchee. If you bring your own bottle the corkage is only 10.00.

Open Tuesday to Friday 11.30 am to 2.30 pm, 5 pm to 10 pm, Saturday 10 am to 2.30 pm (brunch), 5 pm to 9 pm, Sunday 10 am to 2.30 pm (brunch). Closed on Monday. Licensed. All cards. No smoking. No reservations. &

HALIFAX   **MAP 87**
STORIES   ☆☆
Halliburton Inn   **$150**
5184 Morris Street
(902) 444-4400

Stories is small, elegant and very well served. Meals begin with beautiful scallops *en papillote* with sesame and ginger, carpaccio of elk with fleur de sel, a sauté of queen crab-cakes and a torchon of foie gras. Next come salmon from the Faroe Islands—when were you last offered salmon from the Faroe Islands?—tenderloin of bison (so much better than beef), exquisite breast of duck and line-caught striped bass. Best of the sweets is the panna cotta, a lovely composition (as they put it) of drunk and sober berries. The wine-list isn't large, but it offers one or two wines from the Okanagan that are seldom seen in the East. At the moment, there's no better restaurant in Halifax.

Open Monday to Friday 5.30 pm to 9 pm, Saturday and Sunday 5.30 pm to 10 pm. Licensed. Amex, Master Card, Visa. No smoking. Book ahead if you can.

HALIFAX   **MAP 87**
TAREK'S   ☞
3045 Robie Street   **$75**
(902) 454-8723

A local newspaper says that Tarek has the best Middle Eastern cooking in Halifax. We agree. It's hard to believe that healthy food can taste this good. The prices have risen a little over the years, but Tarek's is still a great bargain. It's in an out-of-the-way location in the North End and they take no reservations—everyone just lines up at the door. Tarek himself is a Syrian who came to Canada as a sailor when he was nineteen years old. He learned to cook in various hotel kitchens in Vancouver and Toronto before settling in Halifax, where he opened Tarek's in 2000. He's succeeded because he always uses the best of fresh local produce. This is a great place for vegetarians. Tarek's falafel is usually thought to be the best in the city. His squid are all marinated and barbecued, never deep fried. He cooks chicken Mediterranean-style or with ochre, tomato sauce and coriander, and he has some fine Middle Eastern salads. His juice-bar serves a variety of freshly-squeezed juices, among them grapefruit, orange, tomato, apple and carrot.

Open Monday to Saturday 11.30 am to 7.30 pm. Closed on Sunday. No liquor, no cards. No smoking. No reservations. &

HALIFAX
See also CHESTER, TANTALLON.

HAMILTON, Ontario   MAP 88
LA CANTINA
60 Walnut Street S $125/$75
(905) 521-8989

The cooking at Vicolo 54, the formal dining-room at La Cantina, has improved this year. The best dish on the menu is, however, still the risotto of porcini and crimini mushrooms. This is a rich but wonderful dish and it's full of flavour. They also have an excellent chicken saltimbocca stuffed with goat-cheese and spinach, as well as a couple of other memorable dishes. One is the grilled French-cut veal chop with caramelized onions, the other the ostrich drizzled with raspberry vincotto. Everybody likes the focaccia and with good reason. La Spiga has a wood-burning pizza oven, but there have been changes in personnel lately that make the pizzas less consistent than they used to be. They still offer nineteen varieties, some with too much oil, some with too little. The margherita pizza, however, is always good, and that's the thing to order. There's a well stocked wine-cellar and

several wines by the glass.
Open Tuesday to Thursday 11.30 am to 2.30 pm, 4 pm to 10 pm, Friday 11.30 am to 2.30 pm, 4 pm to 11 pm, Saturday 4 pm to 11 pm. Closed on Sunday and Monday. Licensed. Amex, Master Card, Visa. No smoking.

HAMILTON   MAP 88
EARTH-TO-TABLE BREAD BAR   🍴
258 Locke Street   **$85**
(905) 522-522-2999

This is a fairly new restaurant that opened in the spring of 2011 and already has attracted a loyal following, mainly because of the lively cooking and the reasonable prices. It's an artisanal bakery by day and a pizzeria by night. The best of the pizzas is the Popeye, which is made with spinach, ricotta cheese and a drizzle of lemon. As well as the pizzas (there are ten of them), there's also spaghetti bolognese and a beef burger, served with brie and pickled onions. They have a fine strawberry short-cake to finish with.
Open Monday to Friday 11.30 am to 4.30 pm, 5 pm to 10 pm, Saturday and Sunday 8 am to 11.30 am (breakfast). Licensed. Master Card, Visa. No smoking. &

HAMILTON   MAP 88
THE HARBOUR DINER   🍴
486 James Street N   **$90**
(905) 523-7373

The Harbour Diner was so successful that Chris Preston, the chef-owner, decided to open a second restaurant, on Locke Street, which has become a trendy location for restaurants. While Preston was busy with the new place (called Chuck's Burger Bar), the cooking and service at the Harbour Diner took a step or two backwards. The regular menu was still available, but it was the blackboard specials that made the restaurant what it was, and they were not. The cooking, however, has been improving in recent months, and they still serve good house-made food

114

at very favourable prices. Meals start with a great salmon-and-dill chowder. Then there are burgers, turkey wings and a pulled-pork poutine, followed by macaroni, shepherd's pie, and a strip-loin steak. A few blackboard specials—among them Thai chicken with basmati rice, baked fish and chips, mussels and squid—are back. Most of the specials change every day and you can check them out on line before you come in. Breakfast—served on weekdays until 11 am and on weekends until 2 pm—brings all kinds of eggs, waffles and pancakes.

Open Tuesday to Thursday 8 am to 8 pm, Friday and Saturday 8 am to 10 pm, Sunday 8 am to 3 pm. Closed on Monday. Licensed. Amex, Master Card, Visa. No smoking. &

HAMILTON   MAP 88
SEVEN WINDOWS
432 Aberdeen Avenue   **$165**
(905) 523-7707

Seven Windows occupies premises that once belonged to the Toronto Dominion Bank. The bank vault is now a private dining-room; a patio has just been added, but there's still no outside sign. The interior, however, is very well appointed and the cooking, though cautious, is accomplished. Meals start well with lobster bisque, chicken-liver pâté with port or a roasted-beet salad, then go on to peppercorn steak or fillet of beef with polenta and wild mushrooms. The kitchen likes red meat, but they also offer roasted breast of duck with smoked yam and port and roasted breast of chicken with glazed apples and calvados. The sweets, which are all made in-house, are the best to be had anywhere in Hamilton. The pavlova is probably the best choice, though they also have a fine flourless-chocolate cake. The service has improved, but nobody has seen anything of Calvin.

Open Wednesday and Thursday 11.30 am to 2.30 pm, 4.30 pm to 10 pm, Friday 11.30 am to 2.30 pm, 4.30 pm to 11.30 pm, Saturday 4.30 pm to 11.30 pm, Sunday 11 am to 3 pm (brunch), 5 pm to 10 pm. Closed on Monday and Tuesday. Licensed. Amex, Master Card, Visa. No smoking. &

HEDLEY, B.C. (*MAP 167*)
THE HITCHING POST ☞
916 Scott Avenue **$75**
(250) 292-8413

Hedley is pure Cartwright country. Ben, Adam, Hoss and Little Joe used to live around here. Hedley was once a mining town, but nowadays it's little more than a gas stop. The Hedley Esso diner was in this guide 40 years ago, but the Hedley Esso is seasonal and maybe you get there out of season and want a place to eat. If so, turn left at the Esso and then take the first left for two blocks, That'll bring you to the Hitching Post, an old frame building with a false front. Here they serve burgers, pasta and pizzas. They also have good Russian borscht, made with cabbage and served not with a package of Christie's crackers but with a big slab of focaccia. The Hitching Post has a licence and offers a dozen wines, mostly local and all well chosen. They're open all day every day but Tuesday, serve liquor and take Master Card and Visa. No smoking.

HOPE, B.C. **MAP 90**
OWL STREET CAFE ☞
19855 Owl Street **$55**
(604) 869-3181

The Owl Street Cafe has a big street number, but in fact it's no distance at all from Exit 168 on the Trans Canada Highway. Look for an A-frame built of pine that came from trees killed by pine beetles in Manning Park. (The tables inside are made of hunks of other dead pine trees.) Graeme and Sonia Blair are a friendly couple who cook everything from scratch, making full use of fresh local produce. There's an all-day breakfast for you to eat while you wait for your laundry to get washed in one of the coin-operated washing-machines. That means bacon and eggs, a good omelette or organic oatmeal porridge with fresh fruit on top. Lunch means one of several soups and

a string of sandwiches and chillies. There's a good chicken club, but the smoked-meat sandwich is even better.
Open Tuesday to Saturday 8.30 pm to 4 pm. Closed on Sunday and Monday. Licensed. Master Card, Visa. No smoking. &

ILE D'ORLEANS, Quebec   **(MAP 164)**
LE CANARD HUPPE   ☆
2198 chemin Royal   **$175**
(418) 828-2292

It's easy to forget that the Ile d'Orléans is only twenty minutes from the heart of Quebec City—it feels a world away. This is a small *hôtel champètre*, run by Philip Rae. He has a regional menu that every year makes more of duck and foie gras. On the table d'hôte, for instance, the meal starts with foie gras with apple or smoked breast of duck en croûte. Then come breast of duck with orange and curried chutney or confit of duck with tarragon in a strawberry vinaigrette. The wine-list is long and ambitious, but offers nothing from either the Niagara Region or Prince Edward County in Ontario.
Open daily 6 pm to 10 pm from late May until the middle of October. Licensed. Master Card, Visa. No smoking.

ILE D'ORLEANS   **(MAP 164)**
FERME AU GOUT D'AUTREFOIS   ☆☆
4311 chemin Royal   **$100**
Sainte-Famille
(418) 829-9888

Jacques Legros, who with his partner, Lise Marcotte, runs this place, was once a candidate for the Green Party, and he and Lise spent years developing their organic garden and poultry farm, where they produce foie gras without force-feeding their ducks and geese. They grow greens and vegetables of all sorts and maintain breeding quarters where ducks, geese and wild turkeys are raised in the open air on an all-natural diet. They cook well too and everything is full of flavour. Dinner costs 35.00 for three courses, 45.00 for four and 125.00 for twelve. All their

dinners feature rillettes of duck and goose, breast of pheasant, guinea-fowl and wild turkey.
Open daily by appointment only. Bring your own bottle. Master Card, Visa. No smoking. You must book ahead.

ILES DE LA MADELEINE, Quebec
See MAGDALEN ISLANDS.

INVERMERE, B.C.   MAP 92
SALIKEN
Eagle Ranch   **$175**
9581 Eagle Ranch Road
(250) 342-0562

This is a sumptuous place, with cathedral ceilings in raw wood and expansive views of the Eagle Ranch golf-course. The service is attentive and obliging, but the prices are high and the cooking, in spite of the presence of Marc LeBlanc, once of Panorama, is not as good as it ought to be. The menu is certainly impressive. It starts with albacore tuna and continues with rack of lamb, wild sockeye salmon and a smoked tofu fritter. There's an equally impressive list of wines, offering such good things as Liberty School, Burrowing Owl, Mouton-Rothschild and an Antinori tignanello. Saliken is hard to find. Look for the Tim Hortons and ask your way from there.
Open Wednesday to Saturday 11 am to 9 pm, Sunday 10 am to 1 pm (brunch), 1 pm to 9 pm. Closed on Monday and Tuesday. Licensed. All cards. No smoking. Free parking. Book ahead if you can.

INVERMERE
See also RADIUM HOT SPRINGS.

This is a guide to Canadian restaurants from coast to coast—the first ever published and the only one of its kind on the market today. Every restaurant in the guide has been personally tested. Our reporters are not allowed to identify themselves or to accept free meals.

IQALUIT, Nunavut   MAP 93
THE GALLERY
Frobisher Inn   **$190**
(867) 979-2222

The Gallery remains the best place to eat in Iqaluit, in spite of the departure of Rick Cole. It gets its name from the wall of prints in the dining-room, which come from the Pangnirtung Print Collection. Prices are pretty high, though that's probably true of almost everything in Iqaluit. But you can count on fresh beef and lamb and fresh greens and vegetables whatever the weather is like outside, because Iqaluit is on the great circle route between Europe and the West Coast. Arctic char, here called maple char, is one of their best dishes. There's always a lot of game. Elk osso buco is served with elderberry juice; musk-ox comes in from Cambridge Bay and appears with caribou, duck confit and game sausage in a dish they call Arctic cassoulet. If you can't afford 50.00 for your main course alone, ask for the pizza menu. There's a good wine-list and it's less expensive than you'd expect. The service is sometimes good, sometimes not. *Open daily 11 am to 2 pm, 5 pm to 9 pm. Licensed. All cards. No smoking. Book ahead.* &

IVY LEA, Ontario   (MAP 98)
THE IVY
61 Shipman's Lane   **$160**
Lansdowne
(613) 659-2486

The Ivy used to be known as the Captain's Table, and before that the Ivy Lea Inn, but patrons from those days will find the place much changed. The upstairs dining-room is large and airy and has a fine view of the river. Robert Gobbo is still the chef, but nowadays he's catering to a more sophisticated (and wealthier) clientele. Gobbo likes to call his menu locally-inspired world cuisine. Dinner might start with lobster salad or shrimp and grits with brandy and cream. The main dishes are more traditional

than they used to be, and you're now quite likely to be offered something like seared scallops with twice-baked potatoes, veal chops with chimichurri, pan-seared rainbow trout or oven-roasted breast of chicken. Sticky-toffee pudding is the best of the sweets. The wine-list is expensive and wines by the glass start at 9.00. Better to ask for a pint of draft. Downstairs there's an informal bistro offering pizzas and sandwiches. They have a good lobster roll, served with homemade Yukon Gold fries.
Open daily 5.30 pm to 9 pm from Victoria Day until Labour Day, Friday and Saturday 5.30 pm to 9 pm from Labour Day until Victoria Day. Closed Sunday to Thursday in winter. Licensed. All cards. No smoking.

JASPER, Alberta   **MAP 95**
KIMCHI
407 Patricia Street   **$65**
(780) 852-5022

You don't have to know a lot about Korean food to have fun at Kimchi. The owner, Monica An, and her staff have so much enthusiasm for their cooking that some of it's bound to rub off on the customers. Everybody will tell you to ask for the beef short-ribs on a sizzling plate. But Monica is also proud of her seafood, especially her spicy squid. Most people like her fried dumplings and her kimchi (Korean pickles). We ourselves admire the kalbi and the sweet-and-sour chicken. Several wines are on offer, but we prefer the Korean beer, which goes well with most of the food. The helpings are huge.
Open daily 11 am to 10 pm. Licensed. Master Card, Visa. No smoking. &

JASPER   **MAP 95**
TEKARRA   ☆☆
Highway 93 S   **$180**
(780) 852-4624

The Jasper Park Lodge occupied this valley for 60 years, so it's no wonder that one comes here with a strong sense of *déja vu*. In recent years chefs have come and gone, but Tekarra got to be known only after the arrival of David George Husereau. Husereau put in 25 years elsewhere before coming back to the home of his boyhood. He still travels the world, bringing home new recipes, usually from southeast Asia. But he's also set up a network of local ranchers and farmers to supply the restaurant. Though he's a highly creative chef, he never loses sight of the importance of regional ingredients. Most people begin with Alberta elk tourtière, a trio of wild salmon or bison, rubbed with juniper berries and served *sous-vide*. We particularly like the Hutterite chicken-noodle soup and the market salad with quinoa and goat-cheese. Vegetarians, if they eat fish, will probably go for the cold-poached Arctic char. Everyone finishes up with the walnut ice cream with maple whisky. Tekarra doesn't serve lunch, but their breakfast buffet is known all over town.

Open daily 8 am to 11 am, 5.30 pm to 10 pm from Victoria Day until Thanksgiving. Licensed. All cards. No smoking. &

KAMLOOPS, B.C.   **MAP 96**
ACCOLADES   ☆☆
Thompson Rivers University   **$135**
900 McGill Road
(250) 828-5354

Accolades offers a five-course tasting menu four nights a week for 45.00. This is a very good buy, considering that the cooking here is about the best in Kamloops. The first course is an Italian chutney seldom seen in Canada. It's made of candied fruit with hot mustard. Soup follows, or pork belly with fennel and apple chutney. Next come Pacific spot prawns topped with saffron foam, or perhaps Qualicum Bay scallops on a bed of lentils in a horseradish vinaigrette. The best main course is the venison from Sidney Island with port, blueberries and caraway. It's cooked *sous-vide* and then lightly pan-seared. Sometimes there's also farm-raised lamb from Diamond Creek and breast of duck from the Fraser Valley. The sweets are served from a cart and they're all made in house, even the lemon tart and the chocolate ganache.

Open Tuesday and Wednesday 6 pm to 7 30 pm, Thursday and Friday 11.30 am to 12.45 pm, 6 pm to 7.30 pm. Closed Saturday to Monday. Licensed. Master Card, Visa. No smoking. You must book ahead.

KAMLOOPS   MAP 96
BROWNSTONE   ☆☆
118 Victoria Street   **$110**
(250) 851-9939

Brownstone occupies an old Bank of Commerce building in downtown Kamloops. The place was built in 1904 and it provides a beautiful setting for Dale Decaire and his wife, Connie. Decaire began his career with Bruno Marti in Ladner. Marti's Belle Auberge has closed now, but his genius lives on here in Kamloops. At noon we recommend the smoked-trout salad, which features crisp green beans, watercress and a lemon-chive aioli, though Decaire will probably want you to try his poutine, made with duck-fat fries, cheese curds and chicken gravy. In the evening they offer an appetizer plate of tempura prawns, lemon-grass satays with peanut sauce and a *québécois* tourtière. To follow we suggest either the char-broiled pork or the sirloin of lamb with glazed cipollini onions in red wine. At dinner the poutine goes up-market with foie gras and white-truffle oil. Decaire also has a first-class treatment of mussels steamed in Crannog ale and served with chorizo. The best of his sweets is the mocha tart with fresh raspberries, or so we think.

Open Monday to Friday 11 am to 2 pm, 5 pm to 9 pm, Saturday and Sunday 5 pm to 9 pm. Licensed. Master Card, Visa. No smoking. Book ahead if you can. &

This is a guide to Canadian restaurants from coast to coast—the first ever published and the only one of its kind on the market today. We accept no advertisements. Nobody can buy his way into this guide and nobody can buy his way out.

KAMLOOPS   **MAP 96**

FELIX ON FOURTH   ☞

260 4 Avenue   **$85**

(250) 434-4766

Felix on Fourth has always been one of our favourite restaurants. The service may be shaky, but the cooking is remarkable and the prices are all very low. We like to start with either the Italian salad or the tuna tartar. The organic breast of chicken is probably the best of the main courses. It's topped with truffled pan jus and served with gnocchi, fennel and roasted carrots. The sablefish is another fine dish. It comes with oven-dried tomato tapenade, pesto risotto and sautéed beets. There's a lovely lemon tart to follow, as well as a honey-thyme crème brûlée. The wines are all priced to sell, which is a welcome change from most restaurants in B.C.

Open Monday to Saturday 5 pm to 9 pm. Closed on Sunday. Licensed. Master Card, Visa. No smoking. &

KELOWNA, B.C.   **MAP 97**

CARVERS

5315 Big White Road   **$140**

(250) 491-2009

Carvers has been operating in Kelowna for several years. Ruby and Allahdin Murji started it as a family restaurant, run by their two children and their parents. They knew enough even then to employ a trained chef. But recently their son, Sayyad, has taken over the kitchen himself. His standards are very high and everything is made in the kitchen, even the salad-dressing. The menu is strong on the classic Indian dishes, but the kitchen is equally at home with things like chicken pot-pie, home-smoked lamb burgers and English trifle. Canadian breakfasts too are a specialty. People write to us about the butter chicken and the vindaloos, but in fact all the curries are carefully spiced. The naan is a delight and the service is caring (especially when children are at the table). The restaurant has big windows from which you can see the hills on all sides. There's a large selection of Okanagan wines and Indian beers in the cellar, but we think you'll do just as well with the sweet lassi.

Open daily 7.30 am to 10 am, 11.30 am to 2.30 pm, 5 pm to 10 pm from 4 July until 30 September. Licensed. Amex, Master Card, Visa. No smoking. &

KELOWNA   **MAP 97**
OLD VINES   ☆☆
Quail's Gate Winery   **$160**
3303 Boucherie Road
(800) 420-9463

Old Vines has expansive views of the lake from the slopes of Boucherie Mountain. It's a stunning location and Roger Sleiman has designed a menu that makes the most of local farm produce, Quail's Gate wines and his own kitchen garden. The menu starts with a spot-prawn risotto, followed by a salad of organic greens filled with walnuts, goat-cheese, raisins and caper-berries. To follow there's a great treatment of Quebec foie gras with warm quince cake, candied walnuts and wine-soaked apple. And though Kelowna is a long way from the sea, Sleiman does a fine job with salmon, sablefish, halibut and cod. There's an impressive wine-list and attentive service.

Open Monday to Saturday 11.30 am to 2.30 pm, 5 pm to 9 pm, Sunday 10.30 am to 2.30 pm (brunch), 5 pm to 9 pm. Licensed. Amex, Master Card, Visa. No smoking. &

KELOWNA   **MAP 97**
RAUDZ   ☆
1560 Water Street   **$145**
(250) 868-8805

Rodney Butters came here from the Wickaninnish Inn in Tofino several years ago. His restaurant in Kelowna is less formal, of course, but it's warm and lively. The salt-spring mussels that come as an appetizer with chorizo and a local ale are, of course, lovely. After that, we suggest the oat-crusted Arctic char or the wild boar topped with a reduction of maple and stout. Others have recommended the steaks, which come with gnocchi in a peppery pesto. Butters is a very good baker and his focaccia is wonderful. So is his flourless-chocolate cake. The restaurant is known for its martinis, but the markups on wine are very steep. Have a martini.

Open daily 5 pm to 10 pm (later on weekends). Licensed. Amex, Master Card, Visa. No smoking. No reservations. &

KELOWNA   MAP 97
THE TERRACE   ☆☆
Mission Hill Winery   **$160**
1730 Mission Hill Road
(250) 768-6467

Matt Batey makes sure that the food here at the Terrace is every bit as good as the view. The ingredients are mostly local, though some come from as far away as Salt Spring Island or Vancouver Island. Visitors find themselves starting lunch with a tart of duck prosciutto or perhaps with a simple green salad made with heritage tomatoes and artisanal cheese. They may then move on to braised venison with figs or pan-seared sablefish. Or they may choose to sample dishes from Batey's *cuisine de terroir*. In the evening the meal starts with a torchon of foie gras with Martin's Lane pears, Sloping Hills pork belly or smoked Pacific tuna with preserved apple and a shiso lemon confit. The best of the main courses, we think, is the bison tenderloin with creamed cabbage and cranberry buckwheat. After that we usually ask for the glazed lemon tart.

Open daily 11 am to 3 pm, 5.30 pm to 8.45 pm from mid-May until mid-September. Licensed. Amex, Master Card, Visa. No smoking. &

🍽 This symbol means that the restaurant is rated a good buy. This & means that there is wheelchair access to both the tables and the washrooms. *Smoking only* means that the restaurant has no area for non-smokers.

THE WATERFRONT   ☆
1180 Sunset Drive $145
(250) 979-1222

The Waterfront in Kelowna is one of our favourite
restaurants. Small, chic and very well served, it has four
stainless-steel half-round tables facing an open kitchen.
There's a big wine-list and a number of good open wines,
among them the Noble Blend from Joie Farm and the
syrah from Church and State. The wonderful braised-
beef short-ribs are still off the menu, so ask instead for
the Quadra Island scallops or the milkfed-veal cheeks. It's
best to start with the masala squid and end with a cup or
two of the wonderful espresso.
Open daily 5 pm to 10 pm (later on weekends). Licensed. Amex,
Master Card, Visa. No smoking. Book ahead. ♿

KELOWNA
See also OKANAGAN CENTRE, OLIVER.

KINGSTON. Ontario   *MAP 98*

There are several restaurants in Kingston, in addition to those
listed in full below, that you should know about. Woodenheads
at 192 Ontario Street (telephone (613) 549-1812) is busy and
noisy, but it serves the best thin-crust pizzas in town. You have
the run of about three dozen different varieties, or you can make
up your own from a big list of ingredients. They also serve tapas
and paninis and such main dishes as breast of chicken and fried
Bay of Quinte perch. There's a big wine-list with more than
twenty wines by the glass and four draft beers. A couple of blocks
away at 369 King Street E (telephone (613) 767-2558) is the
Red House, which stands out among the city's pub-style restau-
rants for its dedication to doing things right. They start butchering
their own meat every morning at 7, and everything on the small
menu is made from scratch, whether it's polenta with gorgonzola,
short-ribs with gremolata or a cassoulet of duck with a garlic panko
crust. The most interesting dish is often the blackboard special,
which if you're lucky may be something like chicken with parme-

san-crusted potatoes in a vodka arrabbiata sauce topped with lemon-pepper crème fraîche and served on a bed of sautéed spinach. Windmills at 184 Princess Street (telephone (613) 544-3948) offers an eclectic menu that includes Thai and Cajun dishes as well as a number of thin-crust pizzas, burgers and stir-fries. Windmills is a good place for breakfast or a weekend brunch, when you can have an omelette with Monterey Jack cheese. At lunch there are salads and sandwiches; in the evening they add lamb osso buco with hoisin sauce and Louisiana gumbo with chorizo and shrimps. All the sweets are made in house and there's a wide array of cakes and cheesecakes. Woodenheads, the Red House and Windmills are open all day every day, have a licence and take all cards.

KINGSTON   MAP 98
AQUATERRA BY CLARK   ☆
Radisson Hotel   **$135**
1 Johnson Street
(613) 549-6243

Clark Day has been a major figure on the restaurant scene in Kingston for a long time. When he was retained to design a restaurant in the Radisson Hotel, he transformed both the space he was given and the menu. Most people thought he would eventually move on to other interests, but both he and his son have chosen to stay here on Johnson Street and AquaTerra is still about as good as it gets in Kingston. Day is interested in both fish and meat—hence the same of his restaurant. So you get to choose between terrine de foie gras and a fricassee of snails, between rack of lamb (or lamb shanks) and a seafood risotto. There's also a *prix-fixe* menu offered at the remarkable price of 30.00 a head. There are four appetizers and four main dishes—rabbit terrine, perhaps, and pork belly (or pork tenderloin), followed by a spicy fruit tart. Lunch is, of course, a simpler meal. There's a three-course *prix-fixe* at noon that costs just 17.00. Clark and his son are both passionate about wine and their wine-list, which is the best in Kingston, is well chosen and well-priced. Wines by the glass start at 3.35 for three ounces, bottles

at 28.00.
Open Monday to Saturday 11 am to 11 pm, Sunday 11 am to 10 pm. Licensed. All cards. No smoking. &

KINGSTON   MAP 98
CASA DOMENICO
35 Brock Street   **$150**
(613) 542-0870

If you want something more than a pizza, try the Casa Domenico. But don't come here looking for new ideas. The cuisine here is traditional Italian. You can begin with a salad, say or with seared scallops with sweet potato, pine-nuts, currants and arugula—or perhaps with shrimps with garlic and capers. The main courses are more conventional— steak, lamb chops or breast of chicken with sautéed spinach and caramelized potatoes and onions. Sweets are familiar too, but the coccinella (hazelnut brownie with caramel ice cream) is well worth the money. There's a useful list of Italian wines, most of them modestly priced. The service is warm and friendly.
Open Monday to Thursday 11 am to 10.30 pm, Friday 11.30 am to 11.30 pm, Saturday noon to 11.30 pm, Sunday noon to 10 pm. Licensed. All cards. No smoking.

KINGSTON   MAP 98
CHEZ PIGGY   ☆
68 (rear) Princess Street   **$135**
(613) 549-7673

Chez Piggy has been loved by Kingston people for nearly 40 years. It was renovated this year, but it still has the same owners and many of the same staff. The cooking is basically French with a noticeable Italian accent, as well as a few Asian words. Old favourites reappear year after year. We like to start our meal with a stilton pâté or perhaps with shrimps brought to the table in the pan with garlic and spices. Our favourite main dishes are the breast of chicken stuffed with truffles, the confit of duck with white beans and roasted vegetables and the lamb shank with orange gremolata. There's also a three-course table d'hôte for only 35.00. They have some good beers on tap and a well-chosen list of wines.

Open Monday to Saturday 11.30 am to midnight, Sunday 10 am to midnight. Licensed. All cards. No smoking. &

KINGSTON   **MAP 98**
CHIEN NOIR
69 Brock Street   **$140**
(613) 549-5635

Chien Noir looks and feels like a Parisian bistro. In the evening you start with a small plate of fried smelts, perhaps, or smoked ribs of bison with green cabbage. Next comes coq au vin, mussels with fries and duck confit with lentils. Sweets are all made in-house, but they're not very exciting. Lunch offers all the same dishes, as well as omelettes and sandwiches. Most of the wines come from France, though there are a few from Prince Edward County as well. They also have ten beers on draft, two of them brewed in Quebec and sold only in this restaurant.

Open Monday to Friday 11.30 am to 2.30 pm, 5 pm to 11 pm, Saturday and Sunday 11 am to 2.30 pm (brunch), 5 pm to 11 pm. Licensed. All cards. No smoking. Book ahead if you can.

KINGSTON   **MAP 98**
THE CURRY ORIGINAL   ☜▯
253A Ontario Street   **$70**
(613) 531-9376

The Curry Original is still about the best Indian (or Bangladeshi) restaurant in Kingston, or so we think. The place was opened by Ali and Weais Afzal more than twenty years ago and they're still in charge of the front of the house. They have all the traditional dishes—curries, kormas, vindaloos, dhansaks, saags, bhoonas and tandooris. Everything is fresh and carefully prepared, but, sad to say, the menu almost never changes. It's best to start with an onion bhaji, a samosa or daal, then go on to tandoori chicken (cooked in a traditional clay oven), chicken tikka, a korma, a vindaloo or dhansak, a bhoona or a biryani. They also offer a number of special dishes like kashmiri chicken, with peanuts, sultanas, coconut and homemade yogurt. Then try the barfi, which is homemade cottage cheese with coconut and pistachio nuts. On weekdays they offer a string of lunch dishes, all priced at less than 10.00. The wine-list majors in wines from Prince Edward County and draft beers from India. *Open Tuesday to Saturday 11.30 am to 2 pm, 5 pm to 9.30 pm, Sunday 5 pm to 9.30 pm. Closed on Monday. Licensed. All cards. No smoking.* &

KINGSTON   MAP 98
PAN CHANCHO
44 Princess Street   **$95**
(613) 544-7790

Zal Yanovsky opened Pan Chancho to supply Chez Piggy (see above) with bread and pastries when there was nothing else of comparable quality in town. Nowadays it's really an upscale bakery and deli with a café at the rear. The café is open every day for breakfast and lunch, but not, except on special occasions, for dinner. Croissants and cakes, soups, charcuterie and cheeses are always available in the deli. In the café at breakfast there's a variety of dishes, some traditional, some not. We particularly like the sweet-potato hash, which comes with mushrooms, spinach and poached eggs. The lunch menu changes often, but there are always a couple of first-class soups, a lamb pita spiced with cumin, a venison burger with bacon, dried cherries, red cabbage and parsnip chips and a poutine with pork perky and crisp corn fritters. The meal ends with cheese or one of the sweets from the deli. Pan Chancho has a licence and maintains a useful wine-list and several draft beers.
Open daily 7 am to 4 pm. Licensed. All cards. No smoking. &

KINGSTON
See also IVY LEA.

KIPLING, Saskatchewan   **MAP 99**
PAPERCLIP COTTAGE
503 Main Street   **$40**
(306) 736-2182

Kyle MacDonald of Montreal traded one big red paperclip for this house and then turned it into a delicatessen
and bakery. All the meats are cooked on site, the cheesecakes are made from scratch and so are the cinnamon
buns. There are fresh-fruit pies and home-style sandwiches on home-baked bread. On Thursday and Friday
you can have supper between 5 o'clock and 7.30. You pay
only about 15.00 for a soup or a salad, roast beef and
Yorkshire pudding, roast pork, turkey or poached haddock, sweet and coffee. There's always a hot dish at noon
and on Sunday they do a real brunch. You'll find Kipling
about 90 minutes from Regina on Highway 48.
Open Monday to Wednesday 5.30 am to 4 pm, Thursday and
Friday 5.30 am to 4 pm, 5 pm to 7.30 pm, Sunday 9 am to 2
pm. Closed on Saturday. No liquor. Master Card, Visa. No
smoking.

KITCHENER, Ontario   **MAP 100**
VERSES   ☆☆☆
182 Victoria Street N   **$185**
(519) 744-0144

Verses opened about ten years ago, when the owners
bought an old church and began to serve upscale meals.
The restaurant was an instant success. Inside it's spectacular. The vaulted ceiling is at least 30 feet high, and most
of the original woodwork and lighting has been retained.
You can take a table on the raised platform where the
altar once stood. Or you can choose to sit in what used
to be the choir or in the nave. The menu covers everything from Peking duck to ostrich. The house soup is
made with wild mushrooms and it's excellent. Wagyu
beef is served tartar as an appetizer, but the restaurant is
most at home with its fish. The cooking is essentially
French, with Asian influences. Tile fish, for instance, is

presented with baby bok choy, cellophane noodles and oyster mushrooms in a citrus coulis. Seafood jambalaya is almost always on the menu, and it comes with generous servings of andouille sausage, mussels, shrimps and crab. All the sweets are made in the kitchen, but the best of the lot is the molten-lava cake, which oozes chocolate and butterscotch. The wines are mostly from the Niagara Region and the prices are all very fair.

Open Tuesday to Friday 11.30 am to 2.30 pm, 5 pm to 9.30 pm, Saturday 5 pm to 9.30 pm. Closed on Sunday and Monday. Licensed. All cards. No smoking. Free parking.

KITCHENER
See also WATERLOO.

LA HAVE, N.S. (MAP 108)
LA HAVE BAKERY
3421 Highway 331 **$25**
(902) 688-2908

The La Have Bakery exudes character and charm. It operates in a ship's outfitters building and they bake and sell the best oatcakes in the province, as well as traditional date squares, Nanaimo bars and Queen Elizabeth cakes. They also sell several kinds of bread, among them potato bread Irish-style and milk-and-honey bread. This year they have a new cappuccino machine that makes nothing but double shots of cappuccino at a time. At noon they serve paninis, pulled-pork sandwiches, falafel burgers, smoked-salmon bagels, lobster rolls and a variety of pizzas. They have a wonderful brunch on Sunday and during the off-season serve themed dinners every-second Thursday evening.

Open daily 8.30 am to 6.30 pm (shorter hours in winter). No liquor. Master Card, Visa. No smoking.

Where an entry is printed in italics this indicates that the restaurant has been listed only because it serves the best food in its area or because it hasn't yet been adequately tested.

LAKE LOUISE, Alberta **MAP 102**
THE POST HOTEL ✯✯✯
200 Pipestone Drive **$300 ($650)**
(800) 661-1586

If you come here for the view of Lake Louise, take a
room at the Fairmont, but make sure to eat at the Post on
Pipestone Drive. The Post was one of the first Relais &
Chateaux in Canada and it's one of the very few remain-
ing mountain lodges built of the original rough-hewn
logs, complete with a wood-burning fireplace in every
room. The wine-cellar has 25,000 bottles, and the Post
Hotel is the winner of one of the *Wine Spectator's* grand
awards, only four of which have ever been won in
Canada. George and André Schwartz bought the place in
1978, when it was little more than a ruin. Over the years
the dining-room has been restored, the wine-cellar re-
stocked and a fabulous new menu created. There's now a
six-course table d'hôte for 105.00 a head, but if you prefer you can order from the à la carte, where they have
such delicacies as carpaccio of caribou with lime mayonnaise, duck consommé with foie gras dumplings, grilled
fillet of wild red spring salmon on a bed of asparagus and
morels and a fillet of ranch-fed bison with herb butter.
They have the largest collection of burgundies in the
country and a selection of old barolos and super-Tuscans
that beggars belief.
*Open daily 11.30 am to 2 pm, 5 pm to 9.30 pm. Licensed. All
cards. No smoking. Book ahead.* ♿

LAKE LOUISE
See also FIELD.

LANIGAN, Saskatchewan **MAP 103**
JAN'S STEAK HOUSE ☞🖐
17 Hoover Street **$75**
(306) 365-4366

Jan still misses her career on Broadway, but she came back
to Lanigan because she missed her family more. Her fa-

ther died recently at 101. Her mother is 92 and worked in the restaurant well into her eighties. Jan still does all the baking herself, and makes 60 different kinds of highball. Her salad bar is as good as any on the Prairies. Her beef is all custom cut. She sells a lot of Black Forest ham with black currants and a lot of roast pork with orange sauce. In October she celebrates Oktoberfest with a set dinner of smoked chops with bratwurst, warm German-style potato salad, red cabbage with apples, pumpernickel bread and chocolate cake. St. Patrick's Day in March brings Irish soda bread and corned beef with cabbage. Since a flood seeped into her basement she's no longer putting on Scandinavian weekends, though if you can get together a party of six she'll make you a Scandinavian dinner. But the fact is, she doesn't charge enough for anything on her menu to make a profit.

Open daily 5 pm to 10.30 pm. Licensed. Master Card, Visa. No smoking. &

LETHBRIDGE, Alberta   **MAP 104**
MIRO'S   ☆
212 5 Street S   **$110**
(403) 394-1961

One correspondent wrote to tell us that he was so impressed by his lunch at Miro's that he brought his wife the next day for dinner. Miro Kyjak was one of the first to take a chance on Lethbridge's downtown district. He began by working in this beautiful old building with his son, thinking to repeat the pattern of his own life, where he worked with his father in their native Czechoslovakia. His son, however, had other ideas, so now Miro works alone. He makes everything from scratch, and that means the bread, the soups and the sweets. Everyone loves his pheasant ravioli. Apart from that, he has five or six entrées, among them beef bourguignon and lamb ragoût with homemade spaetzle. His wine-list is at its best with local and imported beers.

Open Tuesday to Friday 11 am to 2 pm, 5 pm to 10 pm, Saturday 5 pm to 10 pm. Closed on Sunday and Monday. Licensed.

All cards. No smoking. &

LETHBRIDGE   **MAP 104**
ROUND STREET CAFE   ☞
427 5 Street S   **$50**
(403) 381-8605

Everybody likes the Round Street Café. Bonny Green-
shields genuinely cares for people and often employs Special Needs personnel in her restaurant. Travellers come
away from the Café saying that they have never encoun-
tered such warmth and friendliness. Bonny taught for ten
years before realizing an old dream of owning her own
place. She and her husband bought the old Wallace Block
in 2004 and moved in upstairs. They make everything on
the premises, often to old family recipes, several of which
are pretty wild. They have some very good sandwiches,
all made on multi-grain bread. Bonny does a lot of baking
and if you think you're tired of carrot cake, just try hers.
Open Monday to Friday 7 am to 5 pm, Saturday 9 am to 5 pm.
Closed on Sunday. No liquor. Master Card, Visa. No smoking.
&

LONDON, Ontario   **MAP 105**
THE ONLY ON KING   ☆☆
172 King Street   **$150**
(519) 936-2064

The Only on King is now the only restaurant we recommend in London. Paul Harding is a wonderful chef, and
everything he cooks tastes as if it had been made half a
minute before. The restaurant is a stone's throw from the
Covent Garden Market and his four-course *prix-fixe* is
built around what they can supply. It may be sea-bass
with lemon and pistachio nuts; it may be pickerel or
pork. Harding is good with pork and serves it with
braised red cabbage, homemade spaetzle and grainy mustard. The soups and salads are all good, especially the
winter-vegetable with fine Tuscan olive-oil. All the bread
and all the sweets, including the chocolate cake, are made

on the premises. The wine-list may not be up to the cooking, but there's a useful selection of wines by the glass.

Open Tuesday to Saturday 5.30 pm to 10 pm, Sunday 11 am to 2 pm (brunch). Closed on Monday. Licensed. Master Card, Visa. No smoking.

LORNEVILLE, N.S   MAP 106
AMHERST SHORE COUNTRY INN   ☆
Highway 366   **$150 ($250)**
(800) 661-2724.

As soon as you reach the front door, you know what this place is all about. There are acres of vegetable gardens growing in the deep, rich, red soil that supply the kitchen. There are three or four luxurious new cottages where you can spend the night, as well as a spacious dining-room facing the sea. Dinners are cooked by Rob Laceby and are served every night of the week from early May until late October. You begin with a garden salad— lettuce, beans, zucchini, carrots, broccoli—and go on to salmon or beautifully tender pork tenderloin with potato cakes, turnip and whatever else is in season. Then comes, if you're lucky, a blueberry flan, made from wild local berries. The wine-list majors in such inexpensive wines as Masi valpolicella, Ruffino chianti and several vintages from Jost. But if you look carefully, there are other things as well. There's a cabernet sauvignon from Mission Hill for 54.00 and another from Joseph Phelps for 129.00. Best of all, there's an Eileen Hardy shiraz from the Clare Valley in Australia. Don't ask the price.

Open daily at 7.30 pm by appointment only from early May until late October, Friday and Saturday at 7.30 pm by appointment only from late October until early May. Closed Sunday to Thursday in winter. Licensed. Master Card, Visa. No smoking.
 ♿

The map number assigned to each city, town or village gives the location of the centre on one or more of the maps at the start of the book.

LOUGHEED, Alberta   MAP 107
HAUS FALKENSTEIN
Lougheed's Hotel   **$65**
4917 51 Avenue
(780) 386-2434

Lougheed is in the middle of nowhere, according to the owner of the Lougheed Hotel himself. It's about 50 miles east of Camrose on Highway 13, and some 250 people live there. The Haus Falkenstein carries more varieties of pan-fried schnitzel than anywhere else in Canada. There are at least 40 of them. Visitors report that the quality of the schnitzels is high and the service always obliging. The Haus Falkenstein is open Tuesday to Friday for lunch and dinner, Saturday for dinner only. They have a licence (and a beer garden) and take Master Card and Visa. No smoking.

LUNENBURG, N.S.   MAP 108
FLEUR DE SEL   ☆☆
53 Montague Street   **$200**
(902) 640-2121

Martin and Sylvie Ruiz Salvador run this place with quiet finesse and genuine flair. Their menu is unusual, majoring in such things as beef heart, pig's head, cherrystone clams and oysters from Eel Lake. Main courses start with beef tenderloin (from Prince Edward Island) and go on to poached lobster, albacore tuna, roast partridge and fried sweetbreads. You should always ask for the pig's head, which makes for brilliant eating. The sweetbreads are too rich for anyone over 30, but the roast partridge is a delight. As for the wine-list, who needs one when they can get a bottle of Benjamin Bridge for the asking? The sparkling wine is always sold out, so we usually ask for the white blend known as Vero. It's a wonderful wine and costs only 40.00 a bottle. The service is exquisite.

Open Thursday to Saturday 5 pm to 9 pm, Sunday 11 am to 2 pm (brunch), 5 pm to 9 pm from 1 April to 30 June, Tuesday to Saturday 5 pm to 9 pm, Sunday 11 am to 2 pm (brunch), 5 pm to 9 pm from 1 July until 31 October. Closed Monday to Wednes-

137

day in the spring, Monday in the fall. Licensed. Amex, Master Card, Visa. No smoking. Book ahead. ♿

LUNENBURG   **MAP 108**
MAGNOLIA'S   🖝
128 Montague Street   **$95**
(902) 634-3287

Magnolia's is a Lunenburg institution. It's been on this site for more than twenty years, and now has a patio at the back from which you can watch the boats in the harbour below. The menu never changes, except for the daily specials. There's always a seafood chowder, as well as peanut soup and French-onion soup. There's always haddock, pan-fried scallops and Alma's vegetarian stew. The meal always ends with key-lime pie. The wine-list is small, perhaps too small. The service is hurried, but friendly, even when the restaurant is packed.
Open Monday to Saturday 11.30 am to 9 pm from 1 April until 31 October. Closed on Sunday. Licensed. Amex, Master Card, Visa. No smoking. Book ahead if you can. ♿

LUNENBURG   **MAP 108**
SALT-SHAKER DELI
124 Montague Street   **$95**
(902) 640-3434

This popular deli has expanded its menu in the last few years and now offers an adventurous Sunday brunch (capicola and spinach Benedict), a wider variety of pizzas (spiced shrimps with basil pesto), more sandwiches and a number of specials (Korean barbecued burrito). They also serve Indian Point mussels with either garlic or sausage Portuguese-style. They have the nicest patio in town, so you can watch the shipping in the harbour while you eat. The service is friendly and knowledgeable and, best of all, they're open year-round.
Open daily 11 am to 9 pm (shorter hours in winter). Licensed. Amex, Master Card, Visa. No smoking. ♿

LUNENBURG
See also LA HAVE, MAHONE BAY, MARTIN'S BROOK.

MAGDALEN ISLANDS, Quebec   MAP 109

There are sixteen islands in the 60-mile arc of the Magdalens.
All but Entry Island are linked by sand dunes. Highway 169,
which is a little over 50 miles long, runs the whole length of the
archipelago. More than half of the total population live on Ile
Cap-aux-Meules. The next largest is the Ile Havre-Aubert,
which is at the southern end of the chain. Everywhere there's fine
hiking, swimming and sailboarding. The Madelon Bakery at
355 chemin Petitpas on Cap-aux-Meules (telephone (418)
986-3409) has a wealth of baked goods, cheeses and made-to-
order sandwiches, and it's a good place to go if you want a packed
lunch. The Islands are known for their soft raw-milk cheese,
which resembles reblochon and is produced by the indigenous breed
of cow, known as Canadienne. You can get it at the Fromagerie
Pied-de-Vent on Havre-aux-Maisons (telephone (418) 969-
9292). The ferry from Souris, P.E.I. takes five hours, but you
can also get here by plane. Few travellers come to the Magdalens,
which is a pity because there are so many pleasures to be had here,
including some very good cooking.

MAGDALEN ISLANDS   MAP 109
AU BOUT DU MONDE   ☆☆
951 route 199   **$150**
Ile Havre-Aubert
(418) 937-2000

Never judge a book by its cover. You might not guess
from the outside that this was an outstanding restaurant.
The chef, Luc Joyal, and his wife, Geneviève, change
their menu every day, making use of whatever is most
plentiful in the garden. Two sisters have been supplying
them with organic vegetables since the day they opened.
For a time they brought in milkfed veal from Montreal,
but now they offer a tartar of young local beef instead.
Cod used to be the mainstay of the menu, but it's pretty
hard to get nowadays. House-smoked salmon and local

crab appear from time to time as appetizers, as does the lemon tart on the sweet list. The highlight of the menu last year, however, was the fresh seal. Luc cooks it very rare and serves it with a sweet sauce. Geneviève buys a lot of Canadian wines, especially the current wines from Mission Hill, which are never off the list. Au Bout du Monde is a small restaurant, but there are expansive seaviews from every window.

Open Tuesday to Sunday 5 pm to 10 pm from 1 June until 30 September. Closed on Monday. Licensed. Master Card, Visa. No smoking.

MAGDALEN ISLANDS   MAP 109
CAFE DE LA GRAVE
Ile Havre-Aubert   **$85**
(418) 937-5765

On the west side of Ile Havre-Aubert there's a village called La Grave, where a number of old fishing boats have been turned into boutiques and restaurants. One of these is the Café de la Grave, which is right next to the theatre. For years we've recommended it for its sandwiches and its wonderful custard cakes. But the fact is, the place does more good things than that. For one thing, it's filled with music all day long, because Sonia Painchaud, the daughter of the house, is a talented musician. Sometimes she plays the accordion alone; sometimes she plays old folk tunes with a three-piece band. The music is magic—nobody criticizes anything they cook, not the bouillabaisse or the boar stew or the mussels or the fries with curried mayonnaise. The dining-room may be small, but it's comfortable and very well appointed. And the music is lovely.

Open Monday to Saturday 9 am to 11 pm, Sunday 10 am to 10 pm from 1 May until 15 October. Licensed. Master Card, Visa. No smoking.

Every restaurant in this guide has been personally tested. Our reporters are not allowed to identify themselves or to accept free meals.

MAGDALEN ISLANDS

MAP 109

CAPITAINE GEDEON

1301 chemin de la Vernière   **$240**
Etang du Nord
(418) 986-5341

*Next year Takanori Serikawa will convert this bed-and-break-
fast into a full-service restaurant, serving meals by appointment
only. Dinner will be at 7 o'clock and there'll be no printed menu.
For nine courses of the chef's choosing you will pay 90.00 plus
tip and taxes. Remember to bring your own bottle, as wine is not
included. The chef is Japanese and most of the dishes will be
Japanese or Japanese-French fusion. This is a superb kitchen and
that's why we've included it in the guide this year. The Capitaine
Gedeon is only five minutes from the ferry to Souris and it's open
all year except in high summer, when it's closed on Sunday and
Monday. It will have a licence and take most cards. No smoking.
You must book ahead.*

MAGDALEN ISLANDS

MAP 109

LA REFECTOIRE   ☆☆

Hôtel Vieux Couvent   **$135**
Ile Havre-aux-Maisons
(418) 969-2233

The old convent has long been one of the most attractive
places to stay in the Magdalens. Now Réginald Gaudet's
wife, Evangeline, is running one of the best kitchens on
the Islands right here in the convent. The Réfectoire is a
gay and lively place with a big menu. Mussels are cultivated in a nearby lagoon and prepared either as an appetizer or as a main course. Evangeline also has cod, halibut,
scallops, clams, herring, mackerel, shrimps and lobster.
A lot of the fish goes into her bouillabaisse, which is
rightly celebrated, but readers speak also of halibut with
a barley risotto, squid with parmesan cheese and salmon
crusted with sesame. If you've had enough seafood for a
while, ask for the local veal or the home-bred boar.
There's also a four-course *prix-fixe* for 16.00 more than
the cost of your main course. There are some good local

cheeses and a variety of fruits and berries. They have only a dozen wines, all sold by the glass and the bottle, but they're all private imports.

Open daily 6 pm to 9 pm from 1 May until 15 June, daily 5 pm to 10 pm from 16 June until 15 September, daily 6 pm to 9 pm from 16 September until 5 October. Licensed. Master Card, Visa. No smoking. Book ahead.

MAGDALEN ISLANDS   MAP 109
LA TABLE DES ROYS   ☆☆☆
1188 route 199   **$250**
Etang du Nord
(418) 986-3004

After being on her own for 25 years, Joanne Vigneault has found a partner. He's not only passionate about her restaurant, but he's also the love of her life. His name is Paul Lemoine and he's responsible for the greenhouse, where he grows such things as Jerusalem artichokes, herbs and greens of all sorts and a variety of edible flowers. The wine-list has been expanded and there are now about 200 labels, many of them organic. La Table des Roys isn't cheap, but an astonishing amount of thought goes into everything they offer. Joanne is one of the best chefs in Quebec, but as she gets older she forgets more and more of her English, so when choosing their meal visitors are more or less on their own. Look for the fresh local seafood. In spring it'll usually be lobster—a whole half-lobster goes into the bouillabaisse, which you'll always find on the menu. Scallops are prepared in five different ways and served as an appetizer, along with mussels, which are always readily available. Lamb was on the menu last year; this year it's more often veal. At the end of the meal there's an exquisite maple soufflé that Joanne has been offering for many years. There's a store on site where you can buy several take-away dishes as well as balsamic vinegar and extra-virgin olive-oil.

Open Tuesday to Saturday at 8 pm by appointment only from 1 June until 30 September. Closed on Sunday and Monday. Licensed. Master Card, Visa. No smoking. Book ahead.

MAHONE BAY, N.S. (MAP 108)
MATEUS ☆
533 Main Street **$95**
(902) 531-3711

Mateus is a real discovery. Opened a year or two ago by
Matthew Krizan, it has some really exciting cooking. The
panko-crusted halibut, for instance, is served with Lunenburg chow. Lunenburg chow is made with onions
soaked in brine, which is allowed to stand overnight and
then brought to the table with fresh tomatoes and
purslane. All this in a small frame restaurant on the south
shore of Nova Scotia? Krizan studied at the cordon bleu
schools in Ottawa and London before he came to Mahone
Bay. He likes curried fishcakes with a house-made blend
of spices. He also likes lobster rolls, seared scallops with
lemon and white wine, Indian Point mussels, and maybe
a quiche or an omelette. There's a nice little wine-list featuring Kim Crawford's sauvignon blanc and the Banrock
shiraz. Mateus is a place to remember.
Open Monday to Friday 11.30 am to 9 pm, Saturday and Sun-
day 10.30 am to 9 pm. Licensed. Master Card, Visa. No smok-
ing. ♿

LA MALBAIE, Quebec **MAP 111**
CHEZ TRUCHON
1065 rue Richelieu **$140 ($275)**
Pointe-au-Pic
(888) 662-4622

Dominique Truchon spent many years at the Auberge des
Peupliers in Cap à l'Aigle (see above), and that's where he
made a name for himself. A year or so ago, he opened his
own restaurant in a handsome old house on rue Richelieu
in Pointe-au-Pic. Here he has a darkly formal dining-
room and several comfortable bedrooms. His menu
makes much of such regional dishes as smoked-salmon
pie, emu pâté, halibut with red peppers and roast beef
with potatoes fried in duck fat. With the sweet, he
splurges on panna cotta, flavoured with basil. His prices

143

are modest—a four-course table d'hôte sells for just 25.00

Open daily 5.30 pm to 9 pm. Licensed. Amex, Master Card, Visa. No smoking. Book ahead if you can.

LA MALBAIE   MAP 111
LE PATRIARCHE   ☆
30 rue du Quai   **$160**
Pointe-au-Pic
(418) 665-9692

The Patriarche occupies an old house that faces the parking-lot of the Café Gare. It's hard to find. Turn south on the chemin du Havre by the museum, then sharply right again on the rue du Quai. Michel Dussuart, thin and very young, hardly looks the part of a *québécois* chef, but he cooks well and his menu of meat and fish, all prepared country-style, gives him plenty of opportunities. He prepares so many shrimps that the restaurant actually smells of shrimp.

Open Tuesday to Sunday 5.30 pm to 8.30 pm. Closed on Monday. Licensed. All cards. No smoking. Book ahead and be on time. ♿

LA MALBAIE
See also CAP A L'AIGLE.

MANITOULIN ISLAND, Ontario   MAP 112
GARDEN'S GATE   ☆
Highway 542   **$90**
Tehkummah
(705) 859-2088

People today are just as enthusiastic about the Garden's Gate as they were the day John and Rosemary Diebold opened the restaurant. If you turn west off Highway 6 in Tehkummah, you'll be at the Garden's Gate in two minutes. The gate opens into a pretty garden, beyond which stands the restaurant, with an old barn and a split-rail fence in the middle distance. Here Rosemary works as her grandmother would have worked, making all her own bread-rolls, her own salad-dressings, even her own hamburger buns. She grows all the fresh vegetables she can and buys her blueberries, organic strawberries and organic raspberries from long-time suppliers. Each year she and John search the vineyards of Niagara for new and exciting wines. They track down local craft beers with the same passion. This year travellers are singing the praises of their Manitoulin lamb with apricots and Moroccan spices. Every evening there are at least ten different sweets, and the Dutch apple pie is known all over the Island. With the sweets they serve fair-trade coffee and loose teas.

Open Tuesday to Sunday 11 am to 8 pm from 1 April until 30 June, daily 11 am to 10 pm from 1 July until 31 August, Tuesday to Sunday 11 am to 8 pm from 1 September until 31 October. Closed on Monday in the spring and fall. Licensed. Master Card, Visa. No smoking. Book ahead if you can. &

MANITOULIN ISLAND   MAP 112
THE SCHOOL HOUSE   ☆
46 McNevin Street   **$115**
Providence Bay
(705) 377-4055

Greg Niven remembers a time when 60 percent of his customers were American. The Americans have gone and people from southern Ontario are gradually moving in, some from the Georgian Bay, some from Muskoka, where property values have become unreal. Niven has sold the fish-and-chips parlour down the road, and is now giving his whole mind to the School House. He gets his vegetables from a neighbour, who has a vegetable garden as big as a tennis-court. A local abattoir opened, then closed again. A new, state-of-the art supplier will open this summer, so Niven will be able once again to get well-hung fresh meat. Most of his customers, however, ask for fresh Lake Huron whitefish, and Niven does what he can with this rather tasteless fish. He also has beef wellington and ravioli stuffed with smoked trout. He trained in

145

France and he knows just how to make a first-class risotto. He's also pretty good with French chocolate. Most of his wines come from the Niagara Region and Niven always goes for the best he can get.

Open daily 5 pm to 9 pm from mid–May until mid–October. Licensed. Master Card, Visa. No smoking. &

MARTINS BROOK, N.S. (MAP 108)
OLD BLACK FOREST CAFE
Highway 3 **$80**
(902) 634-3600

This unassuming little restaurant is a gem. There's no view to speak of, but the cooking and service are both excellent. The maultaschen (German-style ravioli) is wonderful. It's stuffed with ground beef and spinach and baked with cheese. They have three varieties of pork schnitzel and they all melt in your mouth. There's pepper steak with green peppercorns and at least three kinds of fish—salmon, haddock and scallops. The Black Forest cake is baked on the premises, as are all the pies and cakes.

Open Tuesday to Sunday 11.30 am to 9 pm from mid–April until mid–December. Closed on Monday. Licensed. Master Card, Visa. No smoking. Book ahead if you can.

MASSEY, Ontario MAP 114
DRAGONFLY
· *205 Imperial Street* **$65**
(705) 865-3456

Massey is on Highway 17, about halfway between Sudbury and Blind River. There are plenty of gas-stations on this stretch of highway, but very few places where you could expect to really enjoy a meal. The Dragonfly isn't a new restaurant, but we think readers might like to know about it. It's quiet and clean and has a large international menu. Burgers are the big seller, but we like the stir-fries best, especially the cashew chicken. They also have pretty good Tuscan sandwiches. Most of the sweets are homemade and the specialty of the house is the deep-

fried cheesecake. Nothing is expensive.
Open Tuesday to Sunday 11 am to 9 pm. Closed on Monday. No liquor. Master Card, Visa. No smoking. Book ahead if you can. &

MATANE, Quebec   MAP 115

Our first choice in Matane was always the Table du Capitaine at 250 avenue du Phare (telephone (800) 463-7468). It's recently been taken over by the Hôtel Riotel next door, but it remains an attractive little café with fine sea views, serving lunch and dinner every day from late May until mid-October. The chef we knew, who used to catch his own lobster, has recently been replaced by a new chef whose experience has been mainly in hotel kitchens. The menu, however, will be much the same, featuring lobster, shrimps, scallops and cod. They offer a table d'hôte every day for 30.00 and there's an all-you-can-eat dinner of mussels and fries on Thursday night. They have a licence and take Master Card and Visa. There's plenty of free parking.

MATTAWA, Ontario   MAP 116
MOOSEHEAD ESTATE   ☆
655 Moosehead Road $125 ($275)
(705) 744-0322

Melanie Viau and Marc Bouthillier spent almost two years restoring this century-old lodge on Lake Champlain before opening it as a bed-and-breakfast. If you want a meal at the Moosehead Estate you have to book the day before—they are open by appointment only. There's no real menu. Melanie will decide what to give you. She does all her shopping at the local store, because there are no farmers or fisherman anywhere near. Sometimes the store gets in some salmon, and they always have plenty of fresh vegetables. In winter they have butternut squash and she uses that to make some first-class soups. One day she found a bin of limes, so she started making chocolate-and-lime mousse. Lamb might be local, but usually it's just what's on the meat counter. She makes all her own bread and serves it with every meal. She works

alone, with one helper, her son, Max. Max is ten.
Open daily by appointment only. Bring your own bottle. No cards. No smoking. You must book ahead.

MATTAWA   **MAP 116**
MYRTS
610 McConnell Street   **$40**
(705) 744-2274

Scott Edworthy advertises something called Scott's Express Pizzas. Since he cooks every day from 6 in the morning until 9 at night, working as fast as he knows how, we're at a loss to know what he means by an express pizza. He makes all his own soups and all his own pies, as well as a chocolate-twirl cheesecake. He makes all his own fish and chips, using nothing but the freshest halibut. He grinds all his own beef for the hamburgers. And he puts on a hot special every day at noon. Bikers on the Temiskaming Loop are told to stop here, and everyone else should do the same.
Open daily 6 am to 9 pm. Licensed. Master Card, Visa. No smoking. &

MEDICINE HAT, Alberta   **MAP 117**
THAI ORCHID ROOM
36 Strachan Court SE   **$80**
(403) 580-8210

The Orchid Room gets its name from the fact that there are fresh orchids on every table. Some travellers have been critical of the service, but local people seem to have made a habit of the place, which is what matters. The kitchen uses nothing but the most authentic Thai recipes, and there's a lively vegetarian menu as well. Sounantha and Ken Ross started out ten years ago on Bow Island and later moved to Medicine Hat. On weekends they offer market-fresh fish; during the week they stick for the most part to frozen tiger prawns, which, however, are always properly cooked and generously served. They also have all the usual chicken, beef and pork yellow, red and green curries. In season they use market-fresh vegetables, even green asparagus when it's available. They have a variety of premium loose teas and a handful of wines.

Open Tuesday to Thursday 11 am to 9 pm, Friday 11 am to 10 pm, Saturday 4.30 pm to 10 pm, Sunday noon to 9 pm. Closed on Monday. Licensed. All cards. No smoking. &

MEDICINE HAT   MAP 117
TWIST
531 3 Street SE   **$65**
(403) 528-2188

Twist was sold in 2012 to Elle Davis' sisters, Melissa and Cheryl-Lynn. They intend to stay with the menu that made Twist's name in the first place. Melissa used to work in the restaurant and she knows all the ropes. The list of tapas dishes has survived intact, though last fall they added a soup and several salads. There are a number of important main dishes. The panko-crusted salmon has been replaced by salmon Spanish-style and the herb-stuffed chicken is now filled with dilled goat-cheese. The butter chicken, the house paella, and the triple-A beef tenderloin are all exactly as they used to be. Melissa makes the sweets now and they're all lovely.

Open Monday to Saturday 11 am to 11 pm. Closed on Sunday. Licensed. Amex, Master Card, Visa. No smoking. &

MIDDLE WEST PUBNICO, N.S.   (MAP 232)
RED CAP   ☆
Highway 335   **$95**
(902) 762-2112

The Red Cap is just the sort of place that makes it essential for all travellers to keep a copy of *Where to Eat in Canada* in their glove compartment. You'll find Middle West Pubnico about 30 miles east of Yarmouth on the South Shore, which makes it a two-hour drive from the Digby ferry. The Pubnicos still have an active fishing fleet, and the fish at the Red Cap is always stunningly fresh. Amy Scott is the chef and she makes everything from scratch—the sauces, the stocks, the soups and even the onion rings, which are as good as any we know of. There's all kinds of fresh fish and shellfish on the menu—haddock, clams, scallops, salmon and boiled lobster. Aside from the fish and shellfish, they have several traditional Acadian dishes like rappie pie. In blueberry season they make fine blueberry pies, as well as a good Acadian-style bread pudding. Most of the wines come from Grand Pré, and they're no better and no worse than others of their kind.

Open Monday to Friday 11 am to 8 pm, Saturday 11 am to 9 pm, Sunday 10 am to 8 pm. Licensed. Amex, Master Card, Visa. No smoking. ♿

MIDLAND, Ontario   **MAP 119**
EXPLORERS CAFE   ☆☆
345 King Street   **$100**
(705) 527-9199

Maybe the menu here should change more often, but the fact is that nothing else in town can compare with it. The cooking, the presentation and the service are all superb. The decorations are intriguing, the walls hung with treasures from Rob and Jennifer's travels. The menu shows the influence of just about every cuisine in the world. They freeze all their fish as soon as it comes in, since neither Rob nor Jennifer likes to take chances. The salmon comes in a maple-chipotle glaze, the Passage-to-India curry with raita and naan. We like to start with the lamb salad, served on a bed of Asian greens, and go on to the curry. At the end of the meal there's a fine peanut-butter pie with chocolate. The wine-list is one of the best north of Toronto.

Open daily noon to 10 pm from Victoria Day until 31 December, Monday to Saturday noon to 10 pm from 1 January until Victoria Day. Closed on Sunday in winter. Licensed. All cards. No smoking. Book ahead if you can.

Our website is at www.oberonpress.ca. Readers wishing to use e-mail should address us at oberon@sympatico.ca

MIDLAND
See also PENETANG.

MILL BAY, B.C. (MAP 62)
AMUSE ON THE VINEYARD ☆
2915 *Cameron Taggart Road* **$125**
(250) 743-3667

Amusé Bistro has moved from Shawnigan Lake to Mill
Bay and acquired a new name. The restaurant now occupies an old farmhouse next to the Unsworth vineyards.
Dinner starts with chilled cucumber soup topped with
coriander and lemon crème fraîche, emu carpaccio with
pickled squash or chanterelles with brandy and cream.
Qualicum Bay scallops are served as a main course, as well
as Cowichan Valley breast of chicken with summer
squash and wild sockeye salmon with a beet-and-radish
salad. There are also table d'hôtes of three, four and five
courses. The wines all come from the Unsworth vineyards, but it's still too soon to say how they will go with
the food.
*Open Wednesday to Sunday 5 pm to 9 pm. Closed on Monday
and Tuesday. Licensed. Master Card, Visa. No smoking. Book
ahead in summer.* ♿

MILL VILLAGE, N.S (MAP 29)
RIVERBANK CAFE 👉
8 *Medway River Road* **$45**
(902) 677-2013

This charming little café is just off Exit 17A on Highway
103. It's in the Riverbank General Store, right on the
Medway River. There are only eight or nine tables and a
lunch menu that's available from Monday to Friday. They
serve homemade soups (apple squash and apple turnip),
salads (Caesar and orange with sesame) and sandwiches
(free-range chicken with grapes, almonds and celery).
There's always one hot special, often chicken pot-pie.
*Open daily 11.30 am to 2.30 pm. No liquor. No smoking. No
reservations.*

MIRAMICHI, N.B.   MAP 122
BISTRO 140
295 Pleasant Street   **$60**
(506) 622-2221

For years it was pretty hard to get a good meal on New
Brunswick's northeast coast. So when someone wrote to
tell us of the great meal they'd had at the Bistro 140 in
Miramichi it came as a big surprise. Recently the restaurant moved from cramped quarters at 140 Ellen Street to
a roomier site on the other side of town. Now that he
can seat 150 people, the chef is more inclined to take a
chance on fresh fish. His pecan chicken is a perennial
favourite, though nowadays the chicken stuffed with
spinach and feta cheese sells even better. The vegetables
are all fresh and the sweets are all made in-house.
Open Monday to Thursday 11 am to 9 pm, Friday 11 am to 11
pm, Saturday 4 pm to 10 pm, Sunday 10 am to 4 pm (brunch).
Licensed. Master Card, Visa. No smoking.

MONCTON, N.B.   MAP 123
THE CHEF'S BISTRO
Crandall Building   **$50**
1133 St. George Boulevard
(506) 854-3030

As a restaurant, the Chef's Bistro is completely implausible. Located in the basement of a high-rise in a suburban
mall, they offer one or two hot dishes every day, as well
as a variety of sandwiches on homemade focaccia, and
one or two cakes and pies. Everything is extraordinarily
cheap. On Thursday afternoons they put on a formal
high tea. The place is run by Wayne Chase and his wife,
who makes everything come alive with her lively chatter.
Sad to say, she's been ill for over a year, and until she gets
back to work the front of the house will no longer be a
gay and vital place. As for her husband, he happens to be
a first-class cook. His pork tenderloin, for instance, is a
masterpiece. His lobster roll is an excellent example of
its kind. So are his fishcake and his pesto cheese sandwich.

The Bistro now has a liquor licence and takes most credit cards.

Open Monday to Thursday 11 am to 4 pm, Friday 11 am to 9 pm. Closed on Saturday and Sunday. Licensed. Master Card, Visa. No smoking. Free parking.

MONCTON   **MAP 123**
L'IDYLLE   ★★★
1788 rue Amirault   **$225**
Dieppe
(506) 860-6641

Emmanuel Charretier and Hélène Legras run the best restaurant this side of St. Andrews. It's in Dieppe, a suburb of Moncton. Look for L'Idylle three and a half miles south of Main Street (here called rue Champlain) on Highway 106. The dining-room is elegant, the menu daring, the cooking superb. Dinner begins with garden-fresh tomato soup with an olive-and-basil mousse, say, followed by ravioli stuffed with seasonal vegetables. The fish course may be salmon served in a sauce *du chef*. Charretier is proud of his rabbit stew, but we haven't tried it. On a recent visit we had a delightful *amuse-bouche* of shredded greens on a bed of foam, but everything Charretier touches is delicate and lovely. Wine service brings you a glass of carefully chosen wine with every course and costs only 30.00 a head. Every reader of this guide should make their way to L'Idylle at least once a week.

Open Tuesday to Saturday 5 pm to 10 pm. Closed on Sunday and Monday. Licensed. All cards. No smoking. ♿

MONCTON   **MAP 123**
THE WINDJAMMER   ★
Hôtel Beauséjour   **$175**
750 rue Principale
(506) 854-4344

The Windjammer is at once friendly and crisply formal. Your car is taken from you at the door and parked free of charge. You are then shown to your table, where they'll provide you with a flashlight if you ask. The menu, you'll find, is exciting. There's foie gras de canard and smoked sturgeon with wild rice. There are oysters on the half-shell and fresh scallops from Digby. The main courses are equally impressive. There's wild boar, Arctic char and rack of lamb from Witfield Farms. There's steamed lobster and beef tenderloin flamed at your table. The cooking is nicely understated. The wine-list, on the other hand, is not what it used to be, though there's still a sauvignon blanc from Yalumba for just 41.00 and a sassicaia from Bolgheri for 200.00, which, believe it or not, is something of a bargain.

Open Monday to Saturday 5.30 pm to 10 pm. Closed on Sunday. Licensed. All cards. No smoking. Valet parking. Book ahead if you can.

MONTAGUE, P.E.I. (MAP 43)
WINDOWS ON THE WATER ☆
106 Sackville Street **$100**
(902) 838-2080

If you're tired of Windows on the Water you're tired of life, as Dr. Johnson once said of London. Lilian Dingwell has a lovely old house (built in about 1880) with a wrap-around deck overlooking the Montague River. The cooking is old-fashioned and features things like boiled carrots, but everything is perfectly fresh and generously served. The prices are all very fair. The seafood linguine, for instance, offers an abundance of seafood (mussels, haddock, scallops and lobster) for just 22.00. Every noon there's a lobster quiche, a garden salad, a haddock bake and blue mussels in a white-wine mirepoix. We usually order the mussels, because they're the best the Island has to offer. In the evening they pair scallops with beef tenderloin and serve salmon with maple syrup. Lilian's sweets are famous, especially her apple crisp and her blueberry cake with brown sugar. The wine-list, however, is lamentable.

Open daily 11.30 am to 9.30 pm from early June until mid-October. Licensed. All cards. No smoking. Book ahead if you can. ♿

MONTREAL, Quebec   **MAP 125**
CHEZ L'EPICIER
311 rue St.-Paul e   **$160**
(514) 878-2232

If you think that the whole point of this restaurant is its interior, which is stacked with extra-virgin olive-oils, vinegars and jams, come in winter or in the evening for dinner. Laurent Godbout is in charge of the kitchen, which means that it's easy-going and informal. You can expect such things as a so-called BLT (bacon, lettuce and trout) with potato chips, a tartine of snails with white cheese, fried squid with peanuts, scallop ceviche, watermelon soup, stuffed dates with chorizo and fish and chips. If you didn't come to Montreal for fish and chips, ask instead for a lobster risotto with citronella and lime or pan-seared foie gras with dates and coriander. The wine-list is full of surprises—a chianti by Mori and a barolo by Michelino, to say nothing of a couple of unusual (and expensive) riojas.
Open Monday to Wednesday 5.30 pm to 10 pm, Thursday and Friday 11.30 am to 2 pm, 5.30 pm to 10 pm, Saturday and Sunday 5.30 pm to 10 pm. Licensed. All cards. No smoking.

MONTREAL   **MAP 125**
LA CHRONIQUE   ☆
99 avenue Laurier o   **$295**
(514) 271-3095

When Normand Laprise and Marc de Canck arrived in Montreal a generation or so ago, the local restaurant scene had little to cheer about. But before long the two men had turned on all the lights in the city. Over the years, however, both Toque! (see below) and La Chronique have lost some of their original excitement. Laprise and de Canck are both still cooking well, but both have become cautious to a fault. La Chronique is extremely expensive, and it's a good idea to come at noon, when prices are much lower. The lunch menu starts with venison tartar, seared scallops, cured salmon and foie gras de canard, and goes on to a side of beef, a fillet of red snapper and a chine of pork. There may no longer be a lot of real excitement in this kitchen, but there are precious few mistakes either. The cooking is correct. The dining-room is small but well served. Marc's stepson, Olivier de Montigny, is now in the kitchen as well, and regulars like to argue about which is the better of the two. (We think the answer is Marc.)

Open Monday 6 pm to 10 pm, Tuesday to Friday 11.30 am to 2 pm, 6 pm to 10 pm, Saturday and Sunday 6 pm to 10 pm. Licensed. All cards. No smoking. Book ahead if you can. &

MONTREAL   **MAP 125**
LE CLUB CHASSE & PECHE   ☆
423 rue St.-Claude   **$200**
(514) 861-1112

The Club Chasse & Pèche is well appointed and extremely well served. The menu is small and very choice. It starts with oysters on the half-shell, chilled octopus, seared scallops and black cod, which is rarely seen as an appetizer. Then come partridge two ways, Gaspé char with salmon caviar and sea-bass. The sea-bass is elegantly cooked, with crisp skin and moist flesh. The meal ends with a lovely lemon-meringue tart, full of wonderful flavour. The wine-list, which is impressive in every area, is at its best with its stunning array of wines by the glass. These aren't just house wines; there's a delightful, sunny sancerre from the Loire and a magnificent St.-Emilion grand-cru from one of the oldest vineyards in Bordeaux.

Open Tuesday to Friday 11.30 am to 2 pm, 6 pm to 11 pm, Saturday 6 pm to 11 pm. Closed on Sunday and Monday. Licensed. Amex, Master Card, Visa. No smoking. Book ahead. &

MONTREAL   **MAP 125**
LE COMPTOIR
4807 boulevard St.-Laurent   **$135**
(514) 844-8467

This is a *bavette* or wine-bar. It majors in organic wines

and charcuterie. A platter of charcuterie can be had for less than 10.00 at noon, when there's a plate of local cheeses as well. Lunch is a simple, inexpensive meal, featuring a light squash soup, salmon tartar with cucumber and duck *sous-vide* with raw onions. In the evening they add lobster tart, beef short-ribs, pork tongue with chanterelles and albacore tuna confit. To follow there's a marvellous morsel of lemon tart, as well as a lovely house-made rice pudding.

Open Monday 5 pm to midnight, Tuesday to Friday noon to 2 pm, 5 pm to midnight, Saturday 5 pm to midnight, Sunday 10.30 am to 2 pm (brunch), 5 pm to midnight. Licensed. Master Card, Visa. No smoking Book ahead if you can. &

MONTREAL   MAP 125
DOMINION SQUARE TAVERN
1243 Metcalfe Street   **$150**
(514) 564-5056

The Dominion Square Tavern was opened in 1927 and later restored, so it still looks much the same as it did 85 years ago. It's a long room with bare tables and hard chairs and a bar running the whole way from front to back. The chef is Eric Dupuis, formerly of Pullman and Leméac. Here he serves traditional pub food in the Parisian style, which really means Montreal-style. The menu starts with smoked mackerel, salmon gravlax and pork terrine, and continues with a Ploughman's Lunch of fish or beef. The beef and fish are both admirable, but we think the braised beef with mashed potatoes is usually better than either. Every Sunday night they put on a dinner roast between 4.30 and midnight. On weeknights there's a lovely lemon tartlet and a wonderfully light sticky-toffee pudding. They have a massive list of red wines, but we think it's usually more fun (and much cheaper) to have a glass of one of their eight on-tap beers. The service is leisurely—allow two hours, even for lunch.

Open Monday to Friday 11.30 am to midnight, Saturday and Sunday 4.30 pm to midnight. Licensed. All cards. No smoking.

MONTREAL

MAP 125

GARDE-MANGER ☆

408 rue St.-François Xavier **$140**

(514) 678-5044

Garde-Manger, with its old brick and big fireplace, is full of rustic charm. The chef, Chuck Hughes, has now become a television celebrity. Viewers like what he has to say and if you come to Garde-Manger you aren't likely to be disappointed. But there are problems. One is that it may take weeks to get a reservation. Another is the noise, which is unbelievable. It's best to come early, when you'll have time to study the blackboard. The kitchen is best known for its seafood platters, which come in three sizes. The biggest is the size of a window-box; the smallest is more than enough for two, crammed as it is with oysters, clams, crab-legs and shrimps. They're also known for their lobster poutine. If you don't want fish, there are beef short-ribs and a bavette of beef with fries. The most popular sweet is a deep-fried Mars bar, which sounds unreal but isn't.

Open Tuesday to Sunday 6 pm to 11 pm. Closed on Monday. Licensed. Amex, Master Card, Visa. No smoking. Book ahead.

MONTREAL

MAP 125

JOE BEEF ☆☆

2491 rue Notre Dame o **$175**

(514) 935-6504

Joe Beef is the most masculine of restaurants. Hormone-bald waiters with big tattoos are everywhere. The shouting and noise are overwhelming. The crowding is unbelievable. There's no printed menu and the dim light makes it hard to read the blackboards. The menu is full of such things as lobster spaghetti, venison, New York steak and roast beef, pork and duck. The cooking is muscular—this is a meal designed for men. The oysters from Colville Bay are huge. The lamb sweetbreads come with sausages. But there's nothing off-hand about Joe Beef. Everything is exactly what the chef wants it to be. The ingredients are regional—there are no avocadoes on the menu and the salads are thick with local parsley. There are wines from Quebec but none from the rest of Canada. In fact, most of the drinking comes from France. The butter is sweet. The sparkling water comes from Eska. The coffee is strong. And as for the sweets, there are always a lot of sundaes. Joe Beef is the creation of David McMillan and it's something you won't soon forget.

Open Tuesday to Saturday 6.30 pm to 10 pm. Closed on Sunday and Monday. Licensed. Master Card, Visa. No smoking. You must book ahead. &

MONTREAL   **MAP 125**
LAWRENCE   ☆
5201 boulevard St.-Laurent   **$140**
(514) 503-1070

Lawrence is all big windows and hard chairs. You take a seat, notice the elegant servers and pick up the menu. Immediately you see things like marinated trout with a potato cake, ox tongue in a green sauce, smoked sausage with endive and fried veal with potato salad. In the evening there's braised octopus, sablefish with green cabbage and bone-marrow pie. A few minutes later you start to notice the cooking, which as it happens is brilliant. Be sure to ask for the marinated trout, which is wonderful. Don't miss the ox-tongue either or the bone-marrow pie. All this on a corner lot in the far reaches of boulevard St.-Laurent. All this and more. Try the tarte tatin to follow. It's baked fresh and brought to the table piping hot.

Open Wednesday to Friday 11.30 am to 3 pm, 5.30 pm to 10 pm, Saturday and Sunday 5.30 pm to 10 pm. Closed on Monday and Tuesday. Licensed. Amex, Master Card, Visa. No smoking. Book ahead. &

This is a guide to Canadian restaurants from coast to coast—the first ever published and the only one of its kind on the market today. Every restaurant in the guide has been personally tested. Our reporters are not allowed to identify themselves or to accept free meals.

MONTREAL

MAP 125

LEMEAC
1045 avenue Laurier o $140
(514) 270-0999

The pan-seared squid here may not be quite so tender as
it used to be, and the rack of lamb with mushy peas may
now seem a little dull, but there's still the ris de veau,
which is a very exciting dish. In fact, the menu is full of
exciting dishes There's house-smoked salmon, crab in
sauce gribiche, homemade blood pudding and foie gras
de canard. We ourselves usually ask for the salmon pot
au feu with sea-salt or the roasted breast of duck with
dried cherries. On the wine-list there are no fewer than
three super-Tuscans (an ornellaia, a solaia and a sassicaia)
as well as many fine pauillacs, one with a price-tag of
1200.00 a bottle. Which is not to say that you have to
spend a fortune on wine here. There's good drinking
from Marlborough and a very attractive cabernet sauvignon from Napa Edge, both for quite a modest price.
Open Monday to Friday noon to midnight, Saturday and Sun-
day 10.45 am to 3 pm (brunch), 6 pm to midnight. Licensed.
Amex, Master Card, Visa. No smoking. &

MONTREAL

MAP 125

THE LIVERPOOL HOUSE   ☆☆
2501 rue Notre-Dame o $160
(514) 313-6049

The Liverpool House, like Joe Beef, is a restaurant made
for men. It's *masculin*. It's Italian. There's plenty of noise.
There are attractive waitresses. The menu is chalked up
on a blackboard. David McMillan believes in integrity
and integrity is what these two restaurants are all about.
The meal here starts with several varieties of oyster, some
from the Pacific and some (like the Colville Bay) from
the Atlantic. Of course, you don't have to start with oysters on the half-shell. There's also ears and tails of bison,
which as a dish is pure David McMillan. Main courses
rise to lobster spaghetti, which is the most expensive dish

on the menu. But you don't have to have lobster spaghetti. There's also chicken under a brick. Everything on the menu is cooked with easy-going style. The sweetbreads, for instance, which are about the best we've had, are never merely rich. The brussels sprouts—a difficult vegetable to handle—are tender but never bitter. Helpings are big, too big for most women. As for wine, there's always plenty to drink. The wine-list covers a whole wall. *Open Tuesday to Saturday 6 pm to 10 pm. Closed on Sunday and Monday. Licensed. Master Card, Visa. No smoking. You must book ahead.* ♿

MONTREAL   MAP 125

MAISON BOULUD   ☆☆

Ritz-Carlton Hotel   **$195**
1228 Sherbrooke Street W
(514) 842-4224

The new dining-room at the Ritz-Carlton, which opened in late 2012, is called Maison Boulud. Daniel Boulud came to Montreal by way of New York, after a brilliant but unsuccessful stop in Vancouver, where he was briefly in charge of the kitchen at Lumière. At the Ritz he has a sumptuous space—all pale teak, overstuffed chairs and a sensational gas-burning fireplace. His menu is cautious to a fault, offering things like Bayonne ham, smoked salmon, ravioli, terrine de foie gras, Arctic char, black cod and grilled entrecôte. The most spectacular dish, oddly enough, is wild fresh snails in garlic butter. Garlic butter is a familiar enough treatment, but wild snails are a rarity. The cooking is light and delicate, the portions small, the service graceful and well informed. As for the wine-list, it's magnificent. The still wines by the glass are not impressive, but for the same money you can have a glass of Roederer champagne from Anderson Valley in California. The list of bottled wines starts with such good things as Grgich Hills and Stag's Leap and ends with a number of premier-cru Mouton-Rothschilds at appropriate prices.
Open daily noon to 2.30 pm, 5 pm to 10 pm. Licensed. Amex,

Master Card, Visa. No smoking. Book ahead. &

MONTREAL   MAP 125
MIRCHI
365 place d'Youville   **$85**
(514) 282-0123

Mirchi is named for the green-chilli spice used in
Bangladesh and India. Here in Old Montreal Khaled
Rahman serves food from the Moghal north of India and
the Hindi south. There are a dozen appetizers, of which
the best is probably the lentil soup. Then come the birya-
nis and the tandooris (beef, lamb, chicken and fish). If you
aren't familiar with the cuisine, ask for an appetizer platter and a combination dinner to follow. You can drink
wine if you like, but it's better to order one of the Indian
beers or maybe even a glass or two of sweet lassi.
Open Monday to Friday 11 am to 2 pm, 5 pm to 10 pm, Satur-
day and Sunday 5 pm to 10.30 pm. Licensed for beer and wine
only. Master Card, Visa. No smoking. Book ahead if you can.

MONTREAL   MAP 125
NORA GRAY
1391 rue St.-Jacques   **$150**
(514) 419-6672

Emma Cardarelli is the chef at Nora Gray, and Ryan
Gray, the owner, decided to couple her grandmother's
first name with his own family name. Emma Cardarelli's
menu is rich and strange, featuring such things as
boulettes, tripe, braised short-ribs, salt-crusted sea-
bream, rabbit stuffed with walnuts, risotto of squid and,
of course, boudin noir. The most successful dish, however, happens to be the plain char-grilled pork chop. The
cooking can be sensible or merely startling—it all depends on your luck. Be careful to listen to the daily specials, because they're often the best things on the menu.
The stuffed clams, for instance, are more appealing than
either the boulettes or the rabbit. There's a big list of bottled wines, but there aren't many wines by the glass. The

dining-room is comfortable, even elegant, and if you like you can have dinner at the bar.

Open Tuesday to Saturday 5.30 pm to 11.30 pm. Closed on Sunday and Monday. Licensed. Amex, Master Card, Visa. No smoking. Book ahead. ♿

MONTREAL   MAP 125
PASTAGA
6389 rue St.-Laurent   **$120**
(438) 381-6389

Pastaga is a new restaurant, just south of Little Italy. It's bright and contemporary, with plenty of white paint and glass and bare, butcher-block tables. Martin Juneau is the chef and he likes to start his meals with Blueberry Bay oysters on the half-shell and go on to grilled white tuna, spice-crusted porcelet, grilled bison and tataki de cheval. Every day he has seven or eight *québécois* cheeses, including riopelle and bleu d'elizabeth. Most of these dishes are served on small plates and it's usual to order three. The wines are all natural, which means unfiltered, and many are organic. The coffee is wonderful, the service great.

Open Monday to Thursday 5 pm to 11 pm, Friday noon to 2 pm, 5 pm to 11 pm, Saturday and Sunday 10 am to 2 pm (brunch), 5 pm to 11 pm. Licensed. Amex, Master Card, Visa. No smoking. ♿

MONTREAL   MAP 125
AU PIED DE COCHON   ☆
536 rue Duluth e   **$150**
(514) 281-1114

Martin Picard seldom changes his menu. His helpings are all enormous. We ourselves usually order something like the tomato tart, the beautiful beet-and-goat-cheese salad or the cromesquis, which are tiny pastries filled with hot foie gras. But many people come here for the huge servings of pig's head or pied de cochon with foie gras or maybe even duck in a can. The last of these is brought to your table in a large can, which is opened and poured onto your plate. We have actually seen many men and some women put away both a pig's head and duck in a can. These are dishes you couldn't find in Toronto or even New York, and people come here from all over the city for one or the other or both. They also have a fine list of burgundies, among them a gevrey-chambertin premier cru at 395.00 a bottle.

Open Tuesday to Sunday 5 pm to midnight. Closed on Monday. Licensed. Amex, Master Card, Visa. No smoking. Book ahead.
&

MONTREAL
LES 400 COUPS
400 rue Notre-Dame e
(514) 985-0400

MAP 125
☆☆
$195

Chef Marc-André Jetté, *pâtissière* Patrice Demers and *sommelier* Marie-Josée Beaudoin worked together at Laloux, that lovely old-world restaurant that readers will remember from early editions of *Where to Eat*. At Les 400 Coups they've opened their own restaurant. Jetté is no believer in making the most of local ingredients. He uses produce from around the world. He flavours his Arctic char with yuzu, his carrots with smoked tea; he serves his steak tartar with mustard ice cream. Les 400 Coups is wild, over the top and very expensive. It's also booked for weeks in advance. We ourselves have been unable to get a table. We aren't booking for July. If you are, go ahead, but remember always to speak French. There's no English spoken on their telephone.

Open Tuesday to Thursday 5.30 pm to 10.30 pm, Friday 11.30 am to 1.30 pm, 5.30 pm to 10.30 pm, Saturday 5.30 pm to 10.30 pm. Closed on Sunday and Monday. Licensed. All cards. No smoking. Book ahead.

This is a guide to Canadian restaurants from coast to coast—the first ever published and the only one of its kind on the market today. We accept no advertisements. Nobody can buy his way into this guide and nobody can buy his way out.

MONTREAL   **MAP 125**
LA SALLE A MANGER   ☆☆
1302 avenue du Mont-Royal e   **$150**
(514) 522-0777

The Salle à Manger may not have any table-cloths, and
they may set their tables with a knife and fork and no
spoon, but make no mistake, it's a first-class restaurant
with an exciting menu, good service and excellent cooking. They start dinner with such things as foie gras with
cranberries, tartar of duck with crème fraîche and salmon
tartar with wasabi cream—a brilliant dish served with a
delicate array of tiny turnip leaves. The meal continues
with sweetbreads, clams steamed in beer, pork tongue,
blood sausage, salt cod and pot au feu with bone marrow.
Ask for a glass of gewurztraminer with your dinner. It
usually goes better with dishes like this than either
chardonnay or cabernet sauvignon. For us, the Salle à
Manger was an important find.
*Open daily 5 pm to midnight. Licensed. Amex, Master Card,
Visa. No smoking.* ♿

MONTREAL   **MAP 125**
TOQUE!   ☆☆☆
900 place Jean-Paul-Riopelle   **$225**
(514) 499-2084

Normand Laprise and Christine Lamarche have created
a three-star dining-room newly dedicated to the fresh,
the original, the imaginative. This is the more remarkable
in that Normand Laprise is no longer a young man. He
has, in fact, been in the kitchen on place Jean-Paul-Riopelle, for at least twenty years. Almost all of his wines,
for instance, are private imports, put down by more or
less obscure wineries. Where else would you find yourself
drinking a bottle of solinou from Les Pervenches? Where
else would you be eating sea snails (with daikon and sage)
or duck tartar, or even a sliced shoulder or pulled leg of
lamb? These things are all part of the pleasure of a meal
at Toqué! It's expensive, of course, but what isn't? If you

want to see this kitchen preparing a traditional dish, ask for the Eton Mess and notice how much better it is than others of its kind.

Open Tuesday to Friday noon to 2 pm, 5.30 pm to 10.30 pm, Saturday 5.30 pm to 10.30 pm. Closed on Sunday and Monday. Licensed. Amex, Master Card, Visa. No smoking. Book ahead. &

MONTREAL	**MAP 125**
LES TROIS PETITS BOUCHONS	☆☆
4669 rue St.-Denis	**$145**
(514) 285-4444	

The Trois Petits Bouchons are Audrey Dufresne, Xavier Burini and Michel Charette, and after all these years they're still together, obviously enjoying their work and their customers. Their café will win your heart at first sight and it'll never let you down. The chef, Audrey Dufresne, buys the best available produce and cooks it in imaginative ways. Her menu changes daily and is posted on a blackboard, which they'll bring to your table if you ask. Certain dishes tend to recur. For instance, there's usually scallops, duck confit, halibut and beef tenderloin. Only the last of these is expensive. All the partners are passionate about wine, and they've prepared a wine-list that's both exciting and unfamiliar.

Open Monday to Saturday 6 pm to 11 pm. Closed on Sunday. Licensed. All cards. No smoking. Book ahead.

MONTREAL	**MAP 125**
VAN HORNE	☆☆
1268 avenue Van Horne	**$150**
(514) 508-0828	

This is a fairly new restaurant. It has only eight or nine tables, with an open kitchen and superb service. The tables are well spaced and there is no hubbub. The menu is small, with only four entrées and four main dishes. The cooking is amazing. We know of no-one in the city who can match Eloi Dion for delicacy of touch. The plates are bone-white, the presentation refined, the flavours stunning. The mussel salad is the most remarkable of all—a tiny salad with one or two mussels in a thick coulis of saffron, celery and apple. Scallops come with blood pudding in a reduction of clementines, endives and sweet potatoes. Sea-bass is served with lentils and ratatouille. Helpings are small, prices modest. The wine-list is small too, but choice. Van Horne is a long way from Sherbrooke Street and farther from Ste.-Catherine, but it's definitely worth the trip.

Open Tuesday to Saturday 6 pm to 10.30 pm. Closed on Sunday and Monday. Licensed. Amex, Master Card, Visa. No smoking. Book ahead. &

MONT TREMBLANT, Quebec   MAP 126
AUX TRUFFES   ☆
Place Saint-Bernard   **$210**
3035 chemin de la Chapelle
(819) 681-4544

Last year we considered that Aux Truffes possessed every virtue. This year we're not so sure. Recently, however, the cooking has been returning to form. We suggest that for the present visitors avoid the 100.00 *menu de dégustation* in favour of the table d'hôte, which is much cheaper. There's also an à la carte, where you'll find shepherd's pie of caribou and profiteroles of braised veal cheeks. The sweets are disappointing, so ask instead for a plate of *québécois* raw-milk cheeses. The wine-list is enormous and offers wines from all over the world—except Canada.

Open daily 6 pm to 10 pm. Licensed. All cards. No smoking. Book ahead. &

MONT TREMBLANT
See also St.-Faustin-Lac-Carre, St.-Jovite.

Where an entry is printed in italics this indicates that the restaurant has been listed only because it serves the best food in its area or because it hasn't yet been adequately tested.

MORRISTON, Ontario   (MAP 84)
ENVER'S   ☆
42 Queen Street $130
(519) 821-2852

Morriston is little more than a scattering of houses along
Highway 6, but for more than 30 years there's been a
restaurant here good enough to take its place with the
best of Stratford and Toronto. Look for an old grey-brick
store front with neo-Gothic windows and doors. Enver
was a one-man band, doing almost everything himself.
Terri Manolis, who bought the place from Enver many
years ago, was happy to sell a share of the business to the
chef, Ken Hodgins. Hodgins does his best to cater to all
comers. His fish, usually Lake Huron pickerel, is always
fresh. His game is all organic. He features bison and Ontario lamb, either roasted or stewed in Wellington stout.
There's a good appetizer plate to start with, followed by
pheasant or bison and at least four sweets. Last winter
people were talking about the sticky-apple upside-down
cake with cream and brown sugar. The wine-list is no
longer small; it's grown enormously and now covers
most of the New World and the Old.
Open Tuesday to Friday 11.30 am to 3 pm, 5 pm to 8.30 pm,
Saturday 5 pm to 8.30 pm. Closed on Sunday and Monday. Li-
censed. Amex, Master Card, Visa. No smoking. Book ahead if
you can. &

NANAIMO, B.C.   MAP 128
BISTRO AT WESTWOOD LAKE   ☆
2367 Arbot Road $135
(250) 753-2866

Gaetan Brousseau has closed the Wesley Street Cafe and
reopened under a new name on Westwood Lake, next
door to the tennis club. Here he has a handsome dining-
room with a fireplace and high ceilings. He also has excellent service and some of the best cooking in town.
Lunch means, if you're lucky, chicken and double-
smoked bacon with brie and caramelized onions, with a

cup of soup or a mixed salad, for only 12.00. Dinner means a braised lamb shank with polenta or coq au vin with a wild-mushroom risotto, followed by a dark-chocolate cheesecake or vanilla crème brûlée.

Open Tuesday to Saturday 11.30 am to 9 pm, Sunday 11 am to 3 pm (brunch), 5 pm to 9 pm (dinner). Closed on Monday. Licensed. Master Card, Visa. No smoking.

NANAIMO   **MAP 128**
GATEWAY TO INDIA   ☞
202 4 Street   **$85**
(250) 755-4037

The premises on 4 Street have been restored and redeco-rated, and everything is now trim and bright. The restau-rant has a good wine-list and a sensible menu, offering such familiar things as shrimp pakoras, aloo gobi, palak gosht, mutter panir and tandoori chicken. The sweet lassi is disappointing, but they have a good Indian beer (Kingfisher) and several wines. If you like, you can drink Kim Crawford's sauvignon blanc or perhaps a bottle of Caymus Conundrum, with your tandoori chicken. The naan is light and lovely, the service obliging.

Open Monday to Friday 11 am to 9 pm, Saturday and Sunday 4 pm to 9 pm. Licensed. Master Card, Visa. No smoking. ♿

NANAIMO   **MAP 128**
THE NEST BISTRO
486A Franklyn Street   **$120**
(250) 591-2721

The Nest is a newcomer to Nanaimo. Nick Brawn and Jen Ash make all the pasta in-house, as well as the spinach gnocchi. Their prices aren't high. Most of the appetizers, even the wild-mushroom tart with brie and the flash-fried prawns in phyllo, cost less than 10.00. The lamb shank is about the best of the entrées. Afterwards there's a wonderful chocolate-ganache cake and a fabulous warm ginger cake with whipped cream and caramel sauce. There are only about ten tables, so it's a good idea to book

ahead.
Open Wednesday to Friday 11 am to 2 pm, 5 pm to 9 pm, Saturday and Sunday 5 pm to 9 pm. Closed on Monday and Tuesday. Licensed. Master Card, Visa. No smoking. Book ahead if you can.

NANAIMO
See also CEDAR.

NELSON, B.C.   MAP 129

We've been writing about the All Seasons Café at 620 Herridge Lane (telephone (250) 352-0101) for so long that we find it pretty hard to say now that we can no longer recommend it. Nelson is a picturesque town, restored to look much as it did during the Gold Rush, and we've been looking hard for other places to eat. We can tell you that The Full Circle at 402 Baker Street: Suite 101 (telephone (250) 354-4458) has a fabulous breakfast. It's open Monday to Saturday 6.30 am to 2.30 pm, Sunday 7 am to 2 pm, but it doesn't serve dinner. We're still looking for a place that does.

NEW GLASGOW, N.S.   MAP 130
BaKED FOOD CAFE
209 Provost Street   **$60**
(902) 755-3107

This is a delightful little café that makes the most of the local, the seasonal, and the healthy. They have a great number of vegetarian dishes and make all their sandwiches with homemade bread. At noon there may also be a butternut-squash quiche, perhaps served with curried chick-peas. All the helpings are small and the sweets are really small—really small but very good. (The best of the lot is the chocolate-banana marquis topped with hazelnuts.) The coffee is made with freshly ground beans, one cup at a time. In the early morning they serve a fine breakfast that starts with an omelette, made with a variety of fillings, among them ham, peppers, green onions, mushrooms and cheese.

Open Tuesday to Saturday 8 am to 5 pm. Closed on Sunday and Monday. Licensed. Master Card, Visa. No smoking.

NEW GLASGOW   MAP 130
THE BISTRO   ☆☆
216 Archimedes Street   **$115**
(902) 752-4988

The French chef who opened the Bistro later sold it and returned to France. It was bought by Robert Vinton and his wife, Heather Poulin. They closed the place for the better part of a year while everything was renovated. Meanwhile, the couple became involved with the local art community and every three months they put on a display of work in progress. There's always a public reception, with an abundance of appetizers supplied by the kitchen. Vinton's meat is all organic and local, and one often sees him in town shopping for one of his daily specials—a soup, perhaps, or some meat or fish. He's particularly good with fish, especially salmon, scallops and mussels, which never leave the menu.
Open Tuesday to Saturday 5 pm to 9 pm. Closed on Sunday and Monday. Licensed. All cards. Book ahead.

NEW GLASGOW
See also PICTOU, STELLARTON, TRENTON.

NIAGARA-ON-THE-LAKE, Ontario   MAP 131
THE CHARLES INN
209 Queen Street   **$150**
(866) 556-8883

The Charles Inn was built in 1832 and restored many years later. They now have twelve good bedrooms and a handsome dining-room. William Brunyansky is no longer in charge of the kitchen. He's been replaced by Steve Sperling, but it'd be hard to tell the difference between the two. Sperling is easily a match for his predecessor and his pan-seared diver scallops with caramelized onions and his pan-roasted sablefish with oyster mushrooms are both very fine dishes. You can eat quite cheaply at the Charles Inn, if you choose the leek-and-potato soup and the pavé of Atlantic salmon. Or you can spend a lot more and have seared foie gras with ginger, honey and orange and Alberta beef tenderloin. The Alaska black cod is an exciting compromise. The best of the sweets, oddly enough, is the plate of farmhouse cheeses, which cost just 11.00 for three. The wines come from the Niagara region and they're all moderately priced. There's at least one interesting dessert wine, a riesling from the Megalomaniac winery. Try it.

Open daily noon to 2.30 pm, 4 pm to 8.30 pm from 1 May until 31 October, Monday to Friday 4 pm to 8.30 pm, Saturday and Sunday noon to 2.30 pm, 4 pm to 8.30 pm from 1 November until 30 April. Licensed. Amex, Master Card, Visa. No smoking. Book ahead if you can.

NIAGARA-ON-THE-LAKE　　　　　MAP 131
EPICUREAN
84 Queen Street　　　　　　　　　　　　$145
(905) 468-0288

Things have been changing at the Epicurean in the last year or two. It used to be a sandwich bar with a few bistro dishes in the evening; now it's a bistro with a few sandwiches at noon. You can still get good, thick, made-to-order sandwiches to eat with a glass or two of wine under the marvellous butternut tree outside. But what you really come for nowadays is an inexpensive dinner of pâté de foie gras, followed by steak frites, lamb shanks with spicy couscous, pan-seared rainbow trout with a new-potato salad and black tiger shrimps with wilted spinach. They now have fifteen Niagara wines by the bottle, many of them sold also by the glass. Look for the Tawse cabernet franc or the Cattail Creek gewurztraminer.

Open daily 9 am to 5 pm (lunch), 5 pm to 8 pm (dinner). Licensed. Amex, Master Card, Visa. No smoking. &

Nobody can buy his way into this guide and nobody can buy his way out.

NIAGARA-ON-THE-LAKE   MAP 131
HILLEBRAND'S VINEYARD   ☆
Highway 55   **$185**
(905) 468-7123

This is a lovely dining-room, overlooking the vineyards where most of the Hillebrand grapes are grown. Frank Dodd was back in the kitchen again last year and he maintains an expansive à la carte that offers wild mushrooms foraged by a man named Marc. The tomato soup is named for a man named Tommy. From Tommy's tomato soup you move on to beets with icewine, diver scallops from the East Coast, green asparagus, salmon cured in icewine, dry-aged rib-eye of beef, fillet of halibut, organic chicken and local spring lamb. All the wines come from the Hillebrand vineyards; the most interesting are the single-barrel chardonnays and cabernet francs. Neither is expensive. The soundtrack, however, is decidedly unpleasant.

Open daily noon to 2.30 pm, 5 pm to 8 pm. Licensed. Amex, Master Card, Visa. No smoking. Book ahead if you can. ♿

NIAGARA-ON-THE-LAKE   MAP 131
LIV   ☆
White Oaks Resort   **$160**
253 Taylor Road
(800) 263-5766

Liv has a lavish setting in a resort complex on the outskirts of Niagara-on-the-Lake. Good cooking is the last thing one would expect. But so it is: the menu is surprising and so is the cooking. For instance, they have a water list, offering bottled water from Voss as well as San Pellegrino. They have 24 wines by the glass and countless draft beers. Most of the wines come from the Niagara Region, but there are several also from California, Australia, New Zealand, Chile and Argentina. The soup of the day may be spiked with bourbon, and there's an avocado salad with chèvre and black beans as well as mussels in dark ale. After that there's lobster agnolotti, grilled Atlantic salmon, Berkshire pork, rack of lamb and, for 42.00, a ten-ounce striploin steak. To top all this off, if you have 50.00 to spare you can drink yellow-label Veuve Cliquot champagne with your meal.

Open Sunday to Thursday 5 pm to 9 pm, Friday and Saturday 5 pm to 10 pm from 1 May until 30 September, Tuesday to Thursday 5 pm to 9 pm, Friday and Saturday 5 pm to 10 pm from 1 October until 30 April. Closed on Sunday and Monday in winter. Licensed. Amex, Master Card, Visa. No smoking. &

NIAGARA-ON-THE-LAKE   MAP 131
RAVINE VINEYARD CAFE
1366 York Road   **$125**
St. David's
(905) 262-8463

Ravine is open all day every day of the week, serving soups, salads and farmyard cheeses, with a glass or two of wine from the Ravine vineyards. The soups come from the garden at the door. The mussels appear in every imaginable shape—there are six in all—with or without french fries. The cheeses come from Ontario and Quebec, and there are seven of them, from Riopelle to Thundering Oak. They all cost just 4.00 an ounce. They have other things as well, of course: coq au vin, croque monsieur, three-egg omelettes, quiches, burgers and Great Lakes pickerel. In a more adventurous mood, the chef will serve poached prawns cold with preserved lemon, chopped raw steak with truffle oil and sautéed snails in a vol-au-vent with chorizo and pearl onions. They have a few wines from Lailey, Henry of Pelham and Stratus, but most of the wines come from the Ravine vineyards. The most interesting of these are the cabernet franc and the unoaked chardonnay. Nothing is expensive.

Open daily 11 am to 9 pm. Licensed. Master Card, Visa. No smoking. &

Our website is at www.oberonpress.ca. Readers wishing to use e-mail should address us at oberon@sympatico.ca.

NIAGARA-ON-THE-LAKE   MAP 131
STONE ROAD   ☆
Garrison Plaza   **$145**
218 Mary Street
(905) 468-3474

Stone Road has been discovered, and prices have risen dramatically. The menu used to be all about soups, salads and sandwiches. Nowadays they're more ambitious. There's prosciutto with melon (a charming if familiar dish), foie gras poutine, mussels, charcuterie, steak frites and meatballs made of the best beef from Cumbrae in Toronto. The sweets too are surprisingly elaborate— cloudberry crème brûlée and brandied-cherry clafoutis. There are three craft beers to drink, several wines by the glass and at least one good gewurztraminer by the bottle. And they still have a lively oyster bar where you can sample several varieties of oyster, among them Kusshis from the Pacific and Malpèques from the Atlantic, all served in the half-shell with preserved lemon and horseradish.
Open Tuesday to Friday 11.30 am to 2 pm, 5 pm to 9 pm (later on Friday), Saturday 5 pm to 10 pm, Sunday 5 pm to 9 pm. Closed on Monday. Licensed. Master Card, Visa. No smoking. Book ahead. &

NOBLETON, Ontario   (MAP 209)
DANIEL'S   ☆
12926 Highway 27   **$130**
(905) 859-0060

Daniel Gilbert, now in his thirty-first year at Nobleton, describes himself as a provider of what he calls Canadian comfort food. He was just out of cooking-school when he opened in Nobleton, but he worked hard, tailoring his menu to his customers, putting on an entertainment every week or so—jazz-and-blues nights, Robbie Burns nights and wine tastings. The service is attentive, the linen starchy and white and the seating comfortable. Customers came and they stayed. The menu still has its clichés—French onion soup, oysters Rockefeller and

Caesar salad. But the monthly specials are where the action begins. There's always fresh fish, wild game and an international dish, such as carbonada criolla from Argentina. The house pâté comes free in the evening (at noon it's 5.50). There's a variety of organic wines and several specialty beers. Nothing is too sophisticated. Just good food carefully cooked and well served at a fair price. *Open Monday to Friday noon to 2.30 pm, 5 pm to 9 pm, Saturday and Sunday 5 pm to 9.30 pm. Licensed. Amex, Master Card, Visa. No smoking.* &

NORANDA, Quebec
See ROUYN.

NORRIS POINT, Newfoundland (MAP 170)
NEDDIE'S HARBOUR INN
(877) 458-2929 **$120 ($265)**

You don't go to Neddie's for fish and brewis or a jiggs dinner. The chef comes from away and he's more interested in lamb tagine than in either jiggs dinner or fish and brewis. Not that he doesn't have plenty of market-fresh fish—cod, halibut, scallops and mussels. Everything is made from scratch in the kitchen. Breast of chicken is served with bread dumplings, lamb with homemade chutney. The vegetables are all local—often parsnips or beets. The best of the sweets, we think, is the rum-and-molasses cheesecake. Norris Point is on Bonne Bay in Gros Morne National Park, where several good new restaurants have opened in recent years. But everyone is partial to this rather luxurious waterfront inn, and they like its prices too. You can get dinner for two with a modest wine for only about $120. If you want to stay the night, they have a small boutique hotel with lovely views of Bonne Bay and the mountains beyond.
Open Tuesday to Sunday 7.30 am to 10 am, 5 pm to 8.30 pm from 15 June until 15 September. Closed on Monday (Monday and Tuesday from 15 May until 14 June and from 16 September until 30 November). Licensed. All cards. No smoking. &

NORTHEAST MARGAREE, N.S.   (MAP 157)
THE DANCING GOAT   🖝
6335 Highway 19   **$45**
Cape Breton
(902) 248-2308

The Dancing Goat is a real find. It's always full, though now that they've enlarged the dining area you can usually find a chair. There's no table service. You go up to the counter, choose what you want from the blackboard and take a number to your table. Every day they have two homemade soups—curried chicken, perhaps, or broccoli with coconut. There's always a quiche and there are also a number of sandwiches, all made on thick, home-baked bread with crusts on. There's usually some Black Forest ham, some roast beef, some egg salad and (the best of the lot) some bacon with avocado. There's espresso and caffe latte to go with your sandwich and they're both good. There may be no liquor but there's just about everything else.

Open Monday to Wednesday 7.30 am to 5 pm, Thursday and Friday 7.30 am to 8 pm, Saturday 7.30 am to 5 pm, Sunday 8 am to 5 pm. No liquor. Master Card, Visa. No smoking. &

NORTH RUSTICO, P.E.I.   (MAP 43)
THE PEARL   ☆☆
7792 Cavendish Road   **$145**
(902) 963-2111

Five years ago, Maxine Delaney opened the Pearl on the lovely stretch of Highway 6 that leads from North Rustico to Cavendish and *Anne of Green Gables* country. After being twice a finalist, she won the Taste of the Island award for her cooking. Local people love the place, and no wonder. Maxine, a former designer, did much of the interior decoration herself. She also organizes a variety of entertainments in the restaurant, starting with silk-screen painters and classical cellists and going on from there. The menu changes often, but you can usually count on Kim Dormaar's smoked salmon and oysters from Raspberry Point, plus a soup from the garden and another from the sea. They usually also have chicken with a tea rub, pan-seared scallops and triple-A beef tenderloin. The Sunday brunch features a poached lobster tart with local asparagus and pecorino cheese. Last fall her chef left, but Maxine quickly found a replacement. Fred Dickiesone is a local boy who has worked in some of the most exciting restaurants in Europe. At the moment, the Pearl is as good as anything in the province. *Open Monday to Saturday 5 pm to 9 pm, Sunday 10 am to 2 pm (brunch), 5 pm to 9 pm from 28 June until 9 October. Closed on Tuesday from 15 until 31 May, on Monday from 1 until 27 June. Licensed. Master Card, Visa. No smoking.*

NOTRE-DAME-DU-LAC, Quebec   (MAP 31)
AUBERGE MARIE-BLANC
1112 rue Commerciale s   **$125**
(418) 899-6747

For years the Marie-Blanc was the only reliable place to break a journey from Fredericton to Quebec. The motel units were simple but clean, the breakfast was excellent (freshly-squeezed orange-juice, wholewheat toast and coffee) and dinner was better than one had any right to expect. The inn was built as a private home in 1905 by a New York lawyer for his mistress, Marie-Blanc Charlier, who lived here until she died in 1949. Guy Sirois and his wife, Jeannine, bought the place in 1960 and ran it for more than 40 years. Their menu began quite simply, but over the years it grew into a four-course table d'hôte. By the time of the millennium, however, Guy was worn out and a few years later his daughter decided to take over. She had never heard of sweetbreads, but her father lived just long enough to teach her. She hired a local chef, Pauline Beaubien, who now has ready access to a wide variety of regional produce, including maple syrup and farmhouse cheeses. We suggest you start your dinner here with venison carpaccio or salmon tartar, followed by a bavette of beef or, yes, sweetbreads with port wine. The best of the sweets is the maple-syrup crème brûlé.

Open Monday to Saturday 7.30 am to 9.30 am, 5.30 pm to 9 pm, Sunday 8 am to 12.30 pm (brunch) from early June until Thanksgiving. Licensed. Master Card, Visa. No smoking.

OKANAGAN CENTRE, B.C. (MAP 97)
GRAPEVINE
Gray Monk Estate Winery **$140**
1055 Camp Road
(250) 766-3405

After all these years, Grapevine is still being run by Willi Franz and René Haudenschild. They have a good seafood duo for lunch. That means Qualicum Bay scallops and poached tiger prawns with arugula and pink peppercorns. It's a familiar dish, but it's as good as ever. Follow that with local venison in a reduction of red wine with home-made pear chutney or Fraser Valley duck confit with cranberry marmalade. Grapevine is quiet and poised and the meatloaf at least is a wonderful dish.
Open daily 11.30 am to 3.30 pm, 5 pm to 9 pm from mid–April until mid–October. Licensed. Master Card, Visa. No smoking.
&

OLIVER, B.C. (MAP 97)
MIRADORO
Tinhorn Creek Vineyard **$135**
32830 Tinhorn Creek Road
(250) 498-3742

Miradoro is run as a partnership by the Tinhorn Creek winery and Manuel Ferreira, owner of the Gavroche in Vancouver. Jeff van Geest is the executive chef. Miradoro has panoramic views of the South Okanagan Valley. Its menu is Mediterranean in inspiration, its cooking rustic in style. Most of the wines come from Tinhorn Creek, though there are some outstanding wines from other vineyards as well. The best thing they do is the beef pap-pardelle bolognese, but try also the Fraser Valley pork belly or the albacore tuna, poached in olive oil and served with lentil vinaigrette, sunchokes and roasted beets.

OLIVER (MAP 97)

TERRAFINA
Hester Creek Estate Winery **$135**
Highway 8
(250) 498-2229

Terrafina has an informal décor, with wooden beams and wrought-iron chandeliers. Jeremy Luypen, the executive chef, has created a menu that reflects the restaurant's Mediterranean feeling. We've tried their wild-boar meatballs with its sauce of forest mushrooms and Spanish onions and their pork belly with a maple-carrot risotto and a house-made apple chutney. We can recommend both, but have yet to try their Fraser Valley breast of duck with green beans, white truffles and crisp pancetta. They also have first-class wood-fired-oven pizzas. The prosciutto with blue cheese and caramelized onions is one of the best. If you haven't had any of the Hester Creek wines, try one. You'll be surprised.

Open Wednesday to Saturday 11.30 am to 9 pm, Sunday 10 am to 4 pm. Closed on Monday and Tuesday. Licensed. Master Card, Visa. No smoking. ♿

ORANGEVILLE, Ontario **MAP 139**

ONE 99
199 Broadway **$140**
(519) 940-3108

Orangeville is growing, perhaps faster than it would like. But at least that means that there are enough people to support this rather ambitious restaurant. The dining-room is bright and colourful and the service is everything it should be and more. We used to find the appetizers more interesting than the main courses, but that's no longer the case. If you want a special experience, book the chef's table in the kitchen for 65.00 a head. It's cheaper, of course, in the dining-room, where you can get things like chicken-liver pâté with truffles and foie gras (for just 9.65), organic greens, dry-aged beef and pineapple salad with ginger and hoisin. The salmon is farmed and so is the venison, which is served with hand-made spaetzle and a pommery demi-glaze. The venison is expensive, but the free-range breast of chicken stuffed with sundried berries costs only 23.45. The sweets are all very likeable.

Open Tuesday to Saturday 5 pm to 9 pm. Closed on Sunday and Monday. Licensed. All cards. No smoking. ♿

ORILLIA, Ontario   **MAP 140**
WEBERS   ☞
8844 Highway 11 N   **$25**
(705) 325-3696

Webers now has sixteen flavours of ice cream, and if you want a real, old-fashioned milkshake you can get it at the ice-cream counter. They're still using Illy coffee beans to make their espresso. More important, they now have a slick, new stainless-steel railway car that houses brand-new washrooms. Webers beef is still all pasteurized by exposing it to a steam-blanket in a pressurized chamber at a temperature of 185°F; it's then stored at 30°F, ground fresh daily and cooked to a temperature of 160°F. Each week in summer they process and sell more than three tons of ground beef—50 tons a summer. Their fries all come from potatoes grown, cut and packed in Prince Edward Island. In fine weather you can eat outside at one of the brightly-painted picnic tables and watch your children playing on the Via Rail coaches. There's even a coach, newly renovated, where you can sit inside when it's raining. Teenagers take your order, make change and see that you get what you want within minutes, no matter how long the lineup may be. On the first Tuesday in August there's free corn on the cob for all comers. There's rock music on the soundtrack and free parking for hundreds of cars on both sides of the highway, with an overhead bridge that connects the southbound lot to the restaurant.

Open daily 10.30 am to 7 pm from 11 until 21 March, Friday to Sunday 10.30 am to 7 pm from 22 March until 14 April, daily 10.30 am to 7 pm (later on weekends) from 15 April until 26 May, daily 10.30 am to 9 pm from 27 May until 23 June, daily 10.30 am to 10 pm from 24 June until 5 September, daily 10.30 am to 7 pm from 6 September until 10 October, Friday to Sunday 10.30 am to 7 pm from 11 October until 10 November. No liquor, no cards. No smoking. &

OSHAWA, Ontario   **MAP 141**
BUSTER RHINO'S
28 King Street E   **$60**
(905) 432-8750

We've come a long way from the elegant dining-room at the Robert McLaughlin Gallery, where good cooking and reasonable prices couldn't deliver a durable tenant. But Darryl Koster, who has worked rough in both Whitby and Oshawa, has opened a first-class restaurant here on downtown King Street. It may not take reservations, but it does have a licence and comfortable seating. The menu offers a poutine of beef brisket, pulled pork, slow-cooked for sixteen hours, which makes it tender and full of flavour, and wonderful smoked ribs rubbed with spices and then slow-cooked until the meat falls off the bone. There's a new kitchen now, so the menu will be expanding. Meanwhile, the cooking is just getting better and better.

Open Monday to Thursday 11 am to 9 pm, Friday 11 am to 11.30 pm, Saturday and Sunday 11 am to 9 pm. Licensed. All cards. No smoking. No reservations. &

OTTAWA, Ontario   **MAP 142**
ALLIUM
87 Holland Avenue   **$140**
(613) 792-1313

Arup Jana runs a small storefront restaurant on Holland Avenue near Wellington Street. The waiters wear old jeans and the washrooms are downstairs, but the chef knows what he's doing. Lunch is simple and straight-forward: squid with pickled red onions, steak frites with smoked chilli, burgers with chipotle, pickled onions and cheddar cheese, shrimp wrap and roasted breast of duck. Dinner is more elaborate, offering such things as scallops from Qualicum Bay and tagliatelle with parmesan cheese, as well as flat-iron steak and fries. On Monday the kitchen spends the whole day preparing a variety of tapas dishes: a soup, several cheeses, scallops with mango, squid with red onions, shrimps with lemon, raw yellow-tail with basil and truffles. The wine-list majors in wines from California and Italy. Monday is the night to come, but for a table on Monday night you have to book ahead. *Open Monday 5 pm to 10 pm, Tuesday to Friday 11.30 am to 2 pm, 5 pm to 10 pm, Saturday 5 pm to 10 pm. Closed on Sunday. Licensed. Amex, Master Card, Visa. No smoking.*

OTTAWA   **MAP 142**
ATELIER   ☆
540 Rochester Street   **$450**
(613) 321 3537

When the celebrated restaurant elBulli closed in Catalonia, we thought the world had said goodbye to molecular gastronomy. Not so. Marc Lepine has made his name at Atelier in Ottawa using many of the same procedures. He offers a tasting menu of twelve courses served either on small plates or in test tubes. The menu is coy, but the waiters are both knowledgeable and friendly, and if you have 450.00 to spare this may be a good place to spend it. (If you're over 30, perhaps not.) The new Canadian food, as Lepine calls it, is all hyper-modern. It's dehydrated, frozen, then put back together again. This is what Ottawa needs? Sadly, we're over 30. *Open Tuesday to Saturday 5 pm to 10 pm. Closed on Sunday and Monday. Licensed. All cards. No smoking. You must book ahead.* ㄴ

If you use an out-of-date edition and find it inaccurate, don't blame us. Buy a new edition.

OTTAWA   **MAP 142**
BECKTA   ☆
226 Nepean Street   **$185**
(613) 238-7063

Michael Moffatt is cooking better this year. He handles
steelhead trout and lobster with equal assurance, and sells
the lobster at bargain prices. He serves duck from Quebec, wall-eye from Lake Erie and beef from Wellington
County, all with easy competence. His oysters come
from New Brunswick or Prince Edward Island and are
served in the half-shell, though without the benefit of
grated horseradish. His foie gras is wonderful and he has
a seldom-seen dry riesling from Lincoln Lakeshore in Niagara, but if you're having the beef you'll find some good
drinking among the reds from France, Italy or Australia.
The setting on Nepean Street is quiet and serene and the
service is poised and elegant.
*Open daily 5.30 pm to 9.30 pm. Licensed. Amex, Master
Card, Visa. No smoking. Book ahead.* &

OTTAWA   **MAP 142**
THE BLACK CAT   ☆☆
428 Preston Street   **$150**
(613) 569-9998

It's been a while now since Stephen Vardy left the Black
Cat to return to Newfoundland. His place was taken by
Trish Larkin, and the remarkable fact is that she's cooking
just as well as Vardy, though in a different style. The
Black Cat seems to have lost little if any ground. Larkin's
tuna tataki is served with radishes, miso and lemon
grass—and it's magic. So is her bison carpaccio with
truffle oil, lemon and dijon mustard. Her king salmon is
wild and served with beans and basil and her steak with
fries is as good as any in the city. The flourless-chocolate
cake is one of a kind and the traditional lemon tart is a
delight. Only the choice of ice wine still needs to be improved.
Open Monday to Saturday 5 pm to 10 pm. Closed on Sunday.

Licensed. Amex, Master Card, Visa. No smoking. Book ahead.
Free parking. &

OTTAWA   **MAP 142**
DOMUS
87 Murray Street   **$175**
(613) 241-6007

Domus made its name by majoring in regional cuisine—
serving baby ginger from Acorn Creek Farm, foie gras
from across the river in Quebec, beef from O'Brien
Farms. The venison is all free-ranched, the rabbit grain-
fed. Fish comes in twice a week from the West Coast.
Everything is carefully cooked. Yukon Gold and fingerling potatoes are still on the menu, but less frequently
than they used to be, and the list of Niagara wines is as
impressive as ever.
Open Monday to Wednesday 11.30 am to 2 pm, 6 pm to 9 pm,
Thursday to Saturday 11.30 am to 2 pm, 5.30 pm to 9.30 pm,
Sunday 11.30 am to 2.30 pm (brunch). Licensed. Amex, Mas-
ter Card, Visa. No smoking. &

OTTAWA   **MAP 142**
EIGHTEEN   ☆☆
18 York Street   **$195**
(613) 244-1188

Matthew Carmichael made Eighteen the best restaurant
in Ottawa. When he left last year to open his own restaurant we were concerned about the future of his kitchen.
It turned out that Eighteen under Carmichael's sous-chef,
Walid El-Tawel, has lost little (perhaps none) of its former polish. The menu is still extraordinary, offering such
things as salt-roasted beet salad, grilled octopus, tuna
sashimi, bison cheeks, lobster consommé and steak tartar.
These are all perfectly cooked and the tuna sashimi is easily the best in the city. The butter-poached lobster that
comes next has few equals, though the lacquered black
cod is also a marvellous dish. The venison can be tough,
and you may be safer with the rack of Ontario lamb. If

185

the enoki mushrooms from Le Coprin are on offer, be sure to ask for them; they're rare and wonderful. The sticky-toffee pudding is lighter than most and better than any of the crème brûlées. The wine flights are now available only on special occasions like New Year's Eve, but there are many good buys on the regular wine-list. Inside, the restaurant is exciting, but the service is leisurely. Allow two hours for dinner.

Open Monday to Saturday 5 pm to 10.30 pm. Closed on Sunday. Licensed. Amex, Master Card, Visa. No smoking. Book ahead.

OTTAWA   MAP 142
FRASER CAFE
7 Springfield Road   **$150**
(613) 749-1444

Ross and Simon Fraser go from strength to strength. Their restaurant on Springfield Road is full every day of the week, and there's no point in going there unless you have a booking. Their style hasn't changed and their menus mix the plain with the sophisticated. They like to serve such things as Pacific halibut with chick-peas, B.C. salmon with white beans, house-smoked trout with beetroot and mustard and albacore tuna with savoy cabbage. Last year they added Jacobson's cheese and charcuterie, as well as oysters from Whalesbone, which they choose with care and serve in impeccable condition. The menu changes with the seasons, but you can usually count on beef with fries, wild salmon, Cornish game hen, halibut, pork belly and tuna, as well as the cheese and charcuterie.

Open Monday to Friday 11.30 am to 2 pm, 5.30 pm to 10 pm, Saturday and Sunday 10 am to 2 pm (brunch), 5.30 pm to 10 pm. Licensed. Amex, Master Card, Visa. No smoking. Book ahead.

The price rating shown opposite the headline of each entry indicates the average cost of dinner for two with a modest wine, tax and tip. The cost of dinner, bed and breakfast (if available) is shown in parentheses.

OTTAWA   **MAP 142**

MURRAY STREET   🍷

110 Murray Street   **$120**

(613) 562-7244

This place started out as a charcuterie, but it was (and still is) open all day, which means that you can come in at 11 o'clock and have some elk kielbasa with a glass or two of wine. In the years since then they've started serving other things as well—things like chicken pot-pie, falafel, charcoutine (fried kielbasa with black-pepper sausage, bologna and homemade spaetzle), corned beef, pulled pork and potato gnocchi. But we suggest that you stick pretty closely to the charcuterie, most of which is made right on the premises. It's good and so are the cheeses (riopelle and bleu d'Elizabeth). The other things are not. The pickerel, for instance, may come from Whalesbone, but it's buried in lentils and flavoured improbably with tartare sauce. The corned beef is served with pickled onions on rye bread, which comes from the Rideau Bakery. The dining area is dark and solemn, and it would take more than a bowl of fries with mayonnaise to make it seem bright and lively.

Open daily 11.30 am to 2.30 pm, 5 pm to 10 pm (11 pm for charcuterie). Licensed. Amex, Master Card, Visa. No smoking.

OTTAWA   **MAP 142**

NAVARRA   ☆

93 Murray Street   **$175**

(613) 241-5500

René Rodriguez grew up in Mexico and at Navarra today he's cooking in the Mexican style. That means salmon cured with ancho, scallop ceviche with lime and a dungeness-crab salad with red grapefruit. The crab salad is certainly a wonderful dish. After that ask for the Oaxacan black mole, which is made in the traditional way with coffee and chocolate. There are other good things too, like the pig's cheeks with bufala mozzarella, lamb's belly with chilli torcados and rabbit confit with fried mushrooms. The bread is a lovely treatment of sweet potato, served warm with herb butter. On the wine-list there's a chardonnay and a cabernet franc from Prince Edward County. Both are bottled especially for Navarra and both are cheap and pleasant. The sauvignon blanc from Appleby costs more and is better. There are only three red wines from Spain and two white, which is disappointing. After all, the restaurant is called Navarra.

Open Tuesday 4 pm to 10 pm, Wednesday to Saturday 5.30 pm to 10 pm, Sunday 10.30 am to 2.30 pm. Closed on Monday. Licensed. Amex, Master Card, Visa. No smoking. Book ahead.

OTTAWA   MAP 142
SIDEDOOR
18B York Street   **$115**
(613) 562-9331

Sidedoor was opened as a cheaper alternative to Eighteen. Like Eighteen, it's all rough stone and glass. The menu is basically Mexican, though the tacos aren't made with corn. They're white and soft and at noon that's about all there is. In the evening there are two or three tacos, served as appetizers, followed by black cod with soya, mirin and truffle oil, white-tuna sashimi, sockeye-salmon ceviche, salt-and-pepper squid, seared scallops, pork belly with mango, cashews and chillies and braised panaeng beef. The beef and the black cod tend to be overcooked, though the sauces, on which the kitchen lavishes a lot of care, are usually pretty good. There's an ambitious wine-list as well as several sakes. There's nothing else like Sidedoor in Ottawa.

Open daily 11.15 am to 2 pm, 5 pm to 9 pm. Licensed. Amex, Master Card, Visa. No smoking.

This is a guide to Canadian restaurants from coast to coast—the first ever published and the only one of its kind on the market today. We accept no advertisements. Nobody can buy his way into this guide and nobody can buy his way out.

OTTAWA   **MAP 142**
SIGNATURES   ★★
453 Laurier Avenue E   **$190**
(613) 236-2499

Prices have been rising at Signatures and you now pay almost 200.00 for dinner for two with wine. But actually,
it's worth it. They start with beef tartar, a quail-and-
mushroom terrine, a lobster bisque with corn and a surprising dish of sautéed snails. You can have a veal chop
to follow, but it's expensive at 38.00. We think it's better
to go for the seared pickerel in brown butter or the Arctic
char in a buckwheat crêpe. The magret de canard is correctly served, but the seared scallops come with beef
cheeks, which don't do anything for the scallops. If
you're looking for beef, forget the scallops and order the
striploin for 33.00. The five-course tasting menu costs
75.00, which is hardly a bargain. They have sparkling
water from Eska on hand and a list of wines that leans
strongly to France. They need more Italian reds and more
Canadian whites on the list. If you have money to spare,
they do have a tignanello for 170.00 and a hermitage
from Paul Jaboulet for 125.00. That's a fair price for a
Jaboulet and we'll hope to have it next time we come.
Open Wednesday to Friday 11.30 am to 1 pm, 5.30 pm to 9
pm, Saturday 5.30 pm to 9 pm. Closed Sunday to Tuesday. Li-
censed. Amex, Master Card, Visa. No smoking. Free parking.
Book ahead. ♿

OTTAWA   **MAP 142**
TAYLOR'S GENUINE FOOD & WINE BAR
1091 Bank Street   **$140**
(613) 730-5672

John Taylor has obviously chosen the name of his new
restaurant with some care. The key word is *genuine*. In
what sense is this restaurant any more genuine than any
other? Because they serve Alberta lamb, Great Lakes pickerel, guinea fowl and triple-A beef? Everybody does that,
so we have to assess the restaurant, like any other, on the

strength of its cooking and service. Jon Svozas has designed a menu that allows him to make the most of what his kitchen does best. Unfortunately, however, the menu—asparagus salad, loin of lamb and striploin of beef—is not at all exciting. The cheeses, however, are well chosen, and diners are encouraged to arrange their own charcuterie board. There's elk salami, beef bresaola, smoked breast of duck, pork terrine, rabbit porchetta, two cow's-milk cheeses from Saint-Elizabeth de Warwick and a goat's-milk cheese from Notre-Dame-du-Lac. If you want to have some fun, spend 40.00 or 50.00 and share a cheese-board. If you want a Canadian wine, there are plenty to choose from. We suggest the Organized Crime fumé blanc or the Painted Rock syrah from the Okanagan, though the Painted Rock syrah is rather expensive at 100.00 or more a bottle.

Open Monday to Saturday 11.30 am to 2 pm, 5.30 pm to 9.30 pm, Sunday 5.30 pm to 9.30 pm. Licensed. Amex, Master Card, Visa. No smoking. Book ahead if you can.

OTTAWA   MAP 142
WELLINGTON GASTROPUB   ☆
1325 Wellington Street   **$125**
(613) 729-1315

If you knew Christopher Deraiche at Eighteen, you'll be quite surprised by his menus at the Wellington Gastropub, which are full of sarnies and frittatas. True he's also a dab hand with pickerel from the Georgian Bay, and almost as good with sea scallops and pork belly. But most of the entrées come with lentils or black and white beans, which aren't to everyone's taste. In the evening, of course, there's more to choose from. One of the best dishes is the scallops in a coulis of roasted cauliflower purée. The evening menu is quite large, the cooking sophisticated. They have a number of craft beers, several of them on tap, and a number of wines that are sold by the glass as well as the bottle. This, after all, is a gastropub.

Open Monday to Friday 11.30 am to 2 pm, 5.30 pm to 10 pm. Saturday 5.30 pm to 10 pm Closed on Sunday. Licensed. Amex,

Master Card, Visa. No smoking. Book ahead if you can.

OTTAWA   **MAP 142**
WHALESBONE
430 Bank Street   **$140**
(613) 231-8569

At Whalesbone they have fresh oysters that come from
the Pacific coast as well as from Prince Edward Island,
Nova Scotia and New Brunswick. The Sea Angels are so
big they could choke a horse, and we wish they'd carry
the smaller Kusshis from the West Coast instead. But
Whalesbone is no longer just a raw bar. They also sell fish
and chips, lobster rolls, seared tuna and Arctic char with
charred tomatoes and fresh local greens. Nowadays,
there's even a four-course tasting menu for 70.00 a head.
The wine-list is quite small, but most of the wines on
offer are sold by the glass as well as the bottle. Whalesbone isn't the sort of place to take your mother-in-law.
It's small, noisy, crowded and very camp. But it's probably the most genuine restaurant in the city.
Open daily 11.30 am to 2 pm, 5 pm to 11 pm. Licensed. Amex,
Master Card, Visa. No smoking. ♿

OTTAWA
See also CHELSEA.

OWEN SOUND, Ontario   *MAP 143*
THE FLYING CHESTNUT
199 Pellisier Street   *$95*
Flesherton
(519) 924-1809

To get to Flesherton, turn off Highway 26 at Thornbury and
continue south on Highway 13 almost to Highway 4. This is
Blue Mountain country, where you can go fishing in Lake Eu-
genia or go to see Eugenia Falls, which after Niagara are the high-
est in Ontario. Shawn Adler has fitted out his restaurant anew
and dedicated the kitchen to regional organic cooking. The beers
are local and even the wines, all of which are organic, are made

191

locally. At the moment he's open Thursday to Sunday for dinner, Saturday and Sunday for brunch. Licensed. No cards. No smoking. Further reports needed.

OWEN SOUND   **MAP 143**
THE ROCKY RACCOON   ☆
941 2 Avenue E   **$95**
(519) 374-0500

Robin Pradhan plans to concentrate on Owen Sound from now on, even if only because that's his wife's home town. Pradhan and Shelley Bentz first met in Europe. Together they came to Canada and began working for the Rocky Raccoon in Dyers Bay. Before long they had taken the place over and moved it to Gore Bay on Manitoulin Island. Soon they moved again, this time to Wiarton, then finally to Owen Sound. In Owen Sound their menu is, as always, a marriage of Asian cuisine and the profusion of fresh produce available on the Bruce Peninsula. They offer fresh fish from sustainable stock, which means whitefish and line-caught lake trout. They get their lamb, wild boar, bison and pheasant from nearby farms. In the evening they serve a lot of Bengali and Burmese curries with hand-crafted chutneys. At noon they put on a buffet lunch, featuring a variety of French crêpes and Nepalese dumplings. Shelley makes a wonderful chocolate mousse and a great tiramisu. The wines all come from Niagara and even the craft beers are local.
Open Monday to Saturday 11 am to 11 pm. Closed on Sunday. Licensed. All cards. No smoking. ♿

PAPINEAUVILLE, Quebec   **MAP 144**
LA TABLE DE PIERRE DELAHAYE   ☆
247 rue Papineau   **$125**
(819) 427-5027

Pierre Delahaye and his wife, Jacqueline, realized a dream back in 1985, when they bought this old house, built a century earlier. Pierre came from Normandy and liked the dishes he'd grown up with. He intended to buy everything locally. And he believed that to cook well you need to be a happy man, which he was. So people now drive 40 miles from Ottawa for brunch here, knowing they'll have a good time. The menu doesn't change much. There are always snails with apples and calvados, and sweetbreads braised with apples and finished with apple cider. There's a three-course dinner for 31.50 that features a fish course, snails with garlic butter and a French pastry. The pick of the sweets, of course, is the French apple tart.

Open Wednesday to Saturday 5.30 pm to 9 pm, Sunday 11.30 am to 2 pm (brunch), 5.30 pm to 9 pm. Closed on Monday and Tuesday. Licensed. Master Card, Visa. No smoking.

PARRSBORO, N.S.   **MAP 145**
HARBOUR VIEW   ☆
476 Pier Road   **$80**
(902) 254-3507

Parrsboro has some of the highest tides in the world, often exceeding 50 feet. The Harbour View has been on this site for more than half a century, but few people seem to know about it. True, it's an unpretentious place with simple country cooking. Their signature dish is the seafood platter, heaped with lobster, shrimps, clams and haddock. They're equally good with Advocate Harbour scallops, Five Islands clams and potato skins loaded with green onions and cheese. You can have your fish pan-fried or deep-fried. Either way, you should begin with their bowl of seafood chowder. Try to make room for a sweet, because they make a great chocolate cake with boiled icing, which is a rare delight in this or any other country.

Open daily 7 am to 9 pm from 1 May until Labour Day, daily 7 am to 8 pm from Labour Day until Thanksgiving. Licensed. All cards. No smoking. ♿

The map number assigned to each city, town or village gives the location of the centre on one or more of the maps at the start of the book.

193

PEMBROKE, Ontario   **MAP 146**

ULLRICH'S ON MAIN
214 Pembroke Street W   **$65**
(613) 735-6025

Pembroke has never been an easy place for a restaurant
with any ambition. The Saffron Bistro tried but failed.
Ullrich's, however, has survived, partly because it serves
also as a deli and a butcher shop. Unfortunately, it's open
only for lunch and has only a few tables. At noon they
usually have two soups, a quesadilla or two, a few salads
and sandwiches, among them a smoked-meat sandwich
Montreal-style. After that, keep an eye open for the
maple-syrup tart and the chocolate torte. The helpings
are huge and the prices low. As for the butcher shop, it's
certainly the best in town.
Open Monday to Saturday 11 am to 2 pm. Closed on Sunday.
Licensed. All cards. No smoking. &

PENETANG, Ontario   **(MAP 119)**
FROTH CAFE   ☆
102 Main Street: Suite 1   **$50**
(705) 549-7199

The Olympia Gardens has unexpectedly closed, so Penetang is left with the Froth Café, which happens to have
an excellent kitchen. They have superb coffee but, more
important than that, they have at least 30 different varieties of bread—hazelnut with pears and figs, pumpkin,
apple pecan—all of them irresistible. People buy their
bread by the armload, giving loaves to anyone they can
think of. They make a very good breakfast too and a fine
lunch of soups, sandwiches, quiches and some really remarkable salads. The best of these is the garden salad with
a poppyseed dressing or the salmon salad in a honey-
lemon vinaigrette. You won't be disappointed in their
sweets either. They have a carrot cake, and a lovely strawberry-rhubarb pie as well.
Open Tuesday to Saturday 8 am to 6 pm, Sunday 9 am to 4 pm.
Closed on Monday. Licensed. No cards. No smoking.

PERCE, Quebec   **MAP 148**
AUBERGE LE COIN DU BANC   ☆
345 route 132 e   **$150**
(418) 645-2907

The Coin du Banc occupies an old frame building four miles north of Percé on route 132. The place is littered with hurricane lanterns, ships' models, wood stoves and primitive artwork. It's open all day and has a wonderful breakfast that features pain doré, foie de morue and the lightest of crêpes, served with real maple syrup. Every day they put on a simple lunch featuring salade des crevettes and croque monsieur. In the evening they add such things as escargots de bourgogne, smoked salmon and a shrimp omelette, followed by cod three ways, scallops with tartare sauce and steamed lobster. If you come in summer and order the *repas complet*, you can even expect cods' tongues, which are a rarity nowadays. There's a short list of familiar wines and a handful of half-bottles, of which the best is probably the riesling Willm.
Open daily 8 am to 10 pm from 1 June until 30 September. Licensed. Amex, Master Card, Visa. No smoking.

PERCE
See also St.-Georges de Malbaie.

PETERBOROUGH, Ontario   *MAP 149*
ELEMENTS
140 King Street   *$125*
(705) 876-1116

Elements has a lovely patio, shaded by spreading locust trees. They also have a fine wine-list, probably the best in Peterborough. Recently we had one of their tapas specialties, called plato misto della casa, which turned out to be a spicy sausage with four cheeses, ham and a variety of olives. It was typical of their tapas dishes, which are all good. Prices are very fair. Elements is open all day every day, has a licence and takes Amex, Master Card and Visa. Further reports needed.

PETERBOROUGH

MAP 149

38 DEGREES
375 Water Street   **$135**
(705) 750-0038

The number over the front door has nothing to do with
degrees of latitude or the street address. It's the temperature on the Fahrenheit scale that's the best for keeping
meat, fish and vegetables. The chefs have joined hands
with Kawartha Choice, the wholesaler, to support local
products. They serve no fewer than six hot vegetables, as
well as potatoes, with every entrée. You might begin
with a charcuterie plate or a pear salad with cranberries
and go on to a full- or half-rack of New Zealand lamb,
marinated breast of duck with maple, scallions and ginger
or perhaps the fish of the day. In season they make a very
good pumpkin pie.
*Open Tuesday to Thursday 4.30 pm to 9 pm, Friday to Sunday
4.30 pm to 10 pm. Closed on Monday. Licensed. All cards. No
smoking.* ⅃

PICTON, Ontario   MAP 150
                                                          ☆
BLUMEN GARDEN
647 Highway 49   **$130**
(613) 476-6841

Blumen Garden is a few miles from Picton, but it's well
worth the effort because it's probably now better than
anything in Picton itself. It's located in a converted house
on Highway 49—follow the signs to Trenton and the
401. Start with crab ravioli in red curry and coconut
broth, pan-seared tuna or house-smoked breast of duck.
The best of the main courses is the braised rabbit with
gnocchi and oyster mushrooms. The chef, Andreas Feller,
is Swiss and he cooks with a pronounced Swiss accent.
There aren't many sweets, and the best of the lot is the
dark-chocolate mousse. Most of the wines come from
Prince Edward County, and there are five draft beers and
Waupoos County cider as well.
Open Monday and Thursday to Sunday 11.30 am to 2 pm,

5 pm to 9.30 pm. Closed on Tuesday and Wednesday. Licensed. All cards. No smoking. &

PICTON   **MAP 150**
GAZEBO
Waupoos Estate Winery   **$145**
3016 County Road 8
(613) 476-1355

This winery restaurant has proved so popular with summer visitors that the old Gazebo has been expanded and the old patio enclosed. The view over the vines to the lake is as lovely as ever and, despite the fact that Jeff Wilson has replaced Scott Ryan in the kitchen, the food is still very good. We admire the soups and the arugula salad with pears and candied pecans. At noon they also have seared scallops and a number of sandwiches. Most of these dishes are available also in the evening. You can begin your dinner quite grandly with Quebec foie gras, followed by breast of duck, rack of Ontario lamb or roasted local chicken. The wines all come from the estate, even the icewines. The Geisenheim costs only 7.00 a glass, and that's a pretty good buy.
Open daily 11 am to 3 pm, 6 pm to 9 pm from mid-May until mid-October. Licensed. Master Card, Visa. No smoking. Book ahead if you can.

PICTON   **MAP 150**
MERRILL INN   ☆
343 Main Street E   **$125 ($350)**
(866) 567-5969

Now that Harvest has gone it may be time to look again at the Merrill Inn. This old Victorian red-brick hotel, with its tall gables and gingerbread trim, has always been a popular favourite, perhaps because it has the only real wine-bar in the county. But there's more to it than that. The Merrill Inn has always been a civilized place, with a handsome dining-room and first-class service. It's not cheap, but if you spend the night the price includes a spectacular breakfast and a late-afternoon wine-tasting event. Michael Sullivan, the chef, has worked in a number of Toronto's leading restaurants (including, among others, the Auberge du Pommier) and his small menu here shows it. We prefer the fish—scallops and blue crab—to the meats, though the lamb is all local. The pastry—asparagus tart with hand-rolled goat-cheese, maple tart with walnuts—is outstanding and so is the cheese board and the coffee. Keep an eye out for any of the Grange wines from Prince Edward County. They're good.

Open Tuesday to Saturday 5.30 pm to 9 pm. Closed on Sunday and Monday. Licensed. Master Card, Visa. No smoking.

PICTON
See also BLOOMFIELD, WELLINGTON.

PICTOU, N.S. (MAP 130)
MRS. MACGREGOR'S TEAROOM
59 Water Street **$60**
(902) 382-1878

Mrs. MacGregor is a dab hand at selling herself. We've said it before and we say it again. She also, of course, knows how to cook and she runs a catering business summer and winter. At lunchtime she makes an excellent seafood chowder and a very good chicken soup, as well as a number of salads and sandwiches on homemade bread. There are also a couple of hot dishes such as quiche Lorraine and fishcakes. In the evening, coq au vin has taken the place of the turkey dinner and there's a vegetarian pasta as well as scallops and haddock. Mrs. MacGregor thinks her lobster roll is about as good as her sticky-toffee pudding, and that may very well be true. If you come for tea—this is a tearoom after all—you'll find that a slice of butterscotch pie goes well with any of the teas.

Open daily 11 am to 3 pm, 5 pm to 9 pm from 15 February until 23 December. Licensed. Master Card, Visa. No smoking. Book ahead if you can. &

PLANTAGENET, Ontario　　　　　**MAP 152**
MARIPOSA FARM
6468 County Road 17　　　　　　　**$90**
(613) 673-5881

Nothing of importance has changed at Mariposa Farm in
the last couple of years. Suzanne Lavoie and Ian Walker
have been raising Embden geese and Barbary duck on
their 175-acre farm east of Ottawa for almost 30 years.
(Recently they've been breeding Berkshire pigs as well.)
They've converted an old barn into a small but charming
dining-room, complete with white-linen table-cloths and
a broad view of the surrounding countryside. Sad to say,
the dining-room is open only two hours a week, on Sunday from 11 am to 1 pm. The chef, Anna March, has a
small menu—three appetizers, three main courses and
two sweets (or a cheese plate), three courses for 38.00.
Foie gras is always on the menu, along with either duck
or goose and home-baked bread. Unfortunately, Mariposa Farm is not licensed, so the char-grilled breast of
duck is marinated in fruit juice. The farm store is in the
same building and it sells everything from duck and geese
to homemade preserves, jams, jellies and pâtés. Look for
the Mariposa Farm sign outside of town, just east of
Wendover.
Open Sunday 11 am to 1 pm. Closed Monday to Saturday. (The
store is open Friday to Sunday 9 am to 4 pm.) Bring your own
bottle. Master Card, Visa. No smoking. Book ahead. ♿

LA POCATIERE, Quebec　　　　　**MAP 153**
CAFE AZIMUT
309 4 Avenue　　　　　　　　　**$120**
(418) 856-2411

The Café Azimut occupies an old house on 4 Avenue in
La Pocatière, a few minutes from Exit 439 on Highway
20 west of Rivière du Loup. They don't really serve
lunch any more—just pizza and pasta—but every day at
about noon they put up a blackboard for the evening
meal. It'll offer such things as mussel-and-shrimp soup

en croûte, tartar of crab, ravioli of beets, feuilleté of shrimp and—best of all—smoked sturgeon. For sweet, there's usually a wonderful tarte au sucre. The wine-list is full of private imports, and among the open wines there's an R.H. Phillips cabernet sauvignon and a Kim Crawford sauvignon blanc. One could hardly hope for more.

Open daily 9 am to 11 am, 4 pm to 10.30 pm. Licensed. Amex, Master Card, Visa. No smoking. &

POCOLOGAN, N.B. MAP 154
BAYBREEZE MOTEL
6410 Highway 1 **$50**
(506) 755-3850

The Baybreeze, which is on Highway 1 between Saint John and St. Andrews, is better than ever this year. John and Maria Lytras have always offered deep-fried clams and deep-fried scallops, and they're the best you'll find anywhere on this shore. But we usually ask instead for the lobster roll or the lobster stew. Others prefer the (excellent) grilled halibut. The vegetables, once quite indifferent, are now always fresh and seasonal. The fries are still frozen, but the coleslaw is homemade. The pastries are all prepared with a light hand, and the olives come from olive trees that grow on the Lytras property in Italy, where John and Maria spend their winters. Here in Pocologan, they have a spacious deck overlooking the Bay of Fundy where you can have a glass of wine before dinner.

Open daily 8 am to 9 pm from early May until late June, daily 7 am to 10 pm from late June until late August, daily 8 am to 9 pm from late August until late October. Licensed. All cards. No smoking.

This is a guide to Canadian restaurants from coast to coast—the first ever published and the only one of its kind on the market today. We accept no advertisements. Nobody can buy his way into this guide and nobody can buy his way out.

PORT CREDIT, Ontario   **(MAP 209)**
BREAKWATER
Waterside Inn   **$175**
15 Stavebank Road S
(905) 891-6225

The Waterside Inn is near the mouth of the Humber River in the heart of Port Credit. The restaurant has big windows on three sides and the tables are widely spaced and laid with fine linen and silver. They have a tapas menu that features grilled chorizo with soft pumpkin, Yukon Gold potato with brie, shrimps sautéed with ginger, salmon gravlax and terrine of foie gras. The main courses—châteaubriand, lamb shanks, pork wiener-schnitzel and Alaska black cod—are (except for the black cod) less exciting. For sweet there's an apple tart tatin and an icewine crème brûlée. Ask for the crème brûlée every time.

Open Monday to Friday 7 am to 11 pm, Saturday and Sunday 8 am to 11 pm. Licensed. Amex, Master Card, Visa. No smoking. Book ahead if you can. Free parking. ♿

PORT ELGIN, N.B.   **MAP 156**
LITTLE SHEMOGUE INN
2361 Highway 955   **$125 ($325)**
(506) 538-2320

The bright-red house overlooking a marshy inlet of Northumberland Strait has been carefully restored and redecorated. Across the inlet, linked to the main house by a foot-bridge, there's a cottage with a spectacular interior. Ask for Room 8 in Log Point, as it's called, when you book. It's expensive, but there's nothing else like it in Atlantic Canada. Dinner is served every evening at 7 o'clock in one of three or four small dining-rooms, but the Sudbracks sold the place in the summer of 2012, so Petra is no longer in the kitchen and her husband, Klaus, no longer serves the wine. That makes all the difference. Over the years, Petra had become a gifted cook. Petra and Klaus—all that has gone now. Come to Little Shemogue, if you come at all, for a room in Log Point and the sight of the Great Blue Herons that fish in the shallows to the west, but not for the cooking.

Open daily at 7 pm by appointment only from 1 May until 31 October. Licensed. Master Card, Visa. You must book ahead. No smoking. &

PORT HOOD, N.S.   MAP 157
HAUS TREUBURG
175 Main Street   **$125 ($250)**
(902) 787-2116

Georg and Elvi Kargoll bought this old house in 1984 and restored it the same year. Georg talks about retiring in five or six years, but there's no tiredness in his voice as he speaks. Their menu seldom changes, their prices never do. Breakfast costs 12.50, dinner 39.00. Dinner comes in four courses and starts with house-smoked salmon or flammkuchen, an Alsatian version of pizza, followed by soup or a Caesar salad. Then there's a choice of meat, fish or a vegetarian dish. The meat might be beef stroganoff or a pork schnitzel, the vegetarian dish might be lasagne. We ourselves usually prefer the fish. The poached Atlantic salmon is about as good as it gets, though they also usually have some haddock or halibut. The meal ends with a fine apple strudel, made to an old family recipe and topped with real whipped cream. If you spend the night—the bedrooms are immaculate—you'll come down in the morning to what they call a German Sunday breakfast, which means farm-fresh eggs, homemade sausages, cereals, grains, hot buttered toast and home-made yogurt. The Haus Treuburg has its own sandy beach and some of the warmest water in Eastern Canada.

Open daily by appointment only from 1 May until 30 November. Licensed. Master Card, Visa. No smoking. You must book ahead.

PORT HOOD
See also GLENVILLE, NORTHEAST MARGAREE.

PORT STANLEY, Ontario MAP 158
ME & SUZIE'S ☆
295 Bridge Street **$120**
(519) 782-3663

If you take the beautiful drive along the north shore of
Lake Erie, pretty soon you'll come across Me & Suzie's
in the village of Port Stanley. It's a small white cottage
on the main street of town. Suzie is now running the
show alone and has redecorated the place inside and out.
She also has a brand-new menu. In season everybody
wants to sit outside on the patio, where the tables are well
spaced and well served. At noon they have hamburgers
made with triple-A beef, squash ravioli and two other
pasta dishes, plus five thin-crust pizzas. In the evening
they now offer pan-fried yellow perch, char-broiled pork
loin with caramelized apple and grilled breast of duck
with dried cherries. Dinners start well with pan-fried
pickerel and end with a buttermilk tart. All the wines are
V.Q.A. listings from Niagara, many of them sold by the
glass as well as the bottle. Everything is surprisingly
cheap. For instance, the yellow perch costs only 18.00,
which is little more than half what it would cost in
Toronto.
Open daily 11 am to 11 pm from Victoria Day until Labour
Day, Wednesday 11.30 am to 9 pm, Thursday to Saturday
11.30 am to 10 pm, Sunday 11.30 am to 9 pm from Labour
Day until Victoria Day. Closed on Monday and Tuesday in
winter. Licensed. All cards. No smoking. &

PORT STANLEY MAP 158
WINDJAMMER INN ☆
324 Smith Street **$125 ($250)**
(519) 782-4173

Kimberley Sanders says she has survived for five years by
virtue of hard work and hard work alone. Her house was
built by a local ship's captain, Sam Shephard, in 1854 and
it makes a fine place to stay. Kimberley has worked in several important Toronto restaurants and she knows how

to cook. Her menu changes every six or eight weeks, always making the most of fresh local produce. She knows all the local farmers and her brother supplies her with fresh herbs, heirloom tomatoes and edible flowers from his garden. Fresh perch and pickerel are always to hand, as well as a number of artisanal cheeses. Dinner starts with the soup of the moment, bison carpaccio or snails with shiitake mushrooms and goes on to slow-braised osso buco with truffled barley or the fish of the day, usually with Asian-style rice pilaf, ginger-snap peas and a citron-wasabi salsa. When it comes to the sweet course, Kimberley often simply improvises and ends up turning out something irresistible. Breakfast, which is served only to resident guests, is a glorious meal. In summer, Sunday brunch comes with live music on the side.

Open daily 11 am to 3 pm, 5.30 pm to 9 pm from Easter to Thanksgiving, Wednesday to Friday 11 am to 3 pm, 5.30 pm to 9 pm, Saturday 9.30 am to 2 pm, 5.30 pm to 9 pm, Sunday 9.30 am to 3 pm from Thanksgiving to Easter. Closed on Monday and Tuesday in winter. Licensed. Amex, Master Card, Visa. No smoking. &

PORTUGAL COVE, Newfoundland   (MAP 182)
FERRY LAST-STOP CAFE   ☆
2 Loop Drive   **$85**
(709) 895-3082

Paulette King runs this little place with the help of her 84-year-old mother, Mercedes. Of this partnership Paulette says simply, "she is my life." The Café overlooks the ferry to Bell Island, and perhaps for that reason is one of a kind in Portugal Cove. The menu is short and seductive. Everything is fresh and organically grown. One diner writes that his salad of local greens was the best in his memory. Bread is made in the kitchen every morning. All the soups and all the sweets are made in-house. If fresh cod is on the menu, be sure to ask for it—you'll be surprised when it comes to the table. There are fifteen to twenty wines on the list, most of them sold by the glass as well as the bottle. A couple of rooms upstairs are kept

for travellers who want to stay for the night. (Those who do will find that breakfast is almost as good as dinner.)
Open Wednesday to Sunday 10 am to 3 pm, 6 pm to 9 pm from early May until early December. Closed on Monday and Tuesday. Licensed. Master Card, Visa. No smoking.

PRINCE ALBERT, Saskatchewan   MAP 160
AMY'S ON SECOND   ☆
2990 2 Avenue W   **$135**
(306) 763-1515

Amy's seems to be the only good restaurant that can survive in this town. Two by Dahlsjo opened to good reviews, but within a year it was reduced to catering. Amy always gave a little more than she had to, of course; she always listened to her customers and allowed for their preferences. When she began to get tired she found an able sous-chef in Klarke Dergoussoff, a graduate of the Stratford Chefs School. He and Amy have been offering bison and duck for so long that they now seem old hat. Fresh salmon has become a staple too, often served in a mango-butter glaze. Halibut and Arctic char come in once a week. Rack of lamb is often on the menu, though it's not Canadian—Canadian lamb is too expensive. The pastry chef has been with Amy for twenty years and makes at least eight different varieties of cheesecake, as well as wonderful crème brûlée. The Great West Coffee Company is gone, but Amy bought enough beans to last her for some time.
Open Monday to Saturday 11 am to 9 pm. Closed on Sunday. Licensed. All cards. No smoking. Free parking. ♿

PRINCE GEORGE, B.C.   MAP 161
THE WHITE GOOSE   ☆
1205 3 Avenue   **$160**
(250) 561-1002

Ryan Cyre spent ten years in Vancouver as sous-chef to Moreno Miotti before he opened the White Goose in Prince George. He knows Moreno's menus like the back of his hand, but he's determined to be his own man, especially with his five-course dinners. His style is essentially Tuscan. Dinners start with several well-known appetizers: spinach salad with brie, pears and almonds, sea-scallops finished with sambuca, wild-mushroom risotto with white truffles and golden-fried lobster ravioli in a fresh-tomato sauce. The duck confit is a memorable dish too and it comes with wonderful shoestring potatoes. Cyre's mother makes the chocolate cake to an old family recipe, and we ourselves prefer it to the house specialty, which is chocolate cheesecake baked en croûte. The wine pairings are skilfully chosen and as for the service, it's almost too quick, especially at noon.

Open Monday to Saturday 11.30 am to 2 pm, 5 pm to 10 pm. Closed on Sunday. Licensed. Master Card, Visa. No smoking. ♿

PRINCE RUPERT, B.C.   MAP 162
COW BAY CAFE   ★★★
205 Cow Bay Road   **$110**
(250) 627-1212

When Adrienne Johnston took over the Cow Bay Café from Richard Davis, it was immediately evident that there would be no decline in standards. Since then in fact, Adrienne has become one of the most accomplished cooks in the province, without losing a particle of her charm. She has only eleven tables, all of them eagerly booked, and she still changes her menu twice a day. You should come here soon because we hear murmurs of retirement. Seafood is the backbone of her menu, but she also loves duck, now served with pomegranates and quajillo chillies. Other newcomers are the rack of lamb with zinfandel jam and jerk pork, which is made from the best pork tenderloin she can get. In the summer she does a lot of wild Pacific salmon, which often comes with red Thai curry and Asian slaw. The celebrated halibut starts in mid-March and is gone by mid-November. The same fleet fishes for Alaska king crab. The halibut is usually served in hot chermoula sauce or with coconut and coriander; the black cod comes in a miso marinade with

Japanese tamarind. Adrienne makes all her own chowders, all her own bread and a number of lovely sweets,
among them a sticky-toffee pudding-cake and a lemon-
buttermilk pudding. Lately she's been taking courses in
wine service and some of her dinners now come with
Okanagan wine pairings.

*Open Tuesday noon to 2.30 pm, Wednesday to Saturday noon
to 2.30 pm, 6 pm to 8.30 pm. Closed on Sunday and Monday.
Licensed. Amex, Master Card, Visa. No smoking. You must
book ahead.* &

PRINCE RUPERT   MAP 162
OPA SUSHI
34 Cow Bay Road   **$90**
(250) 627-4560

Customers at Opa Sushi are asking for sashimi these days
instead of tempura. The kitchen is still offering kaiseki
dinners every so often, but the chef is now more interested in his bi-weekly fresh sheet. A couple of new items
will be on the sheet this year. One of these is the so-called
Green Dragon, which means pickled asparagus with avocado, carrots and cucumber in barbecue sauce. The
other is the Manila Vanilla, which is named after the Fil-
ipino chef. It combines crab with cucumber, avocado and
curried honey. They never use anything in the kitchen
but fresh local salmon, squid, octopus, eel and sweet
shrimps, and they have the only sake bar in the Pacific
Northwest. You'll find the place on the second floor of
an old net loft, one of the last of its kind on this coast.
It's right on the water and has 35 seats. If you take a table
outside on the patio you should be able to watch sea-ea-
gles nesting overhead.

*Open daily 11.30 am to 2 pm, 5 pm to 9 pm. Licensed. Master
Card, Visa. No smoking.*

The price rating shown opposite the headline of each
entry indicates the average cost of dinner for two with a
modest wine, tax and tip. The cost of dinner, bed and
breakfast (if available) is shown in parentheses.

PRINCE RUPERT   MAP 162
SMILE'S
113 Cow Bay Road $75
(250) 624-3072

You don't usually expect good cooking from a restaurant with a history like Smile's. There's been a café on this site, hidden away among railroad sidings and fish plants, for more than 70 years. People who used to come here with their children come today with their grandchildren. It's true, the cooks still use the old-fashioned deep-fry, but changes are on the way. Already, salmon, sole, red snapper and black cod can be had poached or pan-fried. Prince Rupert used to be the halibut capital of the world. Eventually the supplies ran out, but now halibut is once again on the menu at Smile's. Halibut is fiercely expensive at the moment, so they may be using snapper or cod in their fish and chips. They have excellent chowders too, as well as club sandwiches made with crab or shrimp. If you want an old-fashioned milkshake, this is the place to get it. Last year we were worried by talk of a complete renovation, but all that meant was a coat or two of fresh paint.
Open daily 10 am to 10 pm from early June until Labour Day (shorter hours in winter). Licensed. Master Card, Visa. No smoking. &

QUALICUM BEACH, B.C.   MAP 163
GIOVANNI'S
180 2 Avenue W: Unit 4 $120
(250) 752-6693

This place is the creation of Giovanni (the chef) and Helen Belcastro (the manager). Every evening in summer they serve a four-course tasting menu of Greek and Italian food in an attractive, comfortable setting. They start with an *amuse bouche* of a bruschetta that goes really well with the chianti riserva they have on the wine-list. (The fact is that a good chianti goes well with almost anything.) Steelhead salad comes next, then a trio of veal with prawns, scallops and sole. The sweet is usually tiramisu, which in our opinion comes in a poor second to the panna cotta. On the à la carte, veal is usually the best choice, though the rack of lamb is good too. The seafood, which is plentiful and correctly cooked, is all local. Recently, Giovanni has expanded his lounge, where he serves pizzas and light meals. Everything comes from the same kitchen—ask for the Italian Combo in the lounge and see for yourself.

Open Monday to Friday 11.30 am to 2 pm, 5pm to 10 pm, Saturday and Sunday 5 pm to 10 pm from 1 June until 30 September, Monday to Thursday 11.30 am to 2 pm, 5 pm to 9 pm, Friday 11.30 am to 2 pm, 5 pm to 10 pm, Saturday 5 pm to 10 pm, Sunday 5 pm to 9 pm from 1 October until 31 May. Licensed. All cards. No smoking. &

QUALICUM BEACH
See also COOMBS.

QUEBEC, Quebec	**MAP 164**
APSARA	
71 rue d'Auteuil	**$85 ($175)**
(418) 694-0232	

The Apsara is now run by Chau Mouy Youk and her husband, a son of Beng an Khuong. Beng an Khuong escaped from Cambodia in 1975, leaving all his possessions behind. Within two years of his arrival in Canada he had bought this fine old house with his sixteen children, several of whom still work in the restaurant. Chau Mouy Youk has been in charge of the kitchen for at least 30 years and she makes a virtue of consistency. The menu includes Thai and Vietnamese dishes as well as Cambodian, and it seldom changes. Everything is amazingly cheap. The lunch menu, which changes daily, costs just 12.95. Ignore the chicken brochette and look for one of the shrimp dishes, which are always good. There's a shrimp stir-fry, for instance, that comes to the table in a nest of fried vermicelli. If you come with a companion, there are several dishes on offer for two or more, among

them an appetizer of spicy pork with crisp noodles from Thailand and a main course of oudong chicken stir-fried with ginger. There are a number of Cambodian pastries and some very good sorbets. They have a few wines, but it's better, we think, to ask for a carafe of hakutsuru sake, which is on draft. It comes cold and clear and it's great.
Open Monday to Friday 11.30 am to 2 pm, 5.30 pm to 11 pm, Saturday and Sunday 5.30 pm to 11 pm. Licensed. Amex, Master Card, Visa. No smoking.

QUEBEC   **MAP 164**
L'INITIALE   ✫✫✫
54 rue St.-Pierre   **$295**
(418) 694-1818

L'Initiale is one of a handful of Relais & Châteaux in Canada. Yvan Lebrun has two seasonal menus, one an eight-course tasting menu, the other a traditional à la carte. The à la carte offers medallions of venison, sea-bass, breast of duck and fresh lobster. Both menus end with a sweet *du jour* and a spectacular plate of fresh berries and cream with cake. The setting is beautiful, the service impeccable, the cooking rich but delicate. The wines are mainly French, with a small selection of Tuscans. Prices are high, but you can drink very well by the glass. Yvan Lebrun is once again at the top of his form.
Open Tuesday to Friday 11.30 am to 2 pm, 6 pm to 9 pm, Saturday 6 pm to 9 pm. Closed on Sunday and Monday. Licensed. All cards. No smoking. Book ahead.

QUEBEC   **MAP 164**
LAURIE RAPHAEL   ✫✫✫
117 rue Dalhousie   **$260**
(418) 692-4555

There's no on-street parking and no valet parking at Laurie Raphael and the car park at the end of the street isn't easy to use, especially after dark. If you have trouble, ask for help at the front desk. The evening meal begins with white sturgeon or Raspberry Point oysters on the half-shell, followed by scallops from Maine and a ballotine of guinea-fowl from a local farm. At noon the menu is much simpler and considerably cheaper, featuring smoked salmon, wild-mushroom crostinis and oysters Rockefeller to start with, followed by curried shrimps, loin of pork and fish of the day. The smoked salmon is exquisite. It's smoked right here and served with ground sumac and cauliflower florets. The fish of the day might come from Hawaii, because Daniel Vézina doesn't limit himself to regional produce, though he uses it whenever he can. There's a well-made apple pie at the end of the meal, though we prefer the lemon cake. The wine-list is expansive, offering no fewer than 24 dessert wines, twelve ports and twenty champagnes, as well as the usual table wines.

Open Tuesday to Friday 11.30 am to 2 pm, 5.30 pm to 10 pm, Saturday 5.30 pm to 10 pm. Closed on Sunday and Monday. Licensed. All cards. No smoking. You must book ahead. &

QUEBEC	**MAP 164**
PANACHE	☆☆
Auberge St.-Antoine	**$250**
(418) 692-1022	

It costs a lot to take a taxi to Panache from almost anywhere in the city, but if you come in your own car there's free valet parking at the hotel door. There's a *prix-fixe* dinner that costs 95.00 for six courses, but the à la carte itself is expansive and very splendid. Dinners begin with yellow beets or sweetbreads, tartar of salmon or foie gras and go on to fillet of sea bream, guinea fowl, scallops (now correctly cooked) and duck from Saint-Apollinaire. The wine-list is splendid too. It may skimp on pauillacs, but it has every other virtue. It's expensive, of course. Everything is expensive at Panache, but this is now a restaurant where you should just ask for the bill, pay it and forget the cost.

Open Monday to Friday 11.30 am to 2 pm, 6 pm to 10 pm, Saturday and Sunday 6 pm to 10 pm. Licensed. All cards. No smoking. Free valet parking. Book ahead. &

QUEBEC   **MAP 164**
LE SAINT-AMOUR   ★★★
48 rue Saint-Ursule   **\$250**
(418) 694-0667

Benoît Larochelle is the *chef de cuisine* here, which gives Jean-Luc Boulay more time to look after his own restaurant, Chez Boulay. But there's certainly been no loss of panache in the menu or the cooking at the Saint-Amour. Rather the reverse. The Saint-Amour may still have a two-star à la carte, but it now has a wonderful, three-star table d'hôte that costs 63.00 and changes every day. The soup with which the meal begins is good beyond belief, and everything that follows is carefully orchestrated, so that each dish comes to the table with an air of authority and grace. The à la carte begins with foie gras, long a specialty of Boulay's, and goes on to such things as lobster bisque, snow-crab ravioli, smoked and salted duck, seabass in a coulis of purple cauliflower, venison, squab and Alberta lamb. Why, one wonders, make so much of snow crab, which hasn't enough flavour to carry the ravioli? Why offer European sea-bass, which is always a disappointing fish? Such questions never arise on the table d'hôte, where the flavours are all compelling. The winelist, of course, is extraordinary. There are three Lafites, two Latours, seven Mouton-Rothschilds and five Pétrus, one of which is now priced at 15,000.00. There are sensible wines too for ordinary drinkers, and most of them are fairly priced.
Open Monday to Friday 11.30 am to 2 pm, 6 pm to 10 pm, Saturday 5.30 pm to 10 pm, Sunday 6 pm to 10 pm. Licensed. All cards. No smoking. Free valet parking. Book ahead.

QUEBEC   **MAP 164**
LA TANIERE   ★★★
2115 rang Ste.-Ange   **\$260**
(418) 872-4386

At La Tanière they offer three *prix-fixe* menus, the Discovery (ten courses for 75.00), the Sensation (fifteen courses for 105.00 and the Revolution (twenty courses for 135.00). If your companion shares your wine pairings the evening will cost you 260.00. If not, you'll have to pay 325.00. (If you don't accept the wine pairing and choose your own wine, the price will be even higher.) We have never tried the Sensation or the Revolution—the guide doesn't pay us enough for that. The Discovery menu begins with foie gras, black truffles, smoky fleur de sel and chives in puff pastry, all served on a small mirror, followed by salmon with baby zucchini and banana foam on a warm pillow. Next comes a scallop in honey foam and a morsel of guinea-fowl coated with cherry. Then partridge with local vegetables in thyme jelly and duck gizzard in parsnip purée. Finally, there's raw wapiti, bison tongue, caramelized apple on a candy-cap mushroom and a lavender macaroon. What can one say about such splendours? If you have the money to spare, spend it here. If you haven't, don't blame us.

Open Wednesday to Saturday 6 pm to 9 pm. Closed Sunday to Tuesday. Licensed. All cards. No smoking. You must book ahead. &

QUEBEC	**MAP 164**
TOAST	☆☆
17 Sault-au-Matelot	**$175**
(418) 692-1334	

Toast spends its summers in a big tent; in winter you eat inside. Christian Lemelin is still in charge of the kitchen and he has an exciting and unusual menu. It lists a dozen small plates and customers usually choose two or three to share. There's tartar of venison, foie gras de canard, mushroom crostini, veal cheeks and entrecôte of bison. They're all cleverly cooked and presented with style. We particularly admire the veal and the bison. The menu is all in French, so if you have any allergies be sure to ask for an English translation. The wine-list, which is fairly priced, concentrates on wines from France and California, and there's an excellent Château Signac from the Côtes du Rhône for only 48.00.

Open Monday to Friday 11.30 am to 2 pm (summer only), 6 pm to 10.30 pm (later on Friday), Saturday 6 pm to 11 pm, Sunday 10 am to 2 pm (brunch), 6 pm to 10.30 pm. Licensed. All cards. No smoking. ♿

QUEBEC
See also ILE D'ORLEANS, ST.-GEORGES-DE-BEAUCE.

RADIUM HOT SPRINGS, B.C. (MAP 92)
HELNA'S STUBE
7547 Main Street W **$160**
(250) 347-0047

Don't try anything else in Radium—Helna's is the place to go. The menu is Austrian and offers an extraordinary variety of potato dishes. There are always daily specials, which might be lake trout or roasted elk with gin or roasted venison with chanterelles. Actually, the chef is at his best with veal and his wienerschnitzel comes, rather dramatically, with cranberries. The restaurant seats 40 inside and 40 outside, but Radium is crowded in summer, so be sure to make a booking.
Open Tuesday to Sunday 5 pm to 10 pm from 1 June until Thanksgiving, Tuesday to Saturday from Thanksgiving to 31 May. Closed on Monday in summer, on Sunday and Monday in winter. Licensed. Master Card, Visa. No smoking. Book ahead.

REGINA, Saskatchewan MAP 166
LA BODEGA
2228 Albert Street **$125**
(306) 546-3660

Adam Sperling is constantly trying out new ideas, which he offers on what he calls his fresh sheet. There you might find his jumbo shrimp in white wine, which has become a specialty of the house. Sometimes he's way over the top, as when he offers twenty ounces of beef spiked on a sabre, and several of his tapas dishes are big enough for a whole meal. But every Monday night there's a spectacular tasting menu. It consists of nine courses for 35.00 a head, and it's one of the best deals in town. There aren't a lot of wines, and you're meant to order one of their 80 martinis instead. Most people do just that.

Open Monday to Saturday 11 am to 2 am, Sunday 10.30 am to 2 am. Licensed. Amex, Master Card, Visa. No smoking. Book ahead if you can. &

REGINA   **MAP 166**
TANGERINE
2234 14 Avenue   **$40**
(306) 522-3500

Tangerine is owned by Evolution Catering, which opened in Regina three or four years ago. It's very, very cool. The whole back wall is covered with a huge chalk-board advertising what they have to offer on any given day. That usually means lasagne, soup, a salad and such unusual sandwiches as roasted-peppers-and-walnuts and chicken with apple and sausage. But the menu changes every day, sometimes (it seems) every five minutes, so call ahead and find out what's on.

Open Monday to Friday 7 am to 6 pm, Saturday 9 am to 4 pm. Closed on Sunday. No liquor. Master Card, Visa. No smoking. &

REGINA   **MAP 166**
WILLOW ON WASCANA   ☆
3000 Wascana Drive   **$160**
(306) 585-3663

Somebody once said that Willow on Wascana was too expensive for Regina. That may be true. The land chowder served for lunch costs 15.00 and that's about the cheapest thing on the menu. But there's nowhere else in town where you can have lunch or dinner overlooking Wascana, the man-made lake right in the centre of the city. What is that worth? Also, the kitchen is known for serving nothing but produce raised in Saskatchewan. How much is that worth? Tim Davies' menu is highly experimental, but nearly everything seems to work. Bison is still important to him, and so is Pacific snapper. If you're looking for a filling lunch, order the wild-boar sausage in a cassoulet of white beans. The wine-list has expanded and there's now plenty of good drinking almost everywhere on the list.

Open Monday to Saturday 11.30 am to 4.30 pm (lunch), 4.30 pm to 9 pm (dinner). Closed on Sunday. Licensed. All cards. No smoking. &

REGINA
See also VIBANK.

REVELSTOKE, B.C.   MAP 167
WOOLSEY CREEK CAFE   ☆
600 2 Street   **$120**
(250) 837-5500

We used to call the Woolsey Creek Café a best buy. It still is, but we now think the cooking good enough to earn it a star. Sylvie Bisson has always made full use of local produce, offering meatballs with local wild mushrooms and crème brûlée made with local goat-cheese. Sylvie buys organic fruits and vegetables whenever she can and tries always to have some fresh fish on hand. Ahi tuna appears in many shapes and sizes; wild salmon might appear with barley and pineapple or with maple and dijon. There are three specialties. One of these is pasta, another duck confit, the third a jambalaya of prawns, chorizo, mussels and chicken in a spicy tomato broth. Don't overlook the sweets. There's a dark-chocolate truffle-cake and a rhubarb-and-pear crumble. There are wines from two or three wineries that you won't find in the liquor store.

Open daily 5 pm to 10 pm. Licensed. Master Card, Visa. No smoking.

REVELSTOKE
See also HEDLEY.

RIMOUSKI, Quebec   **MAP 168**
LE CREPE CHIGNON
140 avenue de la cathédrale   **$90**
(418) 724-0400

This is one of the very few places to eat in Rimouski it-self (see also Bic). Basically, it's a crêperie with a con-science—everything is either recyclable or biodegradable. The big, colourful menu offers fifteen or sixteen of their favourite crêpes, as well as the crêpe Breton, for which you choose your own filling from a list of several meats, vegetables and cheeses. They make all their own jams and their own yogurt and bake all their own bread. They also make fine omelettes and several Mexican dishes, but you're usually better with one of the crêpes. They have a licence, and you can have a glass or two of Orpailleur if you like, but we usually ask for the fresh-squeezed orange-juice or even a cup of the excellent coffee. The Cathedral of Saint-Germain is just down the street and its dazzling white interior looks like a painting by Sanredam. It's worth a visit.

Open Monday 7 am to 9 pm, Tuesday to Thursday 7 am to 10 pm, Friday 7 am to 11 pm, Saturday 8 am to 10 pm, Sunday 8 am to 9 pm. Licensed. All cards. No smoking. ♿

RIMOUSKI
See also LE BIC

RIVIERE DU LOUP, Quebec   **MAP 169**
CHEZ ANTOINE   ☆
433 rue Lafontaine   **$145**
(418) 862-6936

Chez Antoine has an astonishing wine-list, filled with the best burgundies and bordeaux and a generous selection of wines from California. There's an especially splendid list of clarets from St.-Julien and an amazing selection of the great Tuscans, with at least ten sassicaias from San Guido and sixteen tignanellos from Antinori. The kitchen makes every effort to prepare appetizers and main courses to match and on the whole it succeeds. The beef tartar with aged balsamic vinegar is a masterpiece and so is the foie gras de canard. The *plats principaux* have improved over the years, and they now serve first-class foie gras de Charlevoix and excellent sea-bass with couscous, shiitake mushrooms and sake. This is a comfortable, stylish restaurant with outstanding service.

Open Monday to Friday 11.30 am to 1.30 pm, 5 pm to 9 pm, Saturday and Sunday 5 pm to 9 pm. Licensed. All cards. No smoking. &

RIVIERE DU LOUP MAP 169
AU PAIN GAMIN
288 rue Lafontaine **$35**
(418) 862-0650

Au Pain Gamin is right across the street from Chez Antoine. We've never been quite sure why Chez Antoine closes its lunch at 1.30, but if you come after that you can pick up a fougasse or a pizza across the street. They make pizzas with goat-cheese and red wine and with mushrooms and fresh tomato, and they're both great. They call their cooking artisanal and use nothing but organic flour in all their sandwiches, the best of which is still the ham-and-cheese. There's some homemade soup every day— perhaps a mushroom or a navy-bean—as well as fine espresso. The interior of the place isn't very prepossessing, but don't be put off by that.

Open Tuesday to Friday 9 am to 6 pm, Saturday 8 am to 5 pm. Closed on Sunday and Monday. No liquor. Visa. No smoking.

ROCKY HARBOUR, Newfoundland MAP 170
JAVA JACK'S ☆
88 Main Street N **$135**
(709) 458-3004

Java Jack's has the only espresso-maker in Rocky Harbour and perhaps the only kitchen without a deep-fry. Jacqui Hunter knows what she's doing. She had a gardener before she had a restaurant, and there's still something from her garden on every plate she serves, even if it's just an edible flower. Her asparagus, all grown from seed, had a great year, and so did her lettuce. Salads are important to her. You'll still find mussels Thai-style, pan-seared cod and salmon en papillote on her menu. But what she's really interested in at the moment is moose meat. Now that moose meat is for sale, she's looking for a suitable entrée. Perhaps it'll be moose-meat shepherd's pie or maybe moose bourguignon. The big change this year was turning the downstairs space into a breakfast room. For breakfast there are now steel-cut oats and smoked-char scrambles with moose sausage. The wine-list is good and growing.

Open daily 8 am to 8 pm from 1 May until 30 June, daily 8 am to 9 pm from 1 July until 30 September. Licensed. All cards. No smoking. No reservations.

ROCKY HARBOUR
See also NORRIS POINT, WOODY POINT.

ROSSEAU, Ontario   (MAP 83)
CROSSROADS
2 Cardwell Road   **$135**
(705) 732-4343

Rosseau is a small village at the northern end of Lake Rosseau. There's not much there except a much-loved general store and Julie and Richard Lalonde's purpose-built restaurant on the other side of the highway. Crossroads, as it's called, has an interesting menu that offers such things as house-smoked Manitoulin Island trout, Georgian Bay pickerel, Berkshire pork and hand-picked Grenville Farms lettuce. The best of these is still the Berkshire pork. The lunch menu is very short, especially as the dry-aged beef burgers are just that. The green-pea soup, however, and the Caesar salad are both lovely dishes. Most of the wines come from California, but there's at least one from Niagara and that's the one to ask for. It's the Peninsula Ridge sauvignon blanc, which shows just how good Canadian wines have become.

Open daily 11.30 am to 10 pm from Victoria Day until Thanks-giving, Thursday to Sunday 11.30 am to 9 pm from Thanks-giving until Victoria Day. Closed Monday to Wednesday in winter. Licensed. Amex, Master Card, Visa. No smoking. &

ROUYN, Quebec　　　　　　　　　　　　**MAP 172**
LA BROCHETTERIE GRECQUE
152 avenue Principale　　　　　　　　　　　**$100**
(819) 797-0086

People used to come to the Brochetterie in Rouyn be-cause it was more genuine than any of the Greek restau-rants in Montreal. That is no longer quite true. Greek dishes have been gradually disappearing from the menu. The lamb has gone and most of the veal has gone, and in-stead of five chocolate cakes there are now only two. (The Chocolate Explosion is still great—try it and see for yourself.) They often used to overcook their fish, but we were sorry to see the salmon and the scallops both disap-pear. There are still good things to eat, however, and most travellers still seem to enjoy themselves here. Veal parmesan, the only veal dish left, is still nicely prepared and so is the souvlaki. The dining-room is too big, of course, but it comes into its own in the evening. The wine-list is largely French, but there are a few interesting vintages from Niagara as well.
Open Monday to Thursday 11 am to 11 pm, Friday and Sat-urday 11 am to midnight, Sunday 9 am to 11 pm. Licensed. All cards. No smoking. &

ST. ANDREWS, N.B.　　　　　　　　　　**MAP 173**
ROSSMOUNT INN　　　　　　　　　　　　☆☆☆
4599 Highway 127　　　　　　　　　　　　**$145**
(506) 529-3351

Chris Aerni is performing brilliantly again this year. He's particularly good with his pan-seared foie gras with cran-berries, walnuts and balsamic vinegar, but you don't have to spend a lot to enjoy Aerni at his best. His most spec-tacular dishes are in fact among his cheapest: salmon tartar with avocado and pickled ginger and steamed quahog clams. Neither dish costs more than 10.00. He's a master of arugula and wild mushrooms, and he's good too with organic beans, which he pairs with grilled striploin of beef. As for his lemon-brûlée tart, it's served in a raspberry coulis and it has few equals anywhere. Aerni has a big wine-list. You can drink a Kim Crawford sauvignon blanc quite cheaply, but nothing—not even a solaia—costs more than 195.00. The Rossmount and the Idylle in Moncton (see above) are without question two of the best restaurants in the country.

Open daily 5.30 pm to 9.30 pm from 9 April until 31 December. Licensed. Amex, Master Card, Visa. No smoking. Book ahead in season. &

ST. CATHARINES, Ontario   MAP 174
WELLINGTON COURT   ☆
11 Wellington Street   **$150**
(905) 682-5518

It's now almost 30 years since Claudia Peacock restored her father's charming little house on Wellington Street and started to run a small, choice restaurant with her son, Erik. Erik has now been on his own for almost ten years, developing an imaginative, even daring menu. The restaurant is plastered with vivid and ever-changing artwork. The service is knowledgeable and efficient; the cooking is reliable. Lunch runs to sandwiches and pizzas, but there's always a homemade soup (wild-mushroom, perhaps) and the fish of the day may be trout or perch or pickerel. In the evening there's homemade ravioli stuffed with Ontario lamb, pappardelle with veal cheeks and chanterelles and confit of duck with white beans and sausage. (If you're looking for a steak, they've got a good one.) We've recommended the sticky-toffee pudding for years, but others think the almond cake with preserved strawberries is even better. Most of the wines come from the Niagara Region and they're all fairly priced. There are nine or ten wines by the glass and there's a fine Peter Lehmann shiraz by the bottle. You can bring your own bottle if you like, and the corkage fee is only 15.00. In summer Erik runs an outdoor restaurant at the Henry of Pelham winery at 1469 Pelham Road (telephone (905) 684-8423).

Open Tuesday to Saturday 11.30 am to 2.30 pm, 5 pm to 9.30 pm. Closed on Sunday and Monday. Licensed. All cards. No smoking. Free parking. Book ahead in summer.

ST. CATHARINES
See also BEAMSVILLE.

ST.-FAUSTIN-LAC-CARRE, Quebec (MAP 126)
LA CABANE A SUCRE MILLETTE
1357 rue St.-Faustin **$60**
(877) 688-2101

St.-Faustin is close to Mont Tremblant and the Cabane à Sucre Millette is a big attraction for the ski crowd, provided the snow lasts until late March or early April, when the sap is rising in the trees. The Cabane has been run by the Millette family on their farm for more than 50 years. Here they serve traditional *habitant* food to up to 300 people at a single sitting. The long tables you share with your neighbours are served by waitresses in period costume, while a fiddler plays traditional reels. Legend has it that the recipes come from the family cook-book. Meals all begin with thick pea soup and crusty homemade bread. Next comes an omelette, baked beans, scrunchions and maple-cured ham or sausage, both garnished with homemade pickles. Sweets mean sugar pie and pancakes with hot cream and sugar. With the meal you're expected to drink maple wine—before the meal there's a caribou cocktail made with maple syrup. It's a lot stronger than you think.

Open Monday to Friday 11.30 am to 1.30 pm, 5.30 pm to 7.30 pm, Saturday and Sunday 11.30 am to 7.30 pm. Licensed. All cards. You must book ahead. No smoking. &

We accept no advertisements. We accept no payment for listings. We depend entirely on you.

STE.-FLAVIE, Quebec   **MAP 176**
LE GASPESIANA
460 rue de la Mer   **$95 ($210)**
(800) 404-8233

The cooking here may not be quite what it used to be, but the place is a godsend for anyone who comes to the Gaspé out of season. The bedrooms, all of which face the beach and the Gulf of St. Lawrence, are immaculate. The dining-room, which is open all year, is expansive and well served. The kitchen majors in fish and shellfish: clam chowder, shrimp bisque, cod meunière and bouil-labaisse. They have a good sugar pie, but otherwise the cooking isn't distinguished. The wine-list, which is rather small and con-ventional, has two great buys: the Kim Crawford sauvignon blanc for 36.00 and the Liberty School cabernet sauvignon for 46.00. They're open Monday to Friday 11 am to 4 pm, 6 pm to 10 pm, Saturday and Sunday 6 am to 10 pm (shorter hours in winter). Licensed. Amex, Master Card, Visa. No smoking. ♿

ST.-GEORGES-DE-BEAUCE, Quebec (MAP 164)
MAISON VINOT   ☆☆
11525 2 Avenue   **$195**
(418) 227-5909

This old house—it was built in 1928—has been restored and refitted as a restaurant. Raymonde and Philippe are an enthusiastic and good-natured couple who like to cook. They've been cooking for five years now and in 2011 were finalists in the Grand Prix du Tourisme. They work with locally grown produce, which means fresh vegetables of all sorts, but little fish. You'll be surprised by the quality and freshness of everything on the menu. The kitchen is particularly interested in grain-fed local turkey, but they also make much of bison and emu and, of course, of beef tenderloin, which must be ordered the day before. At the end of the meal, you can expect Que-bec cheeses and a number of first-class maple-syrup sweets. Dinners are all *prix-fixe* and the price of the main course includes an appetizer and coffee. Nothing is ex-pensive except the beef, which is hard to get in these parts. The wine-list consists mainly of private imports and it keeps changing. The Maison Vinot is in a lovely part of the Eastern Townships and it's well worth a visit. *Open Tuesday to Friday 11.30 am to 1.30 pm, 6 pm to 9 pm, Saturday 6 pm to 9 pm. Closed on Sunday and Monday. Licensed. Master Card, Visa. No smoking. Book ahead.*

ST.-GEORGES DE MALBAIE, (MAP 148)
Quebec
AUBERGE FORT PREVEL ☞
2053 boulevard Douglas **$115**
(418) 368-2281

The same chefs have been in charge of the kitchen here for nearly ten years, the son taking over from the father. The menu seldom changes, but the bouillabaisse is full of beautiful lobster, cod, shrimps, salmon and scallops. Many people admire the foie gras de canard, considering it the best dish on the menu. The kitchen smokes its own salmon and regularly offers Rivière-au-Renard shrimps with white wine and dill. Salmon might come in a lobster coulis, cods' tongues with pancetta. All the seafood is perfectly fresh and in the fall there's usually some game as well. In season they always have plenty of fresh fruit. The hotel has a magnificent situation on a headland between Gaspé and Percé, with a beach, a swimming-pool, a tennis-court and a nine-hole golf course. The dining-room itself is beautiful and there are several modern chalets.
Open daily 6 pm to 8 pm from mid-June until mid-September. Licensed. All cards. No smoking. ♿

ST.-HYACINTHE, Quebec MAP 179
LE PARVIS
1295 rue Girouard o **$75**
(450) 774-0007

You can't miss Le Parvis. It's located in an old church that's painted pink and doubles as an art gallery. Denis Coté, the owner and chef, has a carefully prepared regional menu. There are specials every day of the week and some unusual appetizers, such as elk terrine in a cranberry coulis, shrimps provençal and a scallop salad with candied ginger. The table d'hôte is really a *menu du terroir* and it's a good example of its kind, offering rabbit kidneys stewed in mustard, pan-fried calf's liver with leeks and fillet of cod beurre blanc. There are three soups and six sweets, the best of which is apple pie made with handpicked apples. The meal costs just 22.00, which is a remarkable buy. Before you leave town, pay a visit to the Casavant organ factory. It's well worth it.

Open Tuesday to Sunday 9 am to 8.30 pm. Closed on Monday. Licensed. Master Card, Visa. No smoking.

ST.-JEAN-PORT-JOLI, Quebec   MAP 180
AUBERGE DU FAUBOURG
280 avenue de Gaspé o   **$120**
(800) 463-7045

This place has been around for ages, but in the last few years the cooking has gone up-market. The inn is right on the river and it has a handsome dining-room with an exceptional collection of wood carvings. If you want something more elaborate than the Boustifaille, this makes a useful alternative. Dinner is an ambitious meal, featuring fresh halibut, quail from Cap Saint-Ignace and Moroccan-style lamb. The most interesting appetizer is a guacamole of shrimps and sweet peppers.

Open daily 11 am to 2 pm, 5 pm to 9 pm (later on weekends) from 1 May until 15 October. Licensed. Amex, Master Card, Visa. No smoking. Book ahead. &

ST.-JEAN-PORT-JOLI   MAP 180
LA BOUSTIFAILLE
547 avenue de Gaspé e   **$60**
(877) 598-7409

The Boustifaille opened in 1965 with the intention of providing *habitant* cooking at reasonable prices. After more than 45 years, the kitchen is still preparing things such as split-pea soup, tourtière, ragoût de pattes et boulettes, fèves au lard and, of course, sugar pie. Nowadays, the daily specials like chicken vol-au-vent are as good as ever, and the sugar pie may be better. But the dishes on the à la carte no longer possess their old magic, though the prices are still surprisingly low. (You can have a three-course table d'hôte for less than 20.00 a head.) They have a handful of serviceable wines and two or three draft beers. Maple syrup is always available to take out, and sometimes sugar pie as well.

Open daily 7 am to 11 pm from 1 June until 12 October (shorter hours in the spring and fall). Licensed for beer and wine only. Master Card, Visa. No smoking. &

SAINT JOHN, N.B.　　　　　　　　MAP 181
THE ALE HOUSE
1 Market Square　　　　　　　　　　　　**$90**
(506) 657-2337

The Ale House looks like a pub, with its brick walls and big windows overlooking the Bay of Fundy. Much of the produce they use comes from Chef Jesse Vergen's back garden. (Vergen has a small farm near Quispamsis.) They call their cuisine progressive pub food. Progressive or not, the crisp pork appetizer is a dish of pork lardons dusted with spice, and it's very good indeed. Then there's a chicken wrap, a cheeseburger and a club sandwich. The steaks at 32.00 are pretty expensive; go instead for the steak frites at less than half that. The pan-seared trout is great too. The best of the sweets are the maple bread pudding and the Guinness cake with chocolate. The Ale House has some 35 craft beers, some on tap, most from small, award-winning micro-breweries. Every Thursday they offer a cask of real ale from Moosehead. Upstairs there's a more formal area for diners, but we prefer the ground-floor pub.

Open Monday to Thursday 11.30 am to midnight, Friday and Saturday 11.30 am to 2 am, Sunday noon to 10 pm. Licensed. All cards. No smoking. No reservations. &

SAINT JOHN

MAP 181

BILLY'S
City Market   **$140**
49-51 Charlotte Street
(506) 672-3474

Billy's offers a wide variety of fresh seafood in a newly renovated dining-room, with competent service and reasonable prices. They serve raw oysters for just over 2.00 a shell (26.00 for twelve), steamed mussels in white wine, fish and chips (a fine dish) and Atlantic salmon (blackened or with cucumber yogurt), Atlantic halibut and whole naked lobster. The lobster is as good as any that can be had, and the fish and chips are better, much better than most. They have a dozen wines in the cellar, among them wines from Kim Crawford, Wolf Blass and Mission Hill. The Monkey Bay sauvignon blanc from Marlborough offers great drinking for only 8.00 a glass.
Open Monday to Thursday 11 am to 10 pm, Friday and Saturday 11 am to 11 pm, Sunday (except in winter) 4 pm to 9 pm. Licensed. All cards. No smoking. ♿

SAINT JOHN

MAP 181

INFUSION TEAROOM
City Market   **$45**
41 Charlotte Street
(506) 693-8327

The Infusion Tearoom is in an out-of-the-way corner of the City Market, but inside it's quite elegant. They do a great breakfast (omelettes and croissants) and a very satisfactory lunch (soups and sandwiches). We particularly like their Reuben sandwich and their smoked-salmon pâté. But tea is what the place is really all about. They offer black, white and green teas, as well as all the familiar varieties, in either a two-cup or four-cup press. If you book the day before, you can have a classic high tea, with sandwiches, scones and Devonshire cream. If you like you can even bring your own bottle of wine; the corkage is only 5.00.

Open Monday to Friday 8 am to 6 pm, Saturday 8 am to 5 pm. Closed on Sunday. Licensed for beer and wine only. Amex, Master Card, Visa. No smoking. ♿

SAINT JOHN   **MAP 181**
SUWANNA   ☆
325 Lancaster Avenue   **$85**
(506) 637-9015

Suwanna has become an institution in Saint John. It's located out on Lancaster Avenue, where it overlooks the Saint John River. They serve traditional curries, stir fries and noodle dishes. There are red and green curries, priced from 17.50 for the pork to 21.50 for the fresh scallops. There's also a fine panaeng curry and a lovely, delicate Matsaman curry made with chicken, sweet potatoes and chopped shrimps. There are several noodle dishes, including the familiar pad Thai and a glass-noodle dish called poey sian. There are at least fifteen stir fries, some of which, like the squid with chillies and garlic, are quite unusual. The most attractive of the appetizers are the curry puffs, which are like potato samosas. Or you can just have a chicken satay with peanut sauce. There's a rudimentary wine-list and a Thai beer that goes well with any of the curries. That's the thing to drink.
Open daily 5 pm to 8 pm. Licensed. Master Card, Visa. No smoking. Free parking. Book ahead.

SAINT JOHN   **MAP 181**
THE URBAN DELI   ☆
68 King Street   **$135/$50**
(506) 652-3354

The big news at the Urban Deli is that from Wednesday night to Saturday night it becomes a restaurant called Italian by Night. Liz Rowe hired Michelle Hooten as chef. Hooten is an old hand with bruschettas, ciabattas, terrines and cannellini beans. She also has an Italian sweet and an Italian cheese of the day. Italian by Night is very popular, so you have to book well in advance. Andrew Brewer continues to cook by day. He has a big menu, featuring such things as smoked-meat sandwiches, reubens, salmon burgers and a meatloaf. Usually there's also a quiche and macaroni and cheese in a double-cheese sauce. There are several local beers that go well with the lemon sour-cream pie.

Open Monday to Friday 11.30 am to 3 pm, Saturday 9 am to 3 pm. Closed on Sunday. Licensed. All cards. No smoking. Book ahead if you can.& Italian by Night is open Wednesday to Saturday 5 pm to 9 pm. Closed Monday, Tuesday and Sunday. Licensed. All cards. No smoking. Book ahead.

ST. JOHN'S, Newfoundland   MAP 182
AQUA   ☆☆
310 Water Street   **$140**
(709) 576-2782

Aqua is a casual place, but there's nothing casual about Chef Mark McCrowe's commitment to regional produce. His menu changes four times a year, but his meals all begin with house-made focaccia and an *amuse-bouche*, which if you're lucky may be cod cheeks. Butternut-squash soup flavoured with maple comes next, then sesame-crusted tuna or pan-seared cod with salt-beef collard greens. The chef loves to mix contrasting flavours, like steelhead trout with fennel or braised lamb shanks with caramelized onions. Salmon is almost always on the menu and everybody loves it. Keep an eye out for the parsnip cake, which is often on offer, and no wonder; it's great.

Open Monday to Friday noon to 2 pm, 5 pm to 10 pm, Saturday and Sunday 5 pm to 10 pm. Licensed. All cards. No smoking. Book ahead if you can. &

ST. JOHN'S   MAP 182
BASHO   ☆
283 Duckworth Street   **$160**
(709) 576-4600

Basho is a Japanese fusion restaurant that's popular with

those who like sushi and with those who don't. All the sushi is prepared at the upstairs sushi bar by the proprietor, Tak Ishiwata, using the freshest possible raw fish. Before he came here, Tak worked for Nobu Matsuhisa in Tokyo and he brought many of Nobu's recipes with him. The sushi is all wonderful, especially the maguro. If you don't want sushi, there's also tuna tartar, snow crab and lobster sashimi. If that all sounds too much like sushi, ask for the panko-crusted rack of lamb. If you want some fun at the end of the meal, order yourself a dessert martini. Basho is fun, whatever you order, though on busy nights the service is apt to be slow.

Open Monday to Friday noon to 2 pm, 6 pm to 10 pm (later for sushi), Saturday 6 pm to 11 pm. Closed on Sunday. Licensed. All cards. No smoking. Book ahead. &

ST. JOHN'S
BISTRO SOFIA
320 Water Street
(709) 738-2060

MAP 182
☆
$125

Sofia is a French-style bistro, just across the street from the Murray Premises. Gregory Bersinski, the chef, is Bulgarian and he makes everything in-house. His menu isn't large, but it's uniformly likeable, offering a glimpse of a relatively unfamiliar cuisine. At noon there's a shopska salad and free-range chicken with red wine on ciabatta. In the evening there's blackened salmon with mango and braised lamb shanks with a vegetable mirepoix. The pastry chefs make what are said to be the best sweets to be had in St. John's. The restaurant has a mini-bakery on site and within a year they hope to have gluten-free options for most of their dishes. The coffee is outstanding.

Open daily 9 am to 11 pm. Licensed. All cards. No smoking. &

This is a guide to Canadian restaurants from coast to coast—the first ever published and the only one of its kind on the market today. We accept no advertisements. Nobody can buy his way into this guide and nobody can buy his way out.

ST. JOHN'S
CHINCHED BISTRO
7 Queen Street
(709) 722-3100

MAP 182
★★
$150

Chinched means full. When Michelle LeBlanc and Shaun Hussey first opened it wasn't so easy to fill every table. The charming little house, which isn't far from the strip-joints on George Street, has a dining-room upstairs. The menu is small and seasonal, but everything on the list is the best and freshest they can find. Start with the sweet-onion bisque with salt beef, but take a look also at the charcuterie platter. Hussey is a charcuterie chef and his charcuterie platters are always interesting. After that there's salt cod wrapped in potato, cornmeal-crusted chicken livers, slow-braised lamb shanks and sometimes an octopus stew. The sweets are all good and it's hard to choose among them, but we like the chinched pavlova with roasted apples, caramel and lemon. There aren't a lot of wines, but at least they're cheap.
Open Tuesday to Saturday 6 pm to 10 pm. Closed on Sunday and Monday. Licensed. Master Card, Visa. No smoking. Book ahead.

ST. JOHN'S
GYPSY TEAROOM
315 Water Street
(709) 739-4766

MAP 182
★
$150

They no longer have the old tapas menu here on week-ends, which is a pity. The regular à la carte offers pork tenderloin, rack of lamb and blackened fresh salmon. For that matter, all the fish is fresh and it's never overcooked. The sweets are all made in-house, and there's something different every night. The Gypsy Tearoom calls itself a tearoom, but really it's all about taking a seat at the bar and having a good time.
Open Monday to Friday 11.30 am to 3 pm, 5.30 pm to 10 pm, Saturday and Sunday 11 am to 3 pm (brunch), 5.30 pm to 10 pm. Licensed. All cards. No smoking. Book ahead. ⅏

ST. JOHN'S   **MAP 182**
THE HUNGRY HEART CAFE
142 Military Road   **$45**
(709) 738-6164

The Hungry Heart is still one of the hottest places in town for lunch, so you need to book ahead. It's one of the enterprises run by Stella Burry Community Services, which means that everything is as cheap as possible. Not that Maurice Boudreau cuts corners. On the contrary, everything is perfectly fresh and locally sourced. Every day Boudreau offers soups, salads, sandwiches and one or two quiches. In his off hours he likes to fish for salmon or go foraging for chanterelles or blueberries. Recently he had a salmon sandwich that was made club-style with naturally cured bacon, wasabi and honey mayonnaise, all on homemade ciabatta bread. The menu has been designed to take care of people with allergies, and they even have a gluten-free chocolate pudding.
Open Monday to Friday 10 am to 2 pm, Saturday 10 am to 4 pm (brunch). Closed on Sunday. No liquor. Master Card, Visa. No smoking. Book ahead. ♿

ST. JOHN'S   **MAP 182**
INTERNATIONAL FLAVOURS
4 Quidi Vidi Road $40
(709) 738-4636

We dropped this place last year, because we objected to the fact that it served only one dish, the same dish day after day and week after week. But many of our readers disagreed, and so it's back in the guide this year. You can order their vegetable curry straight up, in which case it costs 9.50. Or you can have it with chicken, lamb or tofu for 10.50. It's a huge dish and it comes with some very good naan. If you want to drink something, help yourself to a bottle of water or a glass of mango juice from the cooler.
Open Tuesday to Saturday noon to 7 pm. Closed on Sunday and Monday. No liquor. Master Card, Visa. No smoking. No reservations.

ST. JOHN'S
MAGNUM & STEINS
329 Duckworth Street
(709) 576-6500

MAP 182
☆
$150

Magnum & Steins was one of the first restaurants to open in St. John's after the oil boom began. The kitchen is full of energy, the cooking full of colour. The regular menu changes every four months, but the daily specials are usually more interesting than anything on the à la carte. Look for the local mussels and the house-made potato gnocchi, the bouillabaisse and the triple-A steaks, followed by the flourless chocolate cake and the triple-nut chocolate in phyllo.

Open Monday to Friday noon to 2 pm, 6 pm to 10 pm, Saturday and Sunday 6 pm to 10 pm. Licensed. All cards. No smoking. Book ahead. ♿

ST. JOHN'S
RAYMONDS
95 Water Street
(709) 579-5800

MAP 182
☆☆
$225

Raymonds opened in late 2010 and it's still hard to get a table. Jeremy Charles and Jeremy Bonia met in Portugal Cove when they were both working at Atlantica. The two men shared a common goal, which was to create a high-end restaurant with fine food, wine and service, while using nothing but regional ingredients bought from local farmers or local suppliers. The dining-room—it's appropriate to call it that—has heavy curtains and thick carpets. There's elegant formal service. The menu opens with a selection of oysters on the half-shell, charcuterie and hand-crafted pasta and goes on to sweetbreads, veal cheeks and belly of lamb. There's also a seven-course tasting menu for 115.00 with a wine pairing for 70.00. The wine-list is very splendid and very expensive.

Open Tuesday to Saturday 5.30 pm to 10 pm. Closed on Sunday and Monday. Licensed. All cards. No smoking. Book ahead. ♿

ST. JOHN'S   **MAP 182**
THE SPROUT
364 Duckworth Street   **$50**
(709) 579-5485

The Sprout is the only vegetarian restaurant in St. John's that we know of. If you want a table you have to come early, because they don't take reservations. They use only the freshest of local ingredients and maintain an extensive menu. They have at least six salads and a variety of sandwiches and burgers. There's also a homemade soup every day and a black-bean chilli. The burgers (lentil, chick-pea and tofu) are always a good bet. Last year they added a cheese plate, several organic wines and a few gluten-free sweets.

Open Tuesday to Thursday 11.30 am to 8 pm, Friday 11.30 am to 9 pm, Saturday 9 am to 9 pm, Sunday 9 am to 3 pm. Closed on Monday. Licensed. Master Card, Visa. No smoking. No reservations.

ST. JOHN'S
See also PORTUGAL COVE.

ST.-JOVITE, Quebec   **(MAP 126)**
LE CHEVAL DE JADE   ★★★
688 rue de St.-Jovite   **$200**
(819) 425-5233

All is well in St.-Jovite. It's been a hard year for Canadian restaurants, but Olivier Tali and Frédérique Pironneau have stuck to their guns. They put all they had into this old farmhouse in St.-Jovite and just a few years later they won the Table d'Or, Quebec's most prestigious honour. Tali is also the only Canadian winner of the Ordre des Canardières, which came to him for his caneton à la Rouennaise, the signature dish of the Tour d'Argent in Paris. It means pressed duck and it's on the menu at the Cheval de Jade every night of the week. It has to be ordered the day before and it costs 99.00 for two. They make their bouillabaisse with seafood they import from

France and serve the same day. Olivier aims to have the freshest and best fish to be had anywhere in the Laurentians and he probably does. He always has a fish soup, a fillet of striped bass en papillote, scallops with vanilla beans and paradise seeds. They buy everything locally, and we especially admire their red deer, their truffled duck and their foie gras. The presentation is always gorgeous, and there's a very good wine-list. The Cheval de Jade is pure magic.

Open Tuesday to Saturday 5 pm to 10 pm. Closed on Sunday and Monday. Licensed. Amex, Master Card, Visa. No smoking. Book ahead. &

ST.-LUNAIRE-GRIQUET, (MAP 6)
Newfoundland
DAILY CATCH
112 Main Street **$75**
(709) 623-2295

This unassuming little restaurant is just a few minutes' drive from L'Anse-aux-Meadows (see above). It was opened several years ago by Pearl Henderson and two of her daughters. They specialize in such local dishes as pan-fried cods' tongues with scrunchions and fish and chips made with freshly-caught haddock. The chips are hand-cut and deep-fried in the kitchen. Local beers come with every meal and every meal ends with partridge-berry or bake-apple cheesecake. They also have a small store that sells locally-prepared bake-apple, blueberry and partridge-berry jams at half the price they charge down the road. If you plan to visit the Viking settlement nearby, the Daily Catch is a handy place to know about.

Open daily 11 am to 9 pm from Victoria Day until 30 September. Licensed. All cards. No smoking. &

This is a guide to Canadian restaurants from coast to coast—the first ever published and the only one of its kind on the market today. Every restaurant in the guide has been personally tested. Our reporters are not allowed to identify themselves or to accept free meals.

ST. MARYS, Ontario   (MAP 199)
WESTOVER INN
300 Thomas Street   **$175 ($350)**
(519) 284-2977

This is a lovely place to stay and it makes an ideal base for the Stratford Festival. Stratford itself is only a few miles away and St. Marys is one of the finest small towns in Ontario. The Westover Inn occupies a wooded estate at the edge of town. The main house was built a hundred years ago of rough stone, and today the dining-room and lounge fill most of the ground floor. The dining-room is handsome and dignified and the service is friendly. But the chef, Anthony Gosselin, doesn't ask enough questions. To him, lamb is lamb and bison bison, though either or both may be tough or tasteless. He's at his best when he relies less on his suppliers. His green salad of baby spinach, for instance, and his ragoût of snails are both very successful dishes. His wines, however, are not cheap and there's nothing much to drink for less than 50.00 a bottle. The Westover Inn is cheaper than, say, Rundles in Stratford, but at 58.00 for a *prix-fixe* dinner it's still fairly expensive.
Open daily 11.30 am to 2 pm, 5 pm to 8 pm. Licensed. All cards. Book ahead. No smoking.

ST. PETER'S, N.S.   MAP 186
BRAS D'OR LAKES INN   ☆
Highway 104   **$125**
(800) 818-5885

Jean-Pierre Gillet ran a resolutely French restaurant in the German town of Kitchener before coming to Cape Breton and settling in St. Peter's, halfway between Sydney and the Canso Causeway. Here he's cooking as well as ever. You can expect a fish knife with your salmon and a hock glass with your gewurztraminer. Your pâté will be made with herbs from the kitchen-garden, your chowder will be filled with fresh seafood, the cream on your sweet will be real and freshly whipped. There's plenty to choose from—lamb bordelaise, day-boat halibut, salmon with mustard and lobster with citrus butter. Believe it or not, the pick of the sweets is a plain apple brown Betty. *Open daily 5 pm to 9 pm from 1 July until 31 August (shorter hours in the spring and fall). Licensed. All cards. No smoking. Free parking.*

ST. PETERS BAY, P.E.I. (MAP 43)
THE INN AT ST. PETERS ☆
1668 Greenwich Road **$140 ($280)**
(800) 818-0925

The great windows of the Inn at St. Peters overlook one of the loveliest views on the Island, soft green fields stretching along the whole length of St. Peters Bay. This year Wes Gallant took over in the kitchen. Gallant uses nothing but local produce, and in fact most of his vegetables and herbs come straight from his own garden. Start with trout in its skin, bacon-wrapped chicken fritters with sweet-potato fries or South Lake oysters on the half-shell. Then there's North Shore lobster in season, seared halibut with grilled asparagus and mango salsa and roasted pork with apple-and-maple chutney. The best of the sweets is probably the raspberry tart with chocolate frangelico, and there's a nice selection of liqueurs on the wine-list. The hostess is Karen Davey. She's in charge of the front of the house and she's a wonder.
Open daily 5 pm to 8.30 pm from 1 May until 30 September. Licensed. All cards. No smoking. ♿

ST.-PIERRE-JOLYS, Manitoba MAP 188
OMA'S SCHNITZEL STUBE 🖐
61 Sabourin Street S **$55**
(204) 433-7726

If you call up this place to book a table, a voice will greet you. "Oma's still here," the voice will say. That's good news, because Oma is a gem. St.-Pierre-Jolys is a pretty village half an hour south of Winnipeg. The Stube is run by the Zimmerman family, who came to Canada from a

small town near Frankfurt in 2007. Oma's has the best German food in the province and some of the lowest prices you'll find anywhere. In the last year or two the buffet price has crept up a dollar or two, so you may have to pay all of 17.00 (less if you're a senior) for rouladen (on Sunday), fresh pollock (on Friday), garlic shrimps with spaetzle (on Saturday) or one of the classic schnitzels, which are on the à la carte every day. After that there's apple strudel and schwartzwalder kirschtorte with cherry brandy or slivowitz. The coffee is great.
Open Wednesday to Sunday 11 am to 9 pm. Closed on Monday and Tuesday. Licensed. Master Card, Visa. No smoking. &

SALT SPRING ISLAND, B.C. (MAP 218)

Salt Spring Island has always been known for its lamb, its cheese and its mussels. More recently it's been known for its wineries, for its abundance of organic produce and for its bakeries. The best way to get to know what's available is to visit the Farmer's Market in Ganges, which is held every Saturday from Easter until Thanksgiving. (There's also an organic Farmer's Market every Tuesday.) Here you can sample David Wood's celebrated goat-cheese and sheep's-milk cheese. If you drive north out of Ganges you'll soon come across the Garry Oaks and the Salt Spring Island wineries. Both offer tours and tastings. A third winery, Mistaken Identity, makes a number of organic wines. Smoked salmon and crab pâté are both available right in Ganges itself from Sea Changes. The restaurant in Hastings House (telephone (250) 537-2362) is, we think, too expensive for readers. Piccolo's (see below, telephone (250) 537-1844) is closer to the mark and attracts visitors by the boatload.

SALT SPRING ISLAND. (MAP 218)
BRUCE'S KITCHEN
115 Fulford Ganges Road: Suite 3106 **$140**
(250) 931-3399

Bruce Wood has moved to Grace Point Square, where he has the room to expand his menu and enlarge his wine-list. He works closely with local farmers to design an ever-changing menu that always features the best of local produce. Homemade soups are on offer at both lunch and dinner. For lunch there may also be a salad of organic greens and a barbecue of pulled pork. You can also have mussels with great, great fries. Bruce is good with pasta and you should try his hand-rolled gnocchi with smoked bacon and moonstruck white grace cheese. If you're looking for seafood, ask for his salmon with green vegetables. *Note:* as this edition went to press, we received reports that Bruce might be planning to close. Call ahead before you go.

Open Tuesday to Saturday 11.30 am to 3 pm, 5.30 pm to 9 pm, Saturday 5.30 pm to 9 pm. Closed on Sunday and Monday. Licensed. Master Card, Visa. No smoking.

SALT SPRING ISLAND (MAP 218)

HOUSE PICCOLO ☆☆
108 Hereford Avenue **$160**
(250) 537-1844

We think this is now the best place to eat on Salt Spring Island. Piccolo Lyytikainen used to price his meals as if the House Piccolo were the Hastings House. This year, however, he has reduced his prices, which makes the restaurant accessible to the ordinary traveller. Piccolo has no sea view, no open-air deck. He has nothing to offer but good food. The best of the appetizers is the gravlax marinated in brandy, though the local goat-cheese salad and the warm gorgonzola tart with red onions and port wine are both impressive dishes too. When it comes to the main course, diners have to choose between Grand Veneur venison with juniper and lingonberries and breast of Muscovy duck with green peppercorns—we usually ask for the venison. Piccolo is good with pastry and his Alsatian pear-and-almond tart is the best of his sweets.

Open Wednesday to Sunday 5 pm to 9 pm. Closed on Monday and Tuesday. Licensed. Master Card, Visa. No smoking.

If you use an out-of-date edition and find it inaccurate, don't blame us. Buy a new edition.

SALT SPRING ISLAND (MAP 218)
MARKETPLACE CAFE
149 Fulford Ganges Road: Suite 103   **$140**
(250) 537-9911

The Marketplace has become a favourite with diners because it's close to all three ferry terminals and has some good things to eat. At noon they offer crisp calamari and a fabulous crab-cake, followed by tiger prawns or mini lamb burgers dressed with either moonstruck feta or curried aioli and spicy mango. In the evening they put on a Basque-style fisherman's stew and end with a wonderful flourless-chocolate cake.
Open Tuesday to Saturday 11.30 am to 4 pm, 5.30 pm to 10 pm (shorter hours in winter). Closed on Sunday and Monday. Licensed. Master Card, Visa. No smoking.

SASKATOON, Saskatchewan   MAP 190
CALORIES
721 Broadway Avenue   **$135**
(306) 665-7991

Calories has an interesting and well presented menu. The chef, Uwe Wedekind, was trained in Germany; his predecessor, Rémi Cousyn, came from France. But they both developed a network of local suppliers when they came to Saskatoon. Wedekind uses nothing but organic produce, much of it grown nearby. His menu changes every month and new ideas come thick and fast. At the moment he's offering rillettes of local pork on a bed of red cabbage, marinated duck with a salad of pea-shoots and eggplant lasagne layered with olives. There are cakes of all sorts—cheesecakes, tortes, pies and cookies, all on display in big glass cases at the front. The wine-list is eccentric at best. Better just ask for a piece of cake and a cup of latte.
Open Monday to Thursday 11 am to 10 pm, Friday and Saturday 10 am to 11 pm, Sunday 10 am to 4 pm. Licensed. Amex, Master Card, Visa. No smoking. Book ahead if you can.

SASKATOON   MAP 190
ST. TROPEZ
238 2 Avenue S   **$135**
(306) 652-1250

Regulars come here because they know exactly what
they'll get. After all, the same chef has been in charge for
twenty years, and his son has been here for at least ten.
The chipotle shrimps and the chicken-liver pâté are both
still on the menu. There have always been two salmon
dinners and two chicken dinners (chicken Cajun-style
and chicken with dijon). There's always filet mignon and
curried lamb. The beef is local, the lamb often not. But
everything is correctly cooked; the vegetables are fresh,
the saskatoons hand picked every summer. At the end of
the meal, crème caramel is always available. There are at
least 70 labels on the wine-list. Almost all of them cost
100.00 a bottle or more, but if you pay cash they give
you a 10% discount on your next meal. If you have tickets for the Persephone Theatre around the corner, they'll
make sure you get there on time.
Open Wednesday to Sunday 5 pm to 10 pm. Closed on Monday
and Tuesday. Licensed. All cards. No smoking. &

SASKATOON   MAP 190
SUSHIRO
737 Broadway Avenue   **$75**
(306) 665-5557

Megan Macdonald moved to Vancouver last year and sold
two thirds of the restaurant to her employees. That didn't
sound like good news, but so far there haven't been any
important changes. The fish is still beautifully fresh, and
the sushi is about as good as it gets. The yam tempura is
still a magical dish and the salads haven't lost their savour.
Their seared tuna tataki with avocado and orange is still
a memorable dish. They have Hakutsuru sake on draft,
as well as two or three premium sakes by the bottle. Inside, the restaurant is decidedly contemporary and everything about the place is very chic indeed.

Open Monday to Saturday 5 pm to 10 pm. Closed on Sunday.
Licensed All cards. No smoking. &

SASKATOON   MAP 190
TRUFFLES   ☆
230 21 Street E   **$125**
(306) 373-7779

Truffles is located in the old Birks building in downtown
Saskatoon. Inside it's bright and *au courant*. This is one
place where the table d'hôte could be regarded as the specialty of the house. There's almost always a first-rate
eight-ounce striploin with wonderful truffled fries on it,
or perhaps steelhead trout from Diefenbaker Lake. But
Lee Helman is a trained French chef and there are those
who think that it would be a mistake to stick to such
things as steak or steelhead trout, even if they are cheap.
If you feel that way, ask for the breast of duck or perhaps
the house-made ravioli. Everything is made from scratch,
even the tomato ketchup. He even makes all his own
bread and all his own sweets. His wine-list, however,
needs to be enlarged, especially the selection of wines by
the glass. The service is all it should be.
Open Monday to Friday 11.30 am to 3 pm, 5 pm to 10 pm,
Saturday 10 am to 2.30 pm (brunch), 5 pm to 10 pm, Sunday
10 am to 2 pm (brunch). Licensed. All cards. No smoking. &

SASKATOON   MAP 190
WECZERIA   ☆☆
820 Broadway Avenue   **$190**
(306) 933-9600

Weczeria means evening meal in Ukrainian. Since the
owner and chef, Dan Walker, is not Ukrainian and serves
lunch as well as dinner, nobody understands (or can pro-
nounce) the name. However that may be, the restaurant
was such a success that, after only a year or so, they were
able to move to larger and grander quarters on Broadway.
The menu changes twice a day and everything is made
from the best and most expensive local produce. Even the

pike and the chicken (that old cliché) are startling and wonderful. Gnocchi is always available as an appetizer, with different toppings every day. There are a number of outstanding sweets, but most people settle for the crème brûlée or (our favourite) the lemon tart. Lunch is a simpler meal, but even at noon everything tastes just as it should. Most of the wines come from the Okanagan or Niagara, and there are also local beers from Paddockwood on tap. Weczeria is now the best restaurant in Saskatoon.

Open Monday to Saturday 11.30 am to 2 pm, 5 pm to 9 pm. Closed on Sunday. Licensed. Master Card, Visa. No smoking. &

SAULT STE.-MARIE, Ontario   **MAP 191**
ARTURO'S   ☆
515 Queen Street E   **$140**
(705) 253-0002

Arturo's is probably the best of the many Italian restaurants in Sault Ste.-Marie. It's been on this site for 30 years, and Arturo has been in charge of the kitchen all that time, assisted first by his brother and later by his children. The menu is pretty familiar, but everything on it is carefully cooked. Arturo is still bringing in milkfed veal and that's what we think you should order. There's piccata limone, saltimbocca, marsala and, if you're really hungry, a twelve-ounce veal chop. If you don't want that much to eat, ask for the mussels, a green salad or the ravioli stuffed with pumpkin. There's always the catch of the day, which may be trout, tuna, red snapper or sea-bass. Most of the wines come from Italy, though there are also wines from Chile and elsewhere in the New World. This has always been a family restaurant and every visitor is made to feel a part of the place.

Open Monday to Saturday 5 pm to 11 pm. Closed on Sunday. Licensed. All cards. No smoking. &

Nobody can buy his way into this guide and nobody can buy his way out.

243

SAULT STE.-MARIE
PANNA
472 Queen Street E
(705) 949-8484

MAP 191
★★
$145

Annelise Wolfe and Erik Nowak settled in the Sault eight or nine years ago and opened this café. Inside it's narrow, noisy and minimalist. One thing you can be sure of and that is that nobody comes here for pasta. The Asian seafood is what gets the most attention, especially the swordfish with chick-peas, the curried shrimp and the pickerel crusted with corn-meal. Theme nights have always been a great success. They have sushi nights, Thai nights, Korean nights and East Indian nights. As for the sweets, once you've had the warm valhrona-chocolate cake you won't be interested in anything else. They have a decent wine-list with an unusual number of open wines.
Open Monday to Saturday 11.30 am to 10 pm. Closed on Sunday. Licensed. Amex, Master Card, Visa. No smoking.

LA SCIE, Newfoundland
THE OUTPORT TEAROOM
Highway 414
(709) 675-2720

MAP 192
$45

This year the Outport Tearoom won the top award for cultural tourism, which inspired Valery Whalen to new heights. She has often said that she and her husband, Larry, would entertain anyone who showed up at their door, no matter what the time of day. And it was true. She did the cooking while Larry played old Newfoundland tunes on his accordion. The Whalens had transformed their family homestead into a museum and then opened a tearoom on the spacious glass verandah that runs the length of the house. At first they just served fruit tarts, tea-buns and rhubarb crumbles. Later they enlarged the menu, adding such local dishes as crab-au-gratin and fishcakes. There's jiggs dinner on Thursday, pea soup on Saturday and codfish on Sunday.

Open daily 8 am to 8 pm from 1 June until 30 September. No liquor, no cards. No smoking.

SHELBURNE, N.S.   MAP 193
CHARLOTTE LANE CAFE   ☆
13 Charlotte Lane   **$135**
(902) 875-3314

Roland Glauser and his wife, Kathleen, have been running the Charlotte Lane for almost twenty years. The restaurant is full of colour and has big windows overlooking the garden. It's a lovely place for dinner in summer. The menu is large and offers a variety of seafood. The best of the appetizers is the seafood chowder or the eggplant piccata, which comes with layers of eggplant and goat-cheese in basil and balsamic vinegar. There's also a South Shore fish sampler for only 9.95. The best of the main dishes has always been rack of lamb with orange and port wine. Roland Glauser cooks well, but he cooks rich. His lobster, for instance, will stagger anyone over 30. If you're over 30, ask for the salmon with honey-mustard and ginger or perhaps the so-called smokehouse salad. There are several luscious sweets, the most exciting of which is the pear cake with chocolate.
Open Tuesday to Saturday 11.30 am to 2.30 pm, 5 pm to 8 pm from the middle of May until late December. Closed on Sunday and Monday. Licensed. Master Card, Visa. No smoking. Book ahead if you can.

SHELBURNE
See also CLARK'S HARBOUR.

SIDNEY, B.C.   (MAP 218)
DEEP COVE CHALET   ☆☆☆
11190 Chalet Road   **$160**
(250) 656-3541

The Deep Cove Chalet is an hour by car from Victoria, but it's worth every mile, even in driving rain. Take Highway 17 from Douglas Street as far as the last exit before Swartz Bay and turn left there on Land's End Road. Pierre Koffel maintains a generous à la carte, but the table-d'hôte menus—there are three, priced from 32.50 to 60.00—offer most of his important dishes. For just 32.50 you can begin with a lovely lobster bisque, go on to a fine cheese soufflé and end with a wedge of flourless-chocolate cake, or, for a few dollars more, with a perfect tarte tatin or a soufflé grand marnier. Everything is perfect. The wine-list is extraordinary. There are eighteen Mouton-Rothschilds dating back to 1967, five Lafites from 1966 and four Latours from 1975. For realistic drinking, there's a useful list of Okanagan wines, of which the best buy is the pinot gris from Burrowing Owl, cheap at 45.00 a bottle. The setting of the Chalet is beautiful and the parking-lot is full of Bentleys and Mercedes-Benzes. No wonder.

Open Wednesday to Sunday noon to 2 pm, 5.30 pm to 9 pm. Closed on Monday and Tuesday. Licensed. All cards. No smoking. Book ahead. &

SINGHAMPTON, Ontario   MAP 195
EIGENSINN FARM   ☆☆☆
Townline 10   **$800**
(519) 922-3128

Michael Stadtländer and his wife, Nobuyo, have been running Eigensinn Farm for nineteen years. This year they plan to be open only on Friday and Sunday, and since there are only twelve seats in the dining-room you should book at least three months in advance and pay when you book. It's a long way to go from almost anywhere, even for an eight-course dinner. The price of a meal is 300.00 a head, plus tip and tax. As for wine, you must bring your own bottle. Michael Stadtländer ranks with the best chefs in the world. He was born the son of a farmer, and here he has a vegetable garden so big that he has had to employ a full-time gardener. He has two farm ponds, where he raises speckled trout and crayfish. He breeds ducks and sheep. He grows fruit trees. All these things eventually find their way onto his table. To get to Eigensinn Farm, head west from Singhampton on Townline 10 and remember to bring your own bottle—there's no charge for corkage.

Open Friday and Sunday at 7 pm by appointment only. Closed Monday to Thursday and on Saturday. Bring your own bottle. No cards. No smoking. You must book ahead.

SINGHAMPTON   **MAP 195**
HAISAI   ★★
794079 County Road 124   **$245**
(705) 445-2748

Michael Stadtländer designed this place for his son, Jonas. But before the job was finished, Jonas and his wife had left Canada for Japan. They've now returned, but not to Singhampton. Michael ran the place himself for a year or so, but the job left him little time for Eigensinn Farm, his main interest (see above). So he decided to hire a top chef from Japan every year. The farm will continue to supply Haisai as well as Eigensinn, which means that all the produce used in both restaurants will be organic and there will be no genetically modified food on either menu. They have a small à la carte menu, as well as two tasting menus, one at 70.00 and a second at 90.00. They also offer a variety of wood-oven pizzas, which they sell for 18.00 each. Haisai also has a short list of Niagara wines. Everything in the room is made by hand, even the wineglasses and the furniture.

Open Wednesday to Friday 5.30 pm to 9 pm, Saturday 1 pm to 3 pm (pizzas only), 5.30 pm to 9 pm, Sunday 11 am to 3 pm (brunch). Closed on Monday and Tuesday. Licensed. No cards. No smoking. Book ahead.

SOOKE, B.C.   **(MAP 218)**
EDGE
6686 Sooke Road   **$110**
(778) 425-3343

Edge gets its name from its two owners, Edward Tuson and Gemma Claridge. In 2010 it was named one of the best restaurants in Canada and it's still living up to its early promise. Edge is a small-town family-style café with a simple décor, a creative menu, good cooking and reasonable prices. The best thing on the menu is (we think) the crisp squid with chilli mayonnaise and home-made coleslaw. Ed also makes a lovely squash soup (in season) and a good organic green salad, as well as a fine array of sweets—flourless-chocolate brownies and crème brûlée with dried Bing cherries. There's usually a lot of fresh seafood on the menu—just try the clams, the mussels steamed in white wine, the steelhead trout or the roasted halibut with Israeli couscous and sweet peppers. Ed raises pigs and uses them to make pulled-pork sandwiches and grilled pork chops with potatoes and cheese. The pasta is all made in house and changes daily. The sauces are pretty plain, but Ed is experimenting with a number of curries, the best of which is the lamb. The salads are all good, especially the Caesar, and this year Ed is starting to make his own charcuterie.

Open Tuesday to Saturday 11.30 am to 2.30 pm, 5 pm to 8 pm. Closed on Sunday and Monday. Licensed. Master Card, Visa. No smoking. No reservations.

SOURIS, P.E.I. (MAP 43)
21 BREAKWATER
21 Breakwater Street **$80**
(902) 687-2556

We liked the old Blue Fin in Souris, but 21 Breakwater is an upscale restaurant, where you can get a good meal while you watch the ferry to the Magdalens come and go. Breakwater opened in June of 2012 and quickly became so busy that you couldn't get in the door without a reservation. The menu is quite small, but everything on it is well and carefully cooked. Pedro Pereira and Betty MacDonald limit themselves to local favourites, plus a daily special or two. One cold winter night we remember that the special was a hot fish chowder, full of mussels, clams and hake. The chowder came with garlic bread and left no room for a sweet, not even the blueberry cobbler that was on offer that night. In the summer they have a splendid chicken salad, as well as Portuguese-style fish and chips. Prices are all reasonable—halibut with corn-on-the-cob costs only 15.95.

Open Monday to Saturday 11.30 am to 5 pm (lunch), 5 pm to 9 pm (dinner) from 1 June until 30 September, Wednesday to Saturday 11.30 am to 5 pm (lunch), 5 pm to 9 pm (dinner) from 1 October until 31 May. Closed on Sunday in summer, Sunday to Tuesday in winter. Licensed. Master Card, Visa. No smoking. Book ahead. ♿

STELLARTON, N.S. (MAP 130)
ANDRE'S SEATS
245 Foord Street **$45**
(902) 752-2700

André started out with a pizza takeout at 243 Foord Street, where business was so good that he expanded next door and opened a full-service restaurant with seats. The menu at André's Seats is enormous. Pizzas aside, there's lots of pasta and a number of salads. The chicken penne with maple is by far the best seller. In the evening they bring on salmon, haddock and several steaks. There are also two great salads: baked goat-cheese and André's salad. A fine oregano dressing comes with both. Most of the sweets are made in the kitchen, and the best of them is the three-layer carrot cake with real whipped cream. There are one or two good wines from Gaspereau, as well as numerous imports. The walls are lined with posters from the eras of Neil Young, Elvis Presley and the Dave Clark Five. The glass-topped tables are covered with ticket stubs from concerts of the time, and there's a real jukebox on the floor.

Open Monday and Tuesday 11 am to 8 pm, Wednesday and Thursday 11 am to 9 pm, Friday and Saturday 11 am to 10 pm, Sunday 4 pm to 8 pm. Licensed. All cards. No smoking. ♿

Every restaurant in this guide has been personally tested. Our reporters are not allowed to identify themselves or to accept free meals.

PAZZO
70 Ontario Street $150
(519) 273-6666

Pazzo comes in two parts: a basement bar serving snacks
and a smart dining-room, which is a seasonal operation,
on the ground floor. This is a well-dressed restaurant
with white table-cloths, accomplished service and an interesting menu. Lunch is a simple meal; dinner is more
ambitious. Everything is carefully prepared. For instance,
the salads come with pea-shoots, which give life and
character to almost any dish. Pan-seared scallops come
next, with peas (in season) and a purée of cauliflower.
There's also loin of pork and (for a *supplément*) dry-aged
rib-eye of beef. The wine-list concentrates on wines from
California, Australia and the Niagara Region and it offers
an unusual number of wines by the glass. There's a bakery
next door at No. 76 (telephone (519) 508-2244) where
you can get a picnic lunch to eat on the grass by the river.
*Open Tuesday to Sunday 11.30 am to 2 pm, 5.30 pm to 9 pm
from Victoria Day until Thanksgiving. Closed on Monday. Licensed. Amex, Master Card, Visa. No smoking. Book ahead if
you can.* &

STRATFORD   **MAP 199**
THE PRUNE   ✩✩
151 Albert Street $230
(519) 271-5052

Eleanor Kane has at last sold the Old Prune, but Bryan
Steele is still very much in charge of the kitchen, so it
isn't easy to tell the difference. The restaurant is beautiful
inside, especially if you choose a table overlooking the
garden. The service is still accomplished and the menu—
set dinners now cost 69.00—is full of good eating.
There's hot-smoked trout, terrine of pork cheeks, a
mousse of chicken livers, duck on a charred pancake, albacore tuna and a saddle of local lamb. The meal usually
ends with a cherry strudel or a chocolate fondant, both

of them beautifully made. Most of the wines come from either Niagara or Prince Edward County, with a few from the Okanagan and California, France and Italy. The best buys, we think, are the Huff chardonnay and the Cattail Creek cabernet sauvignon.

Open Tuesday to Saturday 5 pm to 8 pm from late May until late October. Closed on Sunday and Monday. Licensed. Amex, Master Card, Visa. No smoking. Free parking. Book ahead.

STRATFORD   **MAP 199**
RUNDLES   ☆☆☆
9 Cobourg Street   **$275/$150**
(519) 271-6442

Rundles is designed for a hot summer day. Inside it's decorated in white on white, relieved only by the tropical flowers on every table. In the kitchen dinners are prepared by Neil Baxter six days a week all summer long. His cooking is at once imaginative and correct, and he's at his best with such things as pan-fried Atlantic halibut with soybeans and ginger dumplings, loin of lamb with a purée of Jerusalem artichokes and dry-aged rib-eye of beef with king oysters. Meals end with a glazed double-lemon tart. The wines are all sold by the glass as well as the bottle. Among the best are a Woolshed sauvignon blanc, a Henry of Pelham barrel-fermented chardonnay and a Rosehall gamay from Prince Edward County. On the ground floor at the back there's a bistro that offers a somewhat simpler menu for about half the price (93.50) in the main dining-room.

Open Tuesday 5 pm to 7 pm, Wednesday to Friday 5 pm to 8.30 pm, Saturday 11.30 am to 1.30 pm, 5 pm to 8.30 pm, Sunday 11.30 am to 1.30 pm, 5 pm to 7 pm from late May until late October. Closed on Monday. Licensed. Amex, Master Card, Visa. No smoking. Book ahead. ♿

STRATFORD
See also ST. MARYS.

SUMMERVILLE BEACH, N.S. *(MAP 29)*
QUARTERDECK GRILL
7499 Highway 3 **$115**
(800) 565-1119

The Quarterdeck has one of the most spectacular seaside views to be found anywhere on the South Shore. There are sixteen tables, eight inside and eight outside, all overlooking the mile-long beach. The service is always cheerful and fairly quick, which means that you can have lunch and still have time for a swim. The cooking isn't remarkable and prices are quite high, but we can't find anything better within an hour's drive. The Quarterdeck is open all day every day from mid–May until mid–October. They have a licence and take all cards. No smoking. ♿

SUNDRIDGE, Ontario MAP 201
DANNY'S JUSTA PASTA ☆
367 Valleyview Road **$90**
(705) 384-5542

Highway 11 by-passed Danny's last summer. So now you have to go half a mile off the highway to get some of the best pasta to be had anywhere. Danny has a real passion for pasta, all of it prepared fresh to order. He has a huge pasta menu and he's constantly adding to it. The flavours are clean and the spicing is always just right. Most people come back for the chicken penne, which is served in a curry or a blush sauce. Danny's prices may seem high, but the helpings are big enough for two. Apart from the pasta, our favourites are the carpaccio and the snails. The sweets change daily, but if it's available ask for the tiramisu.
Open Monday to Thursday 11 am to 8 pm, Friday and Saturday 11 am to 9 pm, Sunday 11 am to 8 pm. Licensed. All cards. No smoking. No reservations. Free parking.

The price rating shown opposite the headline of each entry indicates the average cost of dinner for two with a modest wine, tax and tip. The cost of dinner, bed and breakfast (if available) is shown in parentheses.

SYDNEY, N.S.   **MAP 202**
AMEDEO'S
100 Townsend Street   **$95**
(902) 270-8008

Amedeo has improved a great deal in the last year or two.
They've added outdoor umbrellas, which make it pleasant to eat on the front patio. They've enlarged their menu
and they no longer bring everything at once on a cold
plate. Their sambuca shrimp still doesn't have enough
sambuca, but their snails in garlic butter are all they
should be and so are the squid and the mussels, which
come perfectly fresh from Aspy Bay. They still do a lot
of pasta, but we prefer the rack of lamb, which is beautifully tender and full of flavour—and very cheap at
30.00. If halibut is offered as a daily special, be sure to
ask for it. It's always fresh and served with a potato
mousse. There's also osso buco (for just 24.00), veal
parmigiana and a New York strip steak that we haven't
tried. The wine-list is small but skilfully chosen. The best
of the red wines is the primitivo; the best of the whites
is the chardonnay from Greg Norman. Both cost only
about 30.00, which is extraordinary. Dinner at Amedeo's
is a wonderful buy.
*Open Monday to Saturday 11 am to 9 pm. Sunday 5 pm to 9
pm. Licensed. Master Card, Visa. No smoking.*

TANTALLON, N.S.   **(MAP 87)**
WHITE SAILS BAKERY
12930 Peggy's Cove Road   **$45**
(902) 826-1966

Look for a bright-yellow building surrounded by a green
lawn and a scattering of picnic tables. Behind is an inlet
of the sea, in front is a parking-lot. The place is always
packed with people filling up on smoked-meat sandwiches. The sandwiches are Montreal-style, but they
don't taste quite the way they did at Schwartz's. They also
have sugar pies, though they don't come with real
whipped cream. You won't do better, however, this side

253

of Halifax.
Open Monday to Saturday 10 am to 7 pm, Sunday 10 am to 6 pm from 1 April until 31 December. No liquor. Master Card, Visa. No smoking. &

TATAMAGOUCHE, N.S.   MAP 204
GREEN GRASS RUNNING WATER
102 Main Street   **$45**
(902) 657-9393

Green Grass is a trim little café on the road to Tata-magouche from the west. It has an interesting art gallery displaying Indian prints and some fascinating furniture by Ken Pierson. The menu, which is posted on a black-board, offers a couple of homemade soups, a garden-fresh salad, a variety of sandwiches and three or four daily spe-cials—a quiche, smoked salmon, a taco and fishcakes. There are always sandwiches (egg, chicken, ham and tuna) as well as several homemade ice creams. If you ar-rive too late for lunch, or are looking for dinner, try the Train Station Inn at 21 Station Road (telephone (902) 657-3222)). It's open late and is a good place to spend the night.
Open daily 10 am to 4 pm. No liquor. All cards. No smoking. &

TERRACE, B.C.   MAP 205
DON DIEGO'S   ☆
3212 Kalum Street   **$100**
(250) 635-2307

Richard and Annalee Davis sold Don Diego's in May of 2010. We should have seen this coming as soon as they started taking Sunday off to play golf. But it seemed that they'd been here forever and would stay forever. They still live upstairs, but the restaurant itself is now owned by Gerran Thorhaug. Thorhaug has done some painting (a good idea) and added a number of dishes to the menu, but there have been no other changes in the kitchen or the front of the house. When the place opened, Davis cooked in the style of Mexico and the American South-west, and this year the cooking is back where it started, though there's an occasional Thai dish on Mondays and an occasional African dish on Wednesdays. There's no printed menu; you just look up at the blackboard to see what's available on any given day. They do a lot of seafood and you should keep an eye out for the Pacific salmon. All the pasta is made in-house, and fresh fruits and vegetables are plentiful in Terrace. Triple-A beef comes in from Alberta and the steaks are all finished with a hot, spicy Southwestern-style sauce. As for sweets, they've always been a big thing here.

Open Monday to Friday 11.30 am to 9 pm, Saturday 9 am to 11.30 am (brunch). 11.30 am to 9 pm. Closed on Sunday. Licensed. Amex, Master Card, Visa. No smoking. Book ahead if you can. &

THUNDER BAY, Ontario   MAP 206
BISTRO ONE   ☆
555 Dunlop Street   **$150**
(807) 622-2478

Jean Robillard may change his menu frequently, but year in and year out his customers seem to know what they want and that's usually the rack of lamb (fresh from Australia) or the confit of duck flamed with cognac and served with black currants and mushrooms. It's customary to begin with the carpaccio of beef. Ahi tuna disappeared from the menu for a while, but nowadays you'll find it again from time to time. The menu touches all the bases of contemporary cooking, and nothing is ever overstated or overcooked. The *pâtissière*, Maria Costanzo, has built a big following over the years, and so you know that her celebrated molten-chocolate cake will stay on the menu forever. Recently she's been offering a sticky-toffee pudding with homemade malt ice cream as well. If you're willing to wait, there's a made-to-order maple-and-orange doughnut served in an espresso cup filled with warm mocha chocolate. The wine-list features wines from the Okanagan as well as Niagara and has an unusual

255

number of half-bottles.
Open Tuesday to Saturday 5 pm to 10 pm. Closed on Sunday and Monday. Licensed. All cards. No smoking. &

THUNDER BAY
MAP 206
SCANDINAVIAN HOME
147 S Algoma Street
$40
(807) 345-7442

Scandinavian Home was opened to meet the needs of the Finnish community, where people were looking for comfort food at a fair price. Don't expect stylish cooking here. What you'll get is good, honest home-style meals. At noon there are always one or two hot specials. The soups are all homemade, the sandwiches all made to order. In the Christmas season they make luttefish and a number of other Scandinavian specialties. Sadly, Nancy Niva retired last year, so there are no more cinnamon buns crusted with cardamom seeds. But there are still wild-blueberry pies and apple pies in season. There's outstanding coffee, but no liquor.
Open Monday to Friday 7 am to 3.30 pm, Saturday 7 am to 2.30 pm, Sunday 9 am to 2 pm. No liquor, Master Card, Visa. No smoking. &

TOBERMORY, Ontario
MAP 207
GRANDVIEW INN
11 Earl Street
$120
(519) 596-2220

The Grandview has been in business for almost half a century. It's not a luxury hotel, but it has a fine view of Little Tub Harbour, at the point where the ferry crosses to Manitoulin Island The Crowley family have always kept a good kitchen that's known for its Georgian Bay whitefish, which they prepare in five different ways: broiled, blackened Cajun-style, grilled with lemon, lime and orange, stuffed with crab and topped with shrimps or Mediterranean-style with tomato, basil and garlic. Meals begin with a nine-green salad. Whenever possible,

they buy their fish and vegetables from local organic suppliers. The kitchen is at its best with seafood, though it
offers a number of pies made to recipes that have been in
the family for generations. The wine-list features some
fine old barolos.
*Open daily 5 pm to 9 pm from 1 May until Thanksgiving. Li-
censed. Master Card, Visa. No smoking.*

TOBERMORY   **MAP 207**
MOLINARI'S
68 Water Drive   **$80 ($220)**
(877) 596-1228

Molinari's was named in honour of Guido Molinari,
Marie-France's uncle. This is basically an (excellent)
espresso bar with a limited menu. Everything is prepared
in-house, using old family recipes. Keep an eye out for
the osso buco, the ravioli and the Italian gelatos, the best
of which is flavoured with strawberries. Visitors have
written to us also about the apple-squash soup and the
chicken cacciatore. The restaurant is right on the shore
of the outer harbour and you can sit outside on the deck
and watch the comings and goings of the shipping. Or
you can book a sunset cruise with the Molinaris, provided you can make up a party of four or more.
*Open Saturday and Sunday noon to 8 pm from late May until
mid-June, Tuesday to Sunday noon to 8 pm from mid-June until
mid-October. Closed on Monday in summer, Monday to Friday
in the spring. Licence pending. All cards. No smoking.* &

TOFINO, B.C.   **MAP 208**
SHELTER
601 Campbell Street   **$150**
(250) 725-3353

At Shelter everything is fresh, most of it organic and
local. The shellfish all comes from the Gulf Islands, the
chicken from the Cowichan Valley and the greens from
Barkley Sound. Start with chowder from Meares Island
or Cortes Island mussels. The chowder, filled with

smoked salmon, surf clams and Yukon Gold potatoes, makes a great lunch. In the evening they add local wild salmon with honey-apple beurre blanc. The free-run Cowichan Valley chicken is remarkable too and goes well with the warm chèvre salad and Okanagan goat-cheese, caramelized onions and roasted garlic.

Open daily 11.30 am to 5 pm (lunch), 5 pm to 10 pm (dinner). Licensed. Amex, Master Card, Visa. No smoking. Book ahead if you can.

TOFINO   **MAP 208**
SOBO   ☆
311 Neill Street   **$130**
(250) 725-2341

Sobo stands for Sophisticated Bohemian, which is what this place was when it was housed in a chip-wagon parked by the side of the road. Today it occupies an elegant but austere new building overlooking the harbour. Some people think the food isn't as good as it used to be, but it probably is—expectations are different now. We've tried many things—the wild-fish chowder, the beet-and-goat-cheese salad and the duck-confit pizza with gorgonzola, caramelized onions and balsamic vinegar. The evening menu features local pink-shrimp cake with crab and avocado in a tomatillo salsa, spot prawns with tequila in a bleu claire dressing, followed by pan-roasted halibut with potato mash and bouillabaisse with local wild fish—mussels, clams, shrimps, scallops and dungeness crab. If you really miss Sobo's old purple truck, look for the bright-orange van of Tacofino Cantina, parked next to the Wildside Grill at 1184 Pacific Rim Highway in Tofino (telephone (250) 925-8228).

Open daily 11 am to 9.30 pm. Licensed. Amex, Master Card, Visa. No smoking. ♿

Where an entry is printed in italics this indicates that the restaurant has been listed only because it serves the best food in its area or because it hasn't yet been adequately tested.

TOFINO   MAP 208
THE SPOTTED BEAR   ☆☆
120 Fourth Street: Unit 101   **$125**
(250) 725-2215

This small bistro gets full early, so it's important to book
ahead. The food is exquisite and the prices are reasonable.
Vincent Fraissange creates imaginative fusion dishes out
of the best local produce he can find. We like his mushroom risotto with truffle aioli and grainy mustard, which
goes beautifully with his beet salad and his splendid naan.
His beef short-ribs are good too and so is his albacore-
tuna pho. Of course, you can always have a shoulder of
lamb or a steak, which are said to be outstanding. There's
a children's menu that offers pizzas and pasta, and this
makes the Spotted Bear an ideal place to bring your family.
Open Tuesday to Sunday 5.30 pm to 9 pm. Closed on Monday.
Licensed. Amex, Master Card, Visa. No smoking. Book ahead.
&

TOFINO
See also UCLUELET.

TORONTO, Ontario   MAP 209
ACADIA   ☆☆
50C Clinton Street   **$160**
(416) 792-6002

Matt Blondin made Acadia what it is—one of the best
restaurants in Toronto. Then, after less than a year, he
left. The owners turned quickly to Patrick Kriss, who
had worked for Daniel Boulud in New York and more
recently at Splendido in Toronto. Here at Acadia he's
doing things that match Matt Blondin at his best. Like
Blondin, he works in the Louisiana style, smoking his
sturgeon, charring his octopus and making the best
hominy grits in history. His celery soup is a marvel, his
organic salmon a glory of salmon roe and mustard. His
sweetbreads are as good as any we've ever tasted. And he

259

has a number of interesting wines by the glass. Try the Dog Point sauvignon blanc or the dry riesling from Organized Crime. They're both cheap. But Acadia has no charm. Go there to eat and drink well, but don't expect to be entertained.

Open Monday and Wednesday to Sunday 5.30 pm to 11 pm. Closed on Tuesday. Licensed. Amex, Master Card, Visa. No smoking. Book ahead if you can. &

TORONTO   **MAP 209**
ARIA
Maple Leaf Square   **$160**
25 York Street
(416) 363-2742

Aria has a stunning interior and marvellous architectural views of the Union Station and nearby buildings. The environment is exciting, the service poised and the cooking competent. Meals begin with a soup *del giorno*, fried squid, carpaccio and prosciutto parmesan. There's breast of chicken to follow, organic salmon and a beautifully light tuna crudo. Many people simply order a frittata, but the tuna crudo is more interesting. There's a whole page of open wines, but the wine-list is really built around its thirteen chiantis and its twelve valpolicellas. You can pay up to 385.00 for one of the chiantis, up to an astonishing 950.00 for one of the valpolicellas. (The solaias and sassicaias are actually cheaper, and of course there are many affordable wines as well.)

Open Monday to Friday 11.30 am to 3 pm, 5 pm to 11 pm (later on Friday), Saturday 5 pm to midnight, Sunday 5 pm to 10 pm. Licensed. Amex, Master Card, Visa. No smoking. Book ahead if you can. &

TORONTO   **MAP 209**
THE BLACK HOOF   ☆
928 Dundas Street W   **$125**
(416) 551-8854

The big news last year at the Black Hoof was that Grant

van Gameren had left the kitchen. His partner, Jen Agg, assured us that there would be no important changes under the new chef, Brandon Olsen, and so far that seems to be true. Everybody here is young and well dressed, their wallets full of folding money. The Black Hoof is for committed carnivores. But the beef served here has little in common with the roast beef of Old England. Here you eat all the parts of the animal that no-one else wants, even the blood. (Once they went looking for a recipe for blood custard.) Everyone's favourite is the roasted bone marrow, but the duck prosciutto and the tuna crudo are just about as good. As for the charcuterie, it's amazing. After that there's an excellent cheese plate and good fresh fruit.

Open Monday 6 pm to 11.30 pm, Thursday to Saturday 6 pm to 1 am, Sunday 6 pm to 11.30 pm. Closed on Tuesday and Wednesday. Licensed. No cards. No smoking. No reservations.

TORONTO MAP 209
BUCA ☆
604 King Street W **$125**
(416) 865-1600

At Buca, an underground restaurant at the far end of a narrow alley off King Street, Rob Gentile cooks in the new Italian style. That means that he cures whole hams to make his prosciutto and pancetta; it means that he makes all his own pasta and bakes all his own breads, including his nodini, which has become famous locally. His pastas are all great and his pizzas are as light as air, but what the restaurant is really all about is its salumi or cured meats, which you can see being prepared in the open kitchen. All the sweets are superb; the best are the pasta stuffed with quince and the torta sanguinaccio, which means chocolate mixed with pork blood. The all-Italian wine-list is extraordinary.

Open Monday to Wednesday 11 am to 3 pm, 5 pm to 10 pm, Thursday and Friday 11 am to 3 pm, 5 pm to 11 pm, Saturday 5 pm to 11 pm. Closed on Sunday. Licensed. Amex, Master Card, Visa. No smoking. Book ahead.

261

TORONTO   **MAP 209**
CAFE BOULUD   ☆
60 Yorkville Avenue   **$200**
(416) 964-0411

After his failure in Vancouver, Daniel Boulud opened
two successful restaurants, one in Montreal (see above),
the other in Toronto. In Toronto, he's taken over the
dining-room of the new Four Seasons Hotel, where his
premises are luxurious and extremely well served. He has
a table d'hôte every day at 32.00 for two courses, as well
as an ambitious à la carte that starts with a soup (sunchoke, say) and goes on to a country terrine and seared
albacore tuna, followed by such main dishes as speckled
trout, loin of lamb, lobster salad, halibut and steak au
poivre. The menu is full of surprises—in fact, surprise is
what Boulud is really all about. Eggplant, zucchini, belly
of lamb, crisp shreds of onion, cucumber, celery, shrimp,
couscous, leeks and chorizo—they all make unexpected
appearances on your plate. Would you believe, even the
plain mashed potatoes come as a masterpiece of hot butter and cream? The sweets are on the whole less successful, but the wine-list is astonishing. The best drinking is
on the list of old-world whites, where there's a Marc
Brédif vouvray for only 69.00. (There's also a first-class
cabernet sauvignon from Tin Barn in Napa that costs just
59.50.) If you really want to spend money, you can;
there's a good Lafite for 3640.00 a bottle.
Open daily 11.30 am to 2.30 pm, 5.30 pm to 10 pm (later on
weekends). Licensed. Amex, Master Card, Visa. No smoking.
Book ahead if you can. ♿

TORONTO   **MAP 209**
CAMPAGNOLO
832 Dundas Street W   **$150**
(416) 364-4785

Campagnolo is Italian and, like most Italian restaurants,
it's warm and very friendly. The waiters laugh a lot and
so does the chef, who spends much of the evening talking

to customers. They have all the familiar things on the menu. There's spaghetti (all'amatriciana), tagliatelle (with water buffalo and honey mushrooms), fettuccine (with white truffles) and veal schnitzels (with sauerkraut). Actually, the two best things on the menu aren't recognizably Italian at all. One is the roasted bone marrow with oxtail and plum marmalade; the other is fresh burrata cheese with whole roasted grapes. (The roasted grapes are the talk of the town, and with good reason.) There's a sensible Norman Hardie pinot noir from Prince Edward County for 69.00); they also have an attractive primitivo from Puglia, but it costs 20.00 more.

Open Wednesday to Sunday 6 pm to 9 pm. Closed on Monday and Tuesday. Licensed. Master Card, Visa. No smoking. Book ahead.

TORONTO   MAP 209
CANOE   ☆☆
Toronto-Dominion Centre   **$225**
66 Wellington Street W
(416) 364-0054

Canoe, like Scaramouche (see below), lives on its view, and of the two Canoe's is probably the more interesting. The whole of Toronto Island is laid out before you from the 54th-floor south windows. The menu may not break important new ground, but the chefs make the most of every opportunity that comes their way. Meals start with maple-poached Pacific salmon, beef tartar and pan-seared Quebec foie gras, followed by skate wing, Alberta lamb and New Brunswick sturgeon, something seldom seen in Canadian restaurants. You can end the meal with panna cotta if you like, but the deconstructed tart is more fun. The wine-list is wonderful.

Open Monday to Friday 11.45 am to 2.30 pm, 5 pm to 9 pm. Closed on Saturday and Sunday. Licensed. All cards. No smoking. Book ahead. &

Our website is at www.oberonpress.ca. Readers wishing to use e-mail should address us at oberon@sympatico.ca.

TORONTO MAP 209
CAVA ☆
1560 Yonge Street **$150**
(416) 979-9918

At Cava Chris McDonald is running a tapas-style restaurant with a remarkable variety of Spanish food and drink. Cava is an exciting restaurant, especially if you spend a few dollars on the wonderful Iberican ham, which is much better than serrano ham. Carved off the bone in front of you, this is a dish of extraordinary delicacy and marvellous complexity. There are many other good things as well, though nothing that matches the Iberican ham. There's tiradito of tuna, a salt-cod cake with piperade, smoked octopus with wheat-berries, grilled sardines and roasted sablefish with black rice. The best wines are the riojas and most of them are very good indeed. So are the sherries from Pedro Ximenez, which make a perfect sweet course.

Open daily 5 pm to 10 pm. Licensed. Amex, Master Card, Visa. No smoking. ♿

TORONTO MAP 209
CENTRO ☆☆
2472 Yonge Street **$215**
(416) 483-2211

Centro last appeared in this guide in 1995, when we said: "the noise, the oversized plates, the menu, the cooking, which is bold and very aggressive, this is food, one would suppose, for men and young men at that. Big helpings, big flavours." The new Centro is a horse of a very different colour. The noise and the brash effects are both gone. Centro today is quiet and elegant. The menu is serious. The cooking is knowledgeable and sophisticated. The front of the house is run by Armando Mano, who calls Franco Prevedello "Pop." Dinner starts with foie gras and black trumpet mushrooms or tuno crudo and goes on to striped bass with white asparagus, rack of lamb with

264

green peas and mint and beef tenderloin with roasted garlic and marrow, that rare and wonderful delicacy. The wine-list is mainly French and Italian, and rises to an extraordinary selection of super-Tuscans and great clarets, all of which cost more than 1000.00 a bottle. If you don't have 1000.00 in your pocket, the thing to do is to ask for a bottle of Three Girls cabernet sauvignon. It's a fabulous little wine and costs only 40.00 a bottle.

Open Monday to Saturday 5 pm to 10 pm. Closed on Sunday. Licensed. Amex, Master Card, Visa. No smoking. Book ahead if you can. க

TORONTO   **MAP 209**
COLBORNE LANE   ☆
45 Colborne Street   **$175**
(416) 368-9009

Colborne Lane has been completely redecorated and, unless you order one of the two tasting menus, now operates on a more modest scale than it used to. The tasting menus are still there. Nine courses cost 119.00 plus 69.00 for wine service, fifteen courses cost 177.00 plus 89.00 for wine service. But the regular à la carte is short and comparatively simple. It offers five appetizers and four main dishes, one of which is a risotto and one a rib-eye of beef. That leaves only pork belly with garlic scapes, sunchokes and old-cheddar polenta and tea-smoked Arctic char, neither of which is of compelling interest. The meal begins, however, in lively fashion with cured trout and preserved lemon, pickled mustard and pressed yogurt, which is a better choice than the seared foie gras with caramelized apple and a quinoa fritter. The foie gras is disappointing and so is the quinoa fritter. There's nothing on the wine-list for less than 52.00, and you have to spend more than that, much more, if you want to drink well.

Open Tuesday to Saturday 5.30 pm to 8 pm. Closed on Sunday and Monday. Licensed. Amex, Master Card, Visa. No smoking. Book ahead.

TORONTO MAP 209

DIDIER
1496 Yonge Street **$175**
(416) 925-8588

Didier Leroy cooks in Parisian style. His favourite dishes are omelettes, not foie gras. He likes to work with flat-iron steak or merguez sausages. He's at home with fried mussels and snails in garlic butter—or perhaps snails bordelaise. If you give him 25 minutes, he'll make you a first-class soufflé or even a fine tarte tatin. He doesn't believe in big, showy wine-lists. He offers only a handful of wines—a few chardonnays and a sauvignon blanc, perhaps a cabernet or two. His prices are modest. These are old-fashioned virtues, simple, straightforward and dignified, like the man.

Open Tuesday to Friday 11.30 am to 2 pm, 5.30 pm to 9 pm, Saturday 5.30 pm to 9 pm. Closed on Sunday and Monday. Licensed. Amex, Master Card, Visa. No smoking.

TORONTO MAP 209

ENOTECA SOCIALE
1288 Dundas Street W **$115**
(416) 534-1200

Rocco Agostino has taken charge of the kitchen here and made the cooking synonymous with that of southern Italy. His pasta is all made in-house—his ravioli with chestnuts, apples and black truffles, his bucatini all'amatriciana, his chicken gizzards with orecchiette—and it's all great. Almost better are his cheeses. There are more than a hundred of them. They're all kept at the correct temperature and humidity—and they show it. The wine-list, however, is less than splendid and many wines that should be there are not.

Open daily 5 pm to 11 pm. Licensed. Amex, Master Card, Visa. No smoking. Book ahead.

If you use an out-of-date edition and find it inaccurate, don't blame us. Buy a new edition.

TORONTO   **MAP 209**

FOXLEY   🐟

207 Ossington Avenue   **$95**

(416) 534-8520

At Foxley Tom Thai has an extraordinary menu. The place is always packed unless you come early, and that's no wonder because the big menu regularly offers such things as water-buffalo steak, ceviche of kingfish, tea-smoked quail, szechuan-style frogs' legs, beef heart, roasted sturgeon, black cod and beef cheeks in red curry. The dining-room is small and dark and the cooking is uneven. (Tom Thai is no longer the Tom Thai of ten years ago at Tempest.) One of the best dishes, as it happens, is one of the most conventional—the ceviche of Nunavut char with green apple and ginger. Whether or not calamari or shrimps go with mango seems never to have occurred to anyone in the kitchen. They arbitrarily yoke together squid with mango, scallops with kumquats and jalapeno, chicken wings with green papaya and, worst of all, Kusshi oysters with lime and chilli. Kusshis with chilli make a dish of splendid awfulness. But Tom Thai has one great virtue—his cooking is always a real eye-opener.

Open Monday to Saturday 6 pm to 11 pm. Closed on Sunday. Licensed. Master Card, Visa. No smoking. Book ahead.

TORONTO   **MAP 209**

FRANK   ☆

Art Gallery of Ontario   **$150**

317 Dundas Street W

(416) 979-6688

Frank was named for Frank Gehry, who designed the space, but over the years it's come a long way. They still begin very plainly with soupe du jour, gravlax with dill, heirloom beets and crab-cakes with aioli. It's with the next course that surprises come thick and fast. The corn-and-cheddar soufflé is about as good as it gets, but the tuna, served rare with lovely young bok choy and sliced fingerling potatoes, is a masterpiece. There's sweet butter, sea-salt and black bread on every table, but the tuna soon makes you forget everything else. Ask for the brown-sugar ice cream to follow—it's almost as good as the tuna. There are many local beers and a splendid variety of Canadian wines to drink, most of them from the Niagara Region. We like the fumé blanc from Cattail Creek, but there's plenty to choose from. The service, once slow, is now both efficient and friendly. Frank is one of the best places for lunch in Toronto, and in the evening they add things like steelhead trout and rack of lamb from Dufferin County. Prices are modest, even in the evening.

Open Tuesday to Friday 11.30 am to 2.30 pm, 5.30 pm to 10.30 pm, Saturday 11.30 am to 3 pm (brunch), 5.30 pm to 10.30 pm, Sunday 11.30 am to 3 pm (brunch). Closed on Monday. Licensed. Amex, Master Card, Visa. No smoking.

TORONTO   MAP 209
THE GALLERY GRILL
Hart House   **$105**
7 Hart House Circle
(416) 978-2445

Everyone knows that the cooking here is top of the line. You may not really want tomato tartar or squash soup, but ask for either and you'll be pleasantly surprised. One day last winter we were offered roasted halibut or calamari schnitzel—a disheartening choice. But just try the calamari schnitzel and you'll be stunned by the flavour and texture of the dish. The sweets are all quite prepossessing. There's a bittersweet chocolate pudding-cake, a roasted apple strudel, a yogurt panna cotta and a maple-syrup crème brûlée. You won't go wrong with any of these, though the wonderful lemon-soufflé tart seems to have vanished.

Open Monday to Friday 11.30 am to 1.30 pm, Sunday 11 am to 2 pm (brunch). Closed on Saturday. Licensed. Amex, Master Card, Visa. No smoking. &

Nobody can buy his way into this guide and nobody can buy his way out.

TORONTO   **MAP 209**
GEORGE   ☆☆
111C Queen Street E   **$180**
(416) 863-6006

Lorenzo Loseto has never quite regained the brilliance
and sophistication of his early days. But he still has a startling menu and he still cooks with delicacy and grace. Try
his wild salmon with seedless watermelon, his Wagyu
beef with carrot mustard, his sea scallops with pea
pastina, his pork tenderloin with succotash or, better yet,
his Pacific halibut with apricots. Such dishes are not
merely rich and luxurious; they are clever. The wine-list
is clever too. If you can afford it, ask for the old barolo
for 295.00; if not, settle for the juliénas for 70.00.
*Open Tuesday to Saturday 5.30 pm to 10.30 pm. Closed on
Sunday and Monday. Licensed. Amex, Master Card, Visa. No
smoking. Book ahead.*

TORONTO   **MAP 209**
THE GLOBE
124 Danforth Avenue   **$160**
(416) 466-2000

The kitchen at the Globe has settled down this year, and
they're doing a lot of very good things. The gnocchi is
one and it's as good as any in the city, if not better. The
sablefish is another, the Cumbrae beef a third. The interior of the restaurant is elegant, the menu small and well
designed. They feature smoked pork belly at noon, along
with halibut from George's Bank, local elk and foie-gras
terrine, as well as the gnocchi, the sablefish and the beef.
In the evening there are scallops, Arctic char and lobster.
The glory of the restaurant, however, is the wine-list,
which features countless wines from the Niagara Region,
a large number from Prince Edward County and a few
from the Okanagan. The whole list is priced at 50 per
cent off on Sunday, which puts almost everything within
easy reach. Half a dozen raw oysters with a bottle of wine
at half-price make a lovely and inexpensive Sunday

brunch.

Open Tuesday to Thursday 6 pm to 10 pm, Friday 11.30 am to 2 pm, 6 pm to 10 pm, Saturday and Sunday 11 am to 2 pm (brunch), 6 pm to 10 pm. Closed on Monday. Licensed. All cards. No smoking. &

TORONTO   MAP 209
THE GROVE   ☆
1214 Dundas Street W   **$150**
(416) 588-2299

The cooking here is deconstructive in spades. Even the parsley-root soup is filled with (overcooked) snails, bacon and fried bread. Cured salmon is more successfully paired with beetroot and apple, scallops (less successfully) with chicken and sunchoke. The main courses are usually more reliable. Cod comes with crab, cabbage and a (brilliant) treatment of black pudding, but the cod itself is seriously overcooked. Arctic char is on the plate with smoked potato and sherry vinegar. What, it has to be asked, does Arctic char do for sherry vinegar, or vice versa? Beef is served, more plausibly, with barley and horseradish. At the end of the meal there's one wonderful pudding. Ben Heaton's Eton mess is so much better than the same dish anywhere else that one wonders what other surprises he's got up his sleeve.

Open Sunday noon to 5 pm, Tuesday to Saturday 6 pm to 11 pm. Closed on Monday. Licensed. Amex. Master Card, Visa. No smoking. Book ahead.

TORONTO   MAP 209
ICI BISTRO   ☆
538 Manning Avenue   **$170**
(416) 536-0079

Jean-Pierre Challet has worked at the Auberge du Pommier and the Inn at Manitou. Now he's settled in downtown Toronto at Ici, which is a small, quiet bistro with 24 seats. Quiet because Challet is a quiet man who runs a quiet kitchen. He's not interested in dramatic effects.

He's interested in good cooking, period. His menu features lobster bisque, foie gras au naturel, braised beef (with black trumpet mushrooms), steak tartar, local lamb and fresh fish. After that he makes a fine soufflé and a lovely trio of lemon. His wine-list, like everything else, is modest and reasonably priced.

Open Wednesday to Saturday 5.30 pm to 9.30 pm. Closed Sunday to Tuesday. Licensed. Amex, Master Card, Visa. No smoking. Book ahead.

TORONTO   **MAP 209**
JACQUES
126A Cumberland Street   **$120**
(416) 961-1893

Jacques does all the cooking himself at this charming, little upstairs restaurant, and he cooks well. His entrecôte maître d'hôtel is as good as you're likely to get anywhere. It's true that the vegetables are very plain and cooked hot raw, but if you like you can have a fricassee of snails with tomatoes and garlic instead. There's also a pretty good quiche *du jour*. The wine-list is small and rather predictable, but the prices are very low. In fact, everything at Jacques is cheap.

Open Monday to Saturday noon to 3 pm, 6 pm to 11 pm, Sunday 5 pm to 10 pm. Licensed. Amex, Master Card, Visa. No smoking. Book ahead if you can.

TORONTO   **MAP 209**
KAISEKI YU-ZEN HASHIMOTO   ☆☆
6 Garamond Court   **$800**
(905) 670-5559

Masaki Hashimoto has designed a new space for his restaurant in the Japanese Cultural Centre in Don Mills. The dining-room is small and holds fewer than ten people and you have to book at least a week in advance. Meals cost 300.00 a head, plus wine or sake, tax and tip. The chef orders everything on the menu from Japan and everything he orders is seasonal. This means, for example, that you'll never be offered conger pike, an eel-like fish that's available only in late summer, during April or May. From the moment you sit down you'll be introduced to new tastes and textures, a new culture and a new history. Hashimoto works in the kitchen alone; his wife is in change of the front of the house and their son, Kei, looks after the closing tea ceremony. There's nothing else like this anywhere in North America. Hashimoto trained for ten years in Japan to qualify as a Kaiseki chef. You must allow at least four hours for a meal here, but for some people it's worth every minute and every dollar. *Open daily at 7.30 pm by appointment only. Licensed. Diners, Master Card, Visa. No smoking. You must book ahead.* ⅜

TORONTO   MAP 209
KAJI   ★★★
860 Queensway   **$310**
Etobicoke
(416) 252-2166

Kaji has always had the best sushi in town, but the dishes cooked by the sous-chef, Takeshi Okada, just get better and more delicate every year. Kaji has been in the kitchen since he was thirteen years old. He started by apprenticing in Japan for more than ten years before coming to Canada in 1980. He's still in the kitchen five nights a week, offering two seasonal menus, seven courses for 100.00, nine courses for 120.00. That means an appetizer, sashimi, a main dish, sushi, soup or a noodle dish and a sweet. Kaji makes all his own soy sauce because the regular soy is, he thinks, too salty. He imports his vinegars from Japan. The menu keeps changing, so you never know exactly what's coming next. It might be pork belly, it might be sea bream, it might be prawns, dandelions, seaweed, bamboo-shoots, udon noodles, ginger, crab, salmon roe or spring onions. The fish is all flown to Canada the day it's caught and it's on your plate the next evening. Before he goes home for the night, Kaji throws away all the leftovers. If you're coming from downtown Toronto, go west on the Gardiner to Islington, exit north

on Islington and turn east on the Queensway.
Open Wednesday to Sunday 5.30 pm to 10.30 pm. Closed on Monday and Tuesday. Licensed. All cards. No smoking. Free parking. Book ahead.

TORONTO   MAP 209
LAI WAH HEEN   ☆
Metropolitan Hotel   **$125**
108 Chestnut Street
(416) 977-9899

The best time to come to Lai Wah Heen is at noon, when Terrence Chan puts on his two *prix-fixe* dim-sum menus, one priced at 48.00, the other at 32.00. The cheaper of the two offers such things as crystal-shrimp dumplings, pan-seared Peking dumplings stuffed with lobster and foie gras with shredded duckling. The other menu offers such costly things as dungeness-crab bisque, Wagyu beef in steamed dumplings and truffled lobster on a bed of noodles. No-one else serves dishes of such subtlety as Terrence Chan and few others maintain a dining-room of such formal elegance. Even the plates are special. They are bone china from Narumi and the silver is weighty. The house tea is, however, without interest. It's best to take a look at the tea menu and order something better. And there's no choice of sakes. There's Gekkeikan, period, though there are a number of quite satisfactory wines.
Open daily 11.30 am to 3 pm, 5.30 pm to 10.30 pm. Licensed. All cards. No smoking. Free parking. Book ahead if you can. &

TORONTO   MAP 209
LOIRE
119 Harbord Street   **$140**
(416) 850-8330

At Loire, Jean-Charles Dupoire runs a bistro with a difference. The prices are modest and the service is casual, but most of the classic bistro dishes are conspicuous by their absence. True, they have steak frites for lunch—and a good steak frites it is—but the dishes that Dupoire has made his own are more apt to be the charcuterie (with excellent chicken-liver terrine), the trout tartar and the mullet, served in its skin with leeks, potatoes and parsley. Prices are low, even in the evening, and there's a useful wine-list offering wines from France and Italy as well as Niagara and the Pacific Rim. If you're tired of Splendido and its unbelievable prices, Loire, just across the street, is a good place to know about.

Open Tuesday to Friday noon to 2 pm, 5.30 pm to 9.30 pm, Saturday 5.30 pm to 9.30 pm. Closed on Sunday and Monday. Licensed. Amex, Master Card, Visa. No smoking. Book ahead if you can. &

TORONTO   MAP 209
LUCIEN
36 Wellington Street E   **$150**
(416) 504-9990

Lucien was one of the few restaurants in Toronto to continue serving elaborate, expensive meals after the financial collapse. We admired them for their courage and said so, but, sad to say, their courage has finally failed them. There's a new chef in the kitchen now and a new menu with somewhat softer prices. Naturally, quality has suffered. Once a brilliant three-star restaurant, asking more than 200.00 for dinner for two with wine, tip and taxes, Lucien has now become a serviceable no-star restaurant that's glad to accept 150.00. It's true, there are still several bright spots. The seared cuttlefish comes as an appetizer with preserved lemon and pork belly; the red-deer tartar is well served with turnips and radishes. The white-radicchio-and-orange salad is cleverly dressed with white anchovies. The Lake Huron whitefish is correctly undercooked and aptly served with parsnips, beets and pickled onions. But such moments of excitement are rarer than they used to be. The black cod that follows is, of course, a fine dish, but when is black cod not a fine dish? The wine-list, of course, is as strong as ever on the best California cabernets and chardonnays. And the coffee is marvellous.

Open Monday to Wednesday 5 pm to 10 pm, Thursday to Saturday 5 pm to 10.30 pm, Sunday 5 pm to 10 pm. Licensed. Amex, Master Card, Visa. No smoking. Book ahead. ♿

TORONTO   **MAP 209**
MISTURA
265 Davenport Road   **$185**
(416) 515-0009

We've said it before and we say it again: the kitchen at Mistura blows hot and cold. The prosciutto is wonderful, but the pickerel is typically overcooked. The crisp fried artichokes are lovely, but the escalope of veal is more beef than veal. The goat-cheese-and-mushroom salad is perfect, but the octopus is tough. The wine-list, on the other hand, unlike the menu, has all the important virtues. It offers many of the best wines from the Old World and the New. There are eight barolos priced from 85.00 to 295.00. There are countless super-Tuscans. There's a Château Pétrus for 2750.00 and a Château Latour for 3600.00. There are, of course, several affordable wines, most of them from the New World. One of the best of these is the J. Lohr chardonnay, which costs only 49.00 a bottle. The restaurant itself looks exactly like the interior of a gentleman's club. As for the service, it's perfect.

Open Monday to Wednesday 5.30 pm to 10 pm, Thursday to Saturday 5.30 pm to 11 pm. Closed on Sunday. Licensed. Amex, Master Card, Visa. No smoking. Book ahead if you can. ♿

TORONTO   **MAP 209**
MODUS
145 King Street W   **$170**
(416) 861-9977

Modus isn't one of your small, cramped, noisy southern Italian bistros. On the contrary, it's big, quiet and northern, its interior lit by huge red standard lamps. Bruce Woods came here from Il Posto and Centro and he's cooking as well as ever. He starts with prosciutto with figs and orange blossom honey, carpaccio with roasted mushrooms and yellowfin tartar with avocado. The main dishes are rather less exciting, but in the evening there's a fine osso buco. Cheese is usually the best of the sweets, and the best of the cheeses is the Blue Elizabeth from Quebec. It's lovely. The wine-list isn't large, but there are some very good things on it, among them the Napa cabernet sauvignon from Edge. It costs 75.00 a bottle, but it's worth it.

Open Monday to Friday 11.30 am to 2 pm, 5.30 pm to 9.30 pm, Saturday 5.30 pm to 9.30 pm. Closed on Sunday. Licensed. Amex, Master Card, Visa. No smoking. Valet parking on weekend evenings only. Book ahead. &

TORONTO   **MAP 209**
MOMOFUKU SHOTO   ☆☆
190 University Avenue   **$485**
(647) 253-8000

David Chang came from New York last year to open three new restaurants in Toronto: Momofuku Shoto, Daisho and Momofuku Noodle Bar. Momofuku Shoto is the flagship restaurant. Reviewers speak of it in hushed tones. They call it spectacular, which it certainly is. Some call it the best restaurant in town. Others speak of Susur Lee and Michael Stadtländer as they would of their grandfather, someone whose day is done. We are not so sure. Shoto had been open only a few months when this edition went to press. The menu changes frequently. What will become, over time, of all that grilled rice, all that crispy shrimp, all that celery-root soup with lamb's belly, all those veal cheeks with green chilli? Dinner for two with wine costs about 485.00. Reservations have to be made online at least two weeks in advance. Does Toronto really need David Chang that much? There are those who think it does. We shall see.

Open Tuesday to Saturday 6 pm to 9 pm. Closed on Sunday and Monday. Licensed. Amex, Master Card, Visa. No smoking. Book ahead.

TORONTO   **MAP 209**
NORTH 44°   ★★
2537 Yonge Street   **$225**
(416) 487-4897

North 44° is as expensive as ever, partly because Mark McEwan insists on buying the best of everything. His red meats are all aged for six weeks. His oysters come from Raspberry Point or Malpèque Bay. His Kusshis may cost 4.95 each, but Kusshis are the best Pacific oyster there is. His foie gras is seared and served with stewed cherries; his shrimps are served tempura-style with yuzu, his lamb chops with curried yellow lentils and white asparagus. When it comes to tenderloin he prefers bison to beef— and he's dead right. There are occasional bargains—the black cod with kohlrabi costs only 40.95, the grilled lobster only 43.95. But it's with his wines that McEwan is at his best. He has 23 chardonnays and two whole pages of cabernet sauvignons, most of them from Napa, with a top price of 695.00 (for a bottle of Groth). Good buys are few and far between, though there's a dry riesling from Cave Spring for only 42.00 a bottle. The spacious dining-room is calm and well appointed, the service serene and poised.

Open Monday to Saturday 5 pm to 10 pm. Closed on Sunday. Licensed. Amex, Master Card, Visa. Valet parking. No smoking. Book ahead. ♿

TORONTO   **MAP 209**
NOTA BENE   ★
180 Queen Street W   **$160**
(416) 977-6400

David Lee has found his feet at Nota Bene. His salads are exquisite and so are his hamachi ceviche, his big-eye tartar and his black-pig salumi. His main courses are on the whole less successful, perhaps because he feels free to ignore regional produce, buying his sea scallops in Digby and his ocean trout in Tasmania. There's a special every day of the week, and they're often the best things on the menu. We were last at Nota Bene on a Wednesday, when we were offered wild striped bass with truffles in a cauliflower purée, a fine, imposing dish. (On Saturdays you can have slow-roasted suckling pig.) The wine-list touches a lot of bases in the mid-price range, where there's a likeable sauvignon blanc from Map-Maker in Marlborough.

Open Monday to Friday noon to 2.30 pm, 5.30 pm to 11 pm, Saturday 5.30 pm to 11 pm. Closed on Sunday. Licensed. Amex, Master Card, Visa. No smoking. Book ahead. &

TORONTO   **MAP 209**
ONE   ☆
Hazelton Hotel   **$225**
118 Yorkville Avenue
(416) 961-9600

One has a luscious setting and superb service. Meals start with yellowfin-tuna sashimi, steak tartar and six raw oysters. The best of these is the yellowfin sashimi, which is a gorgeous dish. Next comes salmon niçoise, seared sea scallops and Alaska black cod. The fish is all expensive here and the meats even more so—high prices are a hallmark of Mark McEwan. For instance, he has a sauvignon from the Loire that sells for 16.00 a glass. Native wines afford no refuge—wines from Niagara and the Okanagan both cost upwards of 80.00 or 100.00 a bottle. Is One worth it? You decide.

Open daily 11.30 am to 4.30 pm (lunch), 4.30 pm to 11 pm (dinner). Licensed. Amex, Master Card, Visa. No smoking. Book ahead. &

TORONTO   **MAP 209**
ORIGIN
109 King Street E   **$130**
(416) 603-8009

You don't go to Origin for foie gras, caviar or a bottle of ornellaia. The tables are bare and there's a lot of noise. Origin is essentially a tapas bar, which means that you can have an adventurous meal at minimum cost. There's also a raw bar where you can have oysters with yuzu, a ceviche of shrimps with coconut and a tuna salad with Asian pears and ponzu. If you opt for table service, you can have chilled sweet-pea soup, crisp calamari with caramelized peanuts and curried shrimps with hot naan. Origin may be no Colborne Lane (see above), but it does show what Claudio Aprile can do without a table-cloth. Recently he's opened two more Origins, one in Liberty Village, the other in Bayview.

Open Monday to Friday 11.30 am to 3 pm, 5 pm to 11 pm, Saturday 5 pm to 11 pm, Sunday 10 am to 3 pm (brunch), 5 pm to 11 pm. Licensed. All cards. No smoking. &

TORONTO   MAP 209
PANGAEA   ☆
1221 Bay Street   **$175**
(416) 920-2323

This lovely restaurant is seldom crowded and never noisy. It has superb service and a large, up-to-the-minute menu, featuring Kunomoto oysters, Cookstown greens, serrano ham, dungeness crab, grilled squid (with garlic and lemon), mussels (with chorizo) and a delightful tart of spinach and feta cheese. There's also a nice selection of charcuterie, followed by provimi liver with ginger and apple, sea-bass with white beans and diver scallops with parsnip and vanilla. Martin Kouprie is at his best with parsnip and vanilla, but he can make almost anything— even white beans with sea-bass and beef tenderloin with seasonal vegetables—interesting and memorable. Most remarkable of all, he makes his own cheeses. There's a cow's milk blue, a truffle tomme, two kinds of goat's milk and three kinds of sheep's milk. If you give him notice, he'll even make you a roquefort or a stilton, but both require ageing and so are not always ready to eat. All of these cheeses are made and aged right on the premises, using traditional farmhouse procedures. There's also a big list of Canadian and European wines, a large number of which are sold by the glass as well as the bottle. As a matter of fact, Pangaea isn't really expensive.

Open Monday to Saturday 11.30 am to 5 pm (lunch), 5 pm to 11 pm (dinner). Closed on Sunday. Licensed. All cards. No smoking. &

TORONTO   **MAP 209**
PASTIS EXPRESS   ☆
1158 Yonge Street   **$145**
(416) 928-2212

The long-time owner, Georges Gurnon, is still in charge of the front of the house at Pastis. His fish soup is unusually delicate and served with a proper rouille and gruyère cheese. The ravioli is made in the kitchen and stuffed with snails with garlic and herb butter—a nice idea. The entrées are on the whole less interesting There's fish and chips, steamed mussels, roasted breast of chicken, grilled lamb chops, calf's liver and steak frites, all of which you've often seen before. Ask instead for the beef ragoût with spicy basil or perhaps the slow-roasted leg of duck with a toulouse sausage. There are some choice sweets, among them a lovely mango ice. The bottled wines are expensive and they need more wines by the glass.

Open Tuesday to Saturday 5.30 pm to 10.30 pm. Closed on Sunday and Monday. Licensed. Amex, Master Card, Visa. No smoking. Book ahead if you can. &

TORONTO   **MAP 209**
SCARAMOUCHE   ☆☆
1 Benvenuto Place   **$240**
(416) 961-8011

Scaramouche has a spectacular view of the city below, a sumptuous interior, a lavish menu and very high prices. It hasn't appeared very often in this guide, because we felt that our readers could do as well elsewhere at considerably lower prices. But if you have a taste for luxury and plenty of money in your pocket, this is the place for you. Dinners begin with tuna sashimi with ginger and caramelized soy, steak tartar with garlic and watercress,

Malpèque oysters on the half-shell or terrine of foie gras, and go on to blue sea-bass in a beautiful coulis of sweet garlic and whipped white beans, steelhead salmon-trout with snap peas, Japanese eggplant and sesame and sea scallops in a leek-and-potato purée. Keith Froggett is a chef who believes in complicated cooking and he has all the virtues except simplicity. Simplicity just isn't what Scaramouche is all about, but there's a lot of excitement on every plate. The selection of wines is surprisingly restrained, but there's plenty of good drinking on the list. The service is exemplary.

Open Monday to Saturday 5.30 pm to 9.30 pm. Closed on Sunday. Licensed. All cards. No smoking. Free valet parking. Book ahead.

TORONTO   MAP 209

SIMPLE BISTRO
619 Mount Pleasant Road   **$125**
(416) 483-8933

Masaguki Tamaru has left the Simple Bistro and been replaced by Da Woon Chae, who so far is cooking about as well as his predecessor. The place is still cheap, though prices have gone up a little in the last year or two. The menu now features such appetizers as salt-cod and a charcuterie platter, followed by Berkshire pork, baked lamb shank and wild Atlantic scallops. The sticky toffee pudding is gone, but you can have a wedge of lovely lemon cake instead. The Norman Hardie wines from Prince Edward County have now priced themselves out of the market and right now the best buy on the list is the Peter Yealands sauvignon blanc, which is sold by the glass as well as the bottle. Simple Bistro is still quiet and extremely well served. All this for about half what you'd have to pay at many Toronto restaurants.

Open Monday and Tuesday 5.30 pm to 10 pm, Wednesday to Friday 11.30 am to 2.30 pm, 5.30 pm to 10 pm, Saturday and Sunday 11 am to 2.30 pm (brunch), 5.30 pm to 10 pm. Licensed. All cards. No smoking.

TORONTO   **MAP 209**
SUPERMARKET
268 Augusta Avenue   **$70**
(416) 840-0501

Supermarket is a good place to go after a day in Kensing-
ton Market. They call their cooking Asian fusion, and in
fact most of the dishes come tapas-style. The dining area
is small and bare, but there's music most nights and dancing on weekends. A lot of the produce comes directly
from the Market, and they always have pork with garlic-
and-chive dumplings, chimichurri calamari or curried-
lamb spring-rolls. If you want something more than that,
go for the Thai shrimps with basil.
Open Tuesday to Thursday 5.30 pm to 10 pm, Friday and Sat-
urday 5.30 pm and 8 pm (two sittings), Sunday 5.30 pm to 10
pm. Closed on Monday. Licensed. Amex, Master Card, Visa.
No smoking. Book ahead.

TORONTO   **MAP 209**
TUTTI MATTI
364 Adelaide Street W   **$110**
(416) 597-8839

Alida Solomon, the chef at Tutti Matti, began her career
at Montalcino in Tuscany and her menu is pure Tuscan.
You can expect in-house pasta (pappardelle with pulled
brisket and tomatoes, tagliatelle with wild boar and
porcini mushrooms), as well as insalata caprese and pâté
con moscato, but it's still the pasta that makes Tutti Matti
what it is—that and the sangioveses from Montalcino.
Nothing—not the pasta nor the wine—is expensive.
Open Monday to Friday noon to 3 pm, 6 pm to 10.30 pm, Sat-
urday 6 pm to 10.30 pm. Closed on Sunday. Licensed. Amex,
Master Card, Visa. No smoking. ♿

The price rating shown opposite the headline of each
entry indicates the average cost of dinner for two with a
modest wine, tax and tip. The cost of dinner, bed and
breakfast (if available) is shown in parentheses.

TORONTO　　　　　　　　　　　　　　　**MAP 209**
YOURS TRULY
229 Ossington Avenue　　　　　　　　　　　**$210**
(416) 533-2243

Yours Truly offers surprise dinners in a small streetfront space on Ossington Avenue. It looks cheap, but it's not. They have a Blue Mountain gamay noir for 60.00 a bottle and that's one of the cheapest wines on the list. The menu looks simple and straightforward, but it isn't either. It reads: carrot, egg, grains, pumpkin, beef, scallop, duck and cheese. What beef or duck mean is anybody's guess. In fact, beef (the best thing on the menu) means tartar of beef nicely served in a shell of raw onion, Duck is less inviting and cheese just means a couple of cheeses we've all seen before. As for the egg, it still keeps its secret. The *amuse bouche* is no lobster or tuna (it's a morsel of mackerel), and the soundtrack is no Mozart, though it's loud enough for Beethoven. The service, one must admit, is crisp and very efficient.

Open Monday and Thursday to Sunday 6 pm to 9 pm. Closed on Tuesday and Wednesday. Licensed. Master Card, Visa. No smoking. Book ahead.

TORONTO　　　　　　　　　　　　　　　**MAP 209**
ZEE GRILL
641 Mount Pleasant Road　　　　　　　　　**$125**
(416) 484-6428

Zee Grill is all about fresh seafood—and low prices. We used to say that the Grill was no longer cheap, but that was a mistake. It is. Sea scallops cost 27.00, black cod, that marvellous fish, 26.00, Ahi tuna 25.00—all very inexpensive by Toronto standards. You can begin with plain raw oysters on the half-shell (there are seven varieties) or, if you want to be more adventurous, with Littleneck clams for 2.75 each. The corn chowder and the lobster fritters are equally inviting, and even cheaper. The wild black cod is, in our opinion, the most exciting of the main courses. There are many good things on the wine-list, but the Mud House sauvignon blanc from Marlborough is, sad to say, not one of them. Choose almost anything else.

Open Monday to Saturday 5.30 pm to 10 pm (later on weekends). Closed on Sunday. Licensed. Amex, Master Card, Visa. No smoking. Book ahead if you can.

TORONTO   MAP 209
ZUCCA
2150 Yonge Street   **$160**
(416) 488-5774

Zucca is Andrew Milne-Allan's creation and, after all these years, he's still in the kitchen. He still makes all the pasta every morning, even the ravioli stuffed with zucchini, ricotta and smoked scamorza. His specialty is whole fish grilled with fresh herbs, lemon and extra-virgin olive-oil. His beef, which comes from Cumbrae around the corner, is all dry-aged and simply grilled. His organic duck is served with spiced orange and wildflower honey. And he now has an impressive list of Italian wines, strong on barolos, barberas, brunellos and chiantis. There's even a tignanello from Antinori for 175.00 a bottle. Prices are modest, not just for the tignanello but for everything on the list.

Open daily 5.30 pm to 10 pm. Licensed. Amex, Master Card, Visa. No smoking.

TORONTO
See also NOBLETON, PORT CREDIT, WHITBY.

TRENTON, N.S.   (MAP 130)
DINE & DASH
102 Main Street   **$70**
(902) 695-3300

Dine & Dash has a new owner, Liz Taylor. The building that houses the restaurant was built in 1892, and at one time was a Sobey's grocery store. The present restaurant has something for everybody. There are six fish dishes, as well as beef, chicken and turkey dinners. At noon they have a wonderful fish chowder and a big selection of sandwiches. The seafood platter consists of a fillet of lightly-battered haddock, scallops, clams, turnips and mashed potatoes. The chicken penne has been a favourite with regulars since day one. People often come in for a cup of coffee and a piece of pie. All the pies are made in-house, and there's usually lemon, apple, butterscotch and coconut cream.

Open Monday to Friday 10 am to 6 pm, Saturday and Sunday 8 am to 8 pm. Licensed for beer and wine only. Master Card, Visa. No smoking.

TRINITY, Newfoundland   **MAP 211**
FISHER'S LOFT INN   ☆☆
3 Mill Road   **$175 ($295)**
Port Rexton
(877) 464-3240

Fisher's has just one set dinner every evening, but travellers who have passed this way all say that their dinner here was better than anything else they had in Newfoundland. Trinity is the oldest settlement in the province. In 1615, only two years after Champlain founded Port Royal, Sir Richard Whitbourne held the first Admiralty Court here. The parish church of St. Paul dates from 1734, and the rest of the town looks much as it did two centuries ago. Fisher's Loft was opened in 1999 by John and Peggy Fisher. It's close to the start of the Skerwink Trail, which is a major destination for visitors. From the dining-room windows you can watch icebergs (and sometimes whales) in Trinity Bay. They now have a greenhouse as well as three open-air gardens where they grow herbs and vegetables for the kitchen. Dinner might begin with a parsnip-and-caramelized-apple soup. Then there'll be garden greens in a partridge-berry vinaigrette. The main course might be cod with brown butter and puréed potato, the sweet, if you're lucky, lemon mousse with a wild berry sauce. They can get lobster from the middle of May until the middle of July and all summer long they forage for wild berries. The wine-list is short and simple; the service is impeccable.

Open daily at 5.30 pm and 7.30 pm (two sittings) by appointment only from 1 May until 31 October. Licensed. Master Card, Visa. No smoking. &

TRINITY   MAP 211
THE TWINE LOFT   ☆
Artisan Inn   **$115**
57 High Street
(877) 464-7700

At the Twine Loft they have an ambitious menu that starts with salmon pâté and shrimps Napoleon, followed by braised lamb shanks, coq au vin with sesame, pork with rhubarb chutney, cod provençale with white beans and Atlantic salmon in a hazelnut crust. Tineke Gow, who owns the place, is also interested in vegetarian dishes and maintains a complete vegetarian menu featuring sun-dried tomato and roasted pine-nut pasta, lentil ragoût, mixed greens in raspberry vinaigrette, partridge-berry sorbet and barren-blends pudding with screech. Tineke's daughter is the *sommelier* and she's developed a remarkable wine-list that offers Yali reserve sauvignon blanc from the Casablanca Valley in Chile and Cockfighter's Ghost pinot noir from Tasmania. The Twine Loft is only five minutes from the summer theatre, and they guarantee that you'll get there before the curtain rises.

Open daily 8 am to 10 pm (pre-theatre dinners at 5.30 pm and 7.45 pm) from 15 May until 15 October. Licensed. Amex, Master Card, Visa. No smoking. Book ahead if you can. &

TROUT RIVER, Newfoundland   MAP 212
THE SEASIDE   🖝
(709) 451-3461   **$95**

The Seaside was opened by May Hann 25 years ago. Maybe more. It used to be a simple place offering nothing but fresh fish and closing early in the evening, so May could go to bed with the sun. The present Seaside, run by May's daughter, Jenny, and her husband, Stan, is a different story. The old place has been greatly enlarged and fitted with big windows overlooking the sea. There's live music and an amazing variety of fresh seafood. But the same dishes, cooked in much the same way, appear on the menu, year after year. That means cod, catfish, sole, flounder, halibut and capelin. Shrimps are brought in from Port-au-Choix, scallops from the Northern Peninsula. Snow crab is to be had in July and August. The cooking is remarkably consistent, though all the family have their fingers in the pie. The best things they do are the poached salmon, the crab, the cods' tongues and the seafood chowders—that and the bake-apple and partridge-berry pies. This is Newfoundland home-style cooking at its very best.

Open daily noon to 10 pm from Victoria Day until Thanksgiving. Licensed. Master Card, Visa. No smoking. &

TYNE VALLEY, P.E.I. (MAP 43)
DOCTOR'S INN
Highway 167 **$135**
(902) 831-3057

The Doctor's Inn is a handsome old place that dates back to the eighteen-sixties. Tyne Valley is a pretty little village not far from the western shore of Malpèque Bay, where it's surrounded by some of the loveliest country in Prince Edward Island. Paul Offer's passion is the two-acre organic vegetable garden behind the house. He may no longer cover the dinner table with vegetables, as he once did, but whatever he puts on your plate will be perfectly fresh. He grows more than 8 varieties of carrot and 28 varieties of lettuce, not to mention the tomatoes, cucumbers, cauliflower, zucchini, beets and onions that he raises to sell at the Farmer's Market in Charlottetown. Paul's wife, Jean, does all the cooking on an old wood stove that came with the house. Her salads are as good as her vegetables and her breads are all freshly baked. Entrées include scallops, Arctic char, salmon, sole and veal. Paul and Jean Offer are genial hosts, and a meal at the

Doctor's Inn is a memorable experience.

Open daily at 7 pm from 1 June until Labour Day, Monday to Thursday and Saturday and Sunday at 7 pm from Labour Day until 31 May. Closed on Friday in winter. Licensed for beer and wine only. Master Card, Visa. You must book ahead. No smoking. &

UCLUELET, B.C.   (MAP 208)
NORWOOD'S ☆☆
1714 Peninsula Road   **$180**
(250) 726-7001

Richard Norwood travelled widely before opening this restaurant in Ucluelet. Here he works closely with farmers, fishermen and cheese-makers to design a menu based exclusively on local ingredients. The restaurant is small and seats only about 25 people. On one side there's an open kitchen; on the other is a small bar. Diners sit at tall tables made of slabs of local fir. Fishermen often call the kitchen a few hours before they reach port to let the chefs know whether they'll have salmon that day or halibut or even octopus. Dinner begins with the tenderest imaginable octopus on a bed of puréed potato with ginger and chilli. Or you can have curried mussels and dungeness crab-cakes with quinoa and lemon. For your main course, you get to choose between braised lamb shanks and albacore tuna wrapped in nori. There's also halibut on a bed of couscous and several steaks. Our favourite sweet is the chocolate mousse with caramel sauce. Wine can be bought by the half-glass, which means that you can have a chenin blanc with your octopus and a pinot noir with your steak.

Open daily 5 pm to 9 pm. Licensed. All cards. No smoking. Book ahead in summer. &

This is a guide to Canadian restaurants from coast to coast—the first ever published and the only one of its kind on the market today. We accept no advertisements. Nobody can buy his way into this guide and nobody can buy his way out.

VAL D'OR, Quebec

HOTEL L'ESCALE
1100 rue de l'Escale
(819) 824-2711

MAP 215

$80

This small hotel has recently been renovated. It's now very attractive and has a lovely setting, just west of town on Highway 117. The kitchen is reliable, the service attentive and warm. Fresh walleye used to be their signature dish, but these days it's likely to be flash frozen, so most travellers now opt for the fillet of beef with black peppercorns. People usually begin with a country terrine or the house-smoked salmon, and end with a chocolate tart or the strawberry shortcake.
Open Monday to Saturday 5.30 pm to 11 pm, Sunday 5 pm to 10 pm. Licensed. All cards. No smoking. &

VANCOUVER, B.C.

L'ABATTOIR
217 Carrall Street
(604) 568-1701

MAP 216

$90

The Abattoir is much too noisy, but the food is good. Always ask for the scallop-and-oxtail dumplings, which are better than any of the salads or terrines. The oxtail is presented as if it were a spring-roll, full of shredded meat and never greasy. After that, we usually order the confit of rabbit, wrapped in bacon and served in a coulis of carrot with pickled radishes and brussels sprouts. Sweetbreads and veal tongue both appear on the menu from time to time. If you find either, go for it. The apple cake with olive-oil is wonderful, the spicy ginger perfectly balancing the bright, sunny taste of the apple.
Open Monday to Saturday 5.30 pm to midnight. Closed on Sunday. Licensed. Master Card, Visa. No smoking. &

Where an entry is printed in italics this indicates that the restaurant has been listed only because it serves the best food in its area or because it hasn't yet been adequately tested.

BANANA LEAF
1096 Denman Street   **$75**
(604) 683-3333

Malaysian cuisine is a blend of the Chinese, Indonesian and Thai styles of cooking. On the West Coast chefs use the extraordinary variety of fresh produce available to display each of these styles to its best advantage. At the three Banana Leaf locations they add great service and a warm atmosphere, and as a result all three have been immediate successes with the critics as well as the general public. Sadly, the Denman Street location doesn't take reservations, though it's always been a good place to recover from a hard walk in Stanley Park. At 820 W Broadway the best things on the menu are usually the dungeness crab with Singapore chilli, the rendang beef and the sambal beans. The beans are often cooked hot raw and if you don't like hot raw ask instead for the mixed seafood, which will bring you Malaysian versions of flat fish, scallops, shrimps, mussels, clams and squid. This is now a much better choice than the appetizer plate, which sometimes comes with soggy spring-rolls. The Kitsilano location, at 3805 W Broadway, has a splendid lunch that starts with roti canal and goes on to boneless shoulder of lamb, stewed in a cumin curry with fennel and coconut milk, or mixed seafood with lemon grass, ginger, garlic, chilli and galangal. In the evening they offer a large variety of fresh seafood—try the crab with garlic and black peppercorns, the prawns with sambal or the red snapper in Assam curry.

Open Monday to Thursday 11.30 am to 2.45 pm, 5 pm to 10.30 pm, Friday 11.30 am to 2.45 pm, 5 pm to 11 pm, Saturday 11.30 am to 11 pm, Sunday 11 am to 10 pm. Licensed. Amex, Master Card, Visa. No smoking. ♿

If you wish to improve the guide send us information about restaurants we have missed. Our mailing address is Oberon Press, 145 Spruce Street: Suite 205, Ottawa, Ontario K1R 6P1.

VANCOUVER

MAP 216

BAO BEI
163 Keefer Street   **$75**
(604) 688-0876

Bao Bei is a post-modern take on the Chinese restaurants
that once flourished all over Canada. It specializes in what
they call schnacks, which in this case means marinated
eggplant braised with soy, garlic and ginger, steamed
prawn dumplings and pork won-tons with arugula in
ham consommé. We particularly like their steamed buns
with pork belly, bean-sprouts, preserved turnip and sug-
ared peanuts, their beef tartar with preserved mustard
root, crisp shallots, watercress and taro chips and their
braised pork meatballs with cabbage in puff pastry.
People write to us about the squid with Chinese sausage
and baby bok choy and the crisp pork belly with sautéed
turnip, Asian cucumber, chilli and garlic. After that
there's Vietnamese coffee and mandarin oranges, or (even
better) panna cotta with lemon gastrique and confit of
kumquat. Bao Bei is still crowded, but it's not half so
noisy as it used to be. Prices are close to their old lows.
Open Tuesday to Saturday 5.30 pm to midnight. Closed on
Sunday and Monday. Licensed. Master Card, Visa. No smok-
ing. No reservations.

VANCOUVER

MAP 216

BIN 941
941 Davie Street   **$85**
(604) 683-1246

Very little has changed at Bin 941. They still offer West
Coast fusion-style tapas, which have little in common
with the real thing. It's a funky place, and when we
go there we usually ask for free-range breast of duck
with sundried cranberries, grilled lamb sirloin with an
heirloom-tomato salad or Digby scallops with bonito
butter. Others tell us that they admire the portobello
mushroom in a reduction of garlic and balsamic vinegar,
the lemon salt-buttered halibut in a Japanese plum

vinaigrette and the mussels steamed with coconut milk, lemon zest and garam masala. Some dishes, like the Yucatan breast of chicken with blue-corn bread and the Chinese five-spice duck with dragon fruit, fragrant pear, watercress and pecans, used to be offered only at Bin 942, which is now closed.

Open daily 5.30 pm to 1.30 am. Licensed. All cards. No smoking. No reservations.

VANCOUVER MAP 216
BISHOP'S ☆
2183 W 4 Avenue **$175**
(604) 738-2025

John Bishop has always been known for his graceful, intimate interiors, his gorgeous flowers (orchids bigger and whiter than most) and his careful, competent service. But he hasn't been known, until now, for a masterpiece like his corn soup with black-pepper squid. His beet salad is such another, his terrine of wild boar still another. His rack of lamb, it's true, is no masterpiece, but it's a pleasing, likeable dish. So is his tenderloin of beef with kale and wild mushrooms. Everything or nearly everything served in the restaurant is organic. Nearly everything comes from nearby farms, many of which are named in the menu. Several of the wines come from either the old World or the Pacific Rim—of course they do. But the bulk of the list is grown next door, in the Okanagan. John Bishop has done an excellent job here on West Fourth, and sometimes he's inspired.

Open daily 5.30 pm to 10.30 pm. Licensed. All cards. No smoking, no cellphones. Book ahead. ♿

VANCOUVER MAP 216
BLUE WATER ☆☆☆
1095 Hamilton Street **$225**
(604) 688-8078

Blue Water is a gorgeous restaurant, with amazing food and expert service. To start with, they have a raw bar with 21 varieties of oyster, two from the State of Washington, four from the Maritime provinces and the rest from the B.C. coast. The best of these, we think, are the oysters from Kusshi and Fanny Bay. There's also a sushi bar, with a short list of sushis and sashimis. Then there's a regular à la carte with an unusual number of such good things as Arctic char, sablefish, white sturgeon, scallops from Qualicum Bay, chinook salmon and Wagyu beef (at market prices). The wine-list is fabulous, offering most of the best wines in the world, as well as local familiars like Burrowing Owl, Blasted Church, See Ya Later and Dirty Laundry. The cooking is magical, the service everything it should be. You won't do better wherever you go.

Open daily 5 pm to midnight. Licensed. All cards. No smoking. Valet parking. &

VANCOUVER   MAP 216
BONETA
12 Water Street   **$185**
(604) 684-1844

Boneta has recently moved to more attractive quarters. The menu, however, is largely unchanged. We've always liked their small plates, which make it possible to have a good time without spending an arm and a leg. The best of these, we think, are the gnocchi with double-smoked bacon and a poached egg and the beef tartar with capers, shallots and egg yolk. Of the main dishes, we like the seabass with preserved-lemon and quinoa and the veal cheeks with kale, hedgehog mushrooms and new potatoes. The tarte tatin is much the best of the sweets. Boneta is open late, which makes it an ideal place for an after-theatre dinner.

Open Monday to Thursday 5.30 pm to 1 am, Friday and Saturday 5.30 pm to 2 am. Closed on Sunday. Licensed. Amex, Master Card, Visa. No smoking. &

If you use an out-of-date edition and find it inaccurate, don't blame us. Buy a new edition.

VANCOUVER   **MAP 216**
LA BRASSERIE   ☆
1091 Davie Street   **$145**
(604) 568-6499

We used to think of this place as a typical French bistro,
but actually it's not and never professed to be. It's a
Franco-German bistro and it's probably more German
than French. The mussels and fries are as good as ever and
so is the salad of organic greens that comes with it. But
too often the chef is offering things like rouladen and
spaetzle, bratwurst and sauerkraut. We didn't come here
for sauerkraut. Instead, try the Alsatian onion tart and
pretend you're in Alsace, with all its bright and lively
colours. There's an excellent selection of wines, most of
them favourably priced, as well as a number of hard-to-
find local beers.

Open Monday to Wednesday 11 am to 11 pm, Thursday to Sat-
urday 11 am to midnight, Sunday 11 am to 10 pm. Licensed.
Master Card, Visa. No smoking. No reservations.

VANCOUVER   **MAP 216**
LA BUCA   ☆
4025 MacDonald Street   **$150**
(604) 730-6988

La Buca serves northern Italian food from a small storefront restaurant on the west side. They start with a specialty of the Friuli region, which is crisply baked Alpine
piave cheese topped with a tomato fonduta and arugula.
The mussels that follow are simply cooked in white wine
and garlic. The tagliatelle is made with chestnut flour
tossed with cabbage, speck and cheese. The Caesar salad
features radicchio with Italian bacon, capers and anchovies. After that, ask for the panna cotta with brandied
plums if it's still on the menu. The wine-list is small but
skilfully chosen.

Open Sunday to Thursday 5 pm to 9.30 pm, Friday and Sat-
urday 5 pm to 10 pm. Licensed. Master Card, Visa. No smok-
ing. Book ahead. ♿

VANCOUVER   **MAP 216**
C   ☆☆
1600 Howe Street   **$210**
(604) 681-1164

C is starting to look dated, even shabby, but their fish and shellfish are still wonderful. Meals start with a "heavenly" wild-mushroom velouté, after which there are "incredible" seared scallops with mushy peas, pancetta and lemonade foam—both words come from our e-mail. Other good things are the home-smoked salmon, the seared albacore tuna with zucchini ribbons and the roasted sablefish with charred octopus and kale. There's a huge list of wines from the Pacific Northwest, but we always ask for the same thing, the Noble Blend from the Naramata Bench. The service is attentive and very well informed.
Open daily 5.30 pm to 10.30 pm. Licensed. All cards. No smoking. Valet parking. Book ahead.

VANCOUVER   **MAP 216**
CAFE KATHMANDU
2779 Commercial Drive   **$85**
(604) 879-9909

Abi Sharma is the chef and owner of Café Kathmandu, and he's as good at talking to customers about politics as he is at preparing choilaa or shredded chicken with lemon, garlic, onion and fresh coriander. Sharma came to Canada after being arrested as a student protester in Nepal. Here in Vancouver, he serves such authentic Nepalese dishes as choilaa, aloo achaar or chilled sesame-and-lemon salad and jhingey maachaa, which means prawns sautéed in garlic. Sharma is at his best with dumplings stuffed with pork or vegetables and served with sesame and cardamom (or sometimes with tomato chutney). If you think that no meal is complete without meat, ask for the goat curry, served with yellow dal and a hot or sweet chutney. Sharma uses no dairy in any of these dishes, unlike most Indian chefs, who use gee for frying. At Kathmandu there's an abundance of such vegetarian dishes as cauliflower infused with turmeric and served with fenugreek potatoes simmered with bamboo-shoots. Nothing here costs more than 15.00.

Open Monday to Saturday 5 pm to 10 pm. Closed on Sunday. Licensed for beer and wine only. Master Card, Visa. No smoking. &

VANCOUVER   **MAP 216**
CAFE MEDINA   ☞
556 Beatty Street   **$60/$85**
(604) 879-3114

Medina is a poor relation of Chambar (see below). It's a small street-front café with bare tables, paper napkins and rough-and-ready service. It's open only for breakfast and lunch. For breakfast they offer a platter heaped with eggs, short-ribs, onions, cheese and potatoes. If that sounds too much for you, ask for the so-called Santé, which means a boiled egg with one perfect, ripe tomato. For lunch there are spicy meatballs, sausages, goat-cheese en croûte and a daily special. There's a handful of wines and several local beers, among them a lovely wheaten lager from Kronenburg. The cooking is good and the place is always packed. They don't take reservations, but if you come in late you can usually find a table.

Open Monday to Friday 9 am to noon (breakfast), noon to 3 pm (lunch), Saturday and Sunday 9 am to 3 pm (brunch). Licensed. Amex, Master Card, Visa. No smoking. No reservations. &

VANCOUVER   **MAP 216**
CAMPAGNOLO
1020 Main Street   **$135**
(604) 484-6018

Campagnolo is a small, shabby Italian restaurant on Main Street. If you come with a companion, it's a good idea to order a salami platter, followed by Sloping Hills pork and the fish of the day, which if you're lucky may be beautifully undercooked trout. The salami is good, but if you don't like charcuterie you can have Sawmill Bay clams or a helping of beef tongue. There's a long list of red wines from Italy that rises unexpectedly to a tignanello for 140.00. On the way down the list there's a Bossi chianti classico for 75.00 and a Fontanafredda barbera for the unbelievable price of 38.00 a bottle. If you choose the barbera, you can spend the money you save on a glass of grappa. They have three grappas by Jacopo Poli, one of which costs only 24.00 a glass.

Open Monday to Friday 11.30 am to 2.30 pm, 5 pm to 11 pm, Saturday 11.30 am to 2.30 pm (brunch), 5 pm to midnight, Sunday 11.30 am to 2.30 pm (brunch), 5 pm to 11 pm. Licensed. Master Card, Visa. No smoking. No reservations.

VANCOUVER   **MAP 216**
CHAMBAR   ☆
562 Beatty Street   **$150**
(604) 879-7119

Chambar is the creation of Nico Schuermans and it's unlike anything else in the city. To begin with, it's dark and noisy and the menu is full of things like bruschetta of peaches and tomatoes, poulpe géant grillée (which means octopus with smoked bacon, watercress, tomatoes and soy vinaigrette), coquotte (mussels in white wine) and culotte au camembert (steak in red wine with black pepper and cheese). Perplexity is part of the game. Conversation is out of the question—borrow a flashlight and concentrate on the menu, where there are a number of good things. One of these is the ragoût of venison. Another is the roasted halibut with saffron and star anise, which they call cassoulet de poisson. Mussels are really what the restaurant is all about, and the most interesting of the mussel dishes is the mussel congolaise, which is mussels with tomatoes, coconut, smoked chilli, lime and cilantro. The beef with chorizo is not a success, however; nor is the octopus, which is overwhelmed by smoked bacon. Take care with the wine-list too. It offers many unfamiliar wines at extraordinary prices. If you want some pleasant drinking at reasonable cost, ask for a bottle of

Coonawarra cabernet sauvignon—it's yours for 59.00.
Open daily 5 pm to midnight. Licensed. Amex, Master Card,
Visa. No smoking. Book ahead. &

VANCOUVER   **MAP 216**
CIBO
Moda Hotel   **$125**
900 Seymour Street
(604) 602-9570

Cibo is located near the Orpheum Theatre on Seymour
Street. Here Neil Taylor cooks in the country Italian
style. In Italian slang, Cibo means festive food, and the
atmosphere in this old building, with its terracotta floors,
high ceilings and exposed beams, is indeed warm, intimate and cheerful. Taylor's menu is simple and changes
with the seasons. His pâté campagnola comes with house-
made pickles and mustard. We usually ask for that, but
his rabbit with tagliatelle and his gnocchi with sage butter
are almost equally good. The chicken under a brick,
served with corn and chanterelles, is about the best of the
main courses, though there are those who prefer the
grilled scallops with crisp artichokes, chilli and mint. The
so-called chocolate nemesis is their best-known sweet,
but we are always tempted by the plum-and-almond tart.
The Italian cabernets are well chosen but expensive.
Open Monday to Saturday 5 pm to 9 pm. Closed on Sunday.
Licensed. Amex, Master Card, Visa. No smoking. &

VANCOUVER   **MAP 216**
CINCIN   ☆
1154 Robson Street   **$190**
(604) 688-7338

CinCin never used to serve lunch, and if you come for
lunch nowadays you may be disappointed—the cooking
at noon blows hot and cold. They have all the usual
dishes: dungeness crab-cakes, lamb sausages, wood-
roasted trout—as well as scallop ceviche with white beetroot, which is probably the best thing on the menu. But

on the whole the cooking is not distinguished. The wine-list, on the other hand, is amazing. Aside from all the Lafites and Mouton-Rothschilds, and the countless ornellaias and solaias, they have no fewer than 78 beautiful grappas, at least two of them from the great Jacopo Poli. We ourselves, whenever we have the money, ask for the grappa ornellaia, which at 28.00 a glass is a marvel of transparent clarity. If you're looking for a gentle white by the glass, ask for the Markus Molitor spatlese riesling from the Mosel. Unfortunately, it isn't cheap.

Open Monday to Friday 11.30 am to 3 pm, 5 pm to 11 pm, Saturday and Sunday 5 pm to 11 pm. Licensed. All cards. No smoking. Book ahead if you can.

VANCOUVER   MAP 216
CIOPPINO   ☆☆☆
1133 Hamilton Street   **$250**
(604) 688-7466

This is an extraordinary restaurant. Pino Posteraro has nothing to offer—and never has had—but superlative cooking. He cooks the familiar dishes of northern Italy and almost nothing but. That means veal, rack of lamb, breast of duck and fresh fish—and he cooks them all with startling perfection. Everything is cooked just as it should be, even the Alaska black cod, which of course is not native to Italy. He starts his meals in traditional fashion too: with prosciutto di Parma, carpaccio of beef, scallops, squid and octopus—the last two both amazingly tender. Last winter we had a bowl of chestnut soup, brilliantly presented in foam, which was an exciting novelty. But usually the excitement comes from the cooking itself. If that isn't enough for you, take a look at the wine-list, which has page after page of ornellaias, solaias, Lafites and Mouton-Rothschilds. If you want to spend less than that, look for the gewurtztraminer from Pfaffenheim or the chianti riserva from Ruffino. Both cost about 30.00 for a half-bottle. The sweets are as remarkable as everything else. Try the lemon tart, the heart-soft chocolate cake or even the maple crème brûlée.

Open Monday to Saturday 5.30 pm to 10.30 pm. Closed on Sunday. Licensed All cards. No smoking. Valet parking. Book ahead if you can. &

VANCOUVER   **MAP 216**
COBRE
52 Powell Street   **$85**
(604) 669-2396

Cobre is located in Gastown and looks like nothing from the outside. Inside, however, all is warmth—exposed brick, dark wood, an inviting bar and friendly service. They have great ceviches, a different selection every day. Small plates are the name of the game. That means wild-boar belly, pulled duck with charred scallions and roasted garlic, wild Mexican sea-prawns, lamb and mole meat-balls with garlic popcorn and roasted elk on a bed of baked squash. Dining here is a memorable experience.
Open daily 5 pm to 2 am. Licensed. Amex, Master Card, Visa. No smoking. Book ahead if you can. &

VANCOUVER   **MAP 216**
CRAVE
3941 Main Street   **$125**
(604) 872-3663

Crave is a small, smart bistro on Main Street at 22 Avenue. It has an attractive menu, agreeable service and low prices. We like to start with the shrimps. The shrimps are lightly battered with a dipping sauce of sweet-chilli mayo. (The tempura of Ahi tuna and the dungeness crab-cakes are both less exciting than the shrimps.) If you pre-fer, you can have Pacific mussels, steak frites or, indeed, a whole roasted chicken. There are only about a dozen wines, but there are several beers, some local, some im-ported. Look for the Kronenburg from France or the Erdinger, a wheaten beer from Germany.
Open Tuesday to Friday 11 am to 10 pm, Saturday 9 am to 10 pm, Sunday 9 am to 9 pm. Closed on Monday. Licensed. Amex, Master Card, Visa. No smoking. No reservations. &

VANCOUVER   **MAP 216**
CRU   ☆
1459 W Broadway   **$115**
(604) 677-4111

Cru is quiet and offers small plates at modest prices. What this means is that you can enjoy impeccable cooking while talking to your friends and listening to their replies. But everyone knows this, so you have to book ahead, especially at lunchtime. We especially recommend the duck-leg confit with bacon vinaigrette, spaetzle and goat-cheese mash and the Alaska black cod with sautéed kale, cauliflower and crushed potatoes. Diners at Cru get a discount at the Arts Club Theatre, which makes it an ideal place for a meal before a performance.
Open daily 6 pm to 10 pm. Licensed. Amex, Master Card, Visa. No smoking. Book ahead. ♿

VANCOUVER   **MAP 216**
DIVA AT THE MET   ☆
645 Howe Street   **$175**
(604) 602-7788

Diva at the Met may not do anything extraordinary or even surprising, but it has an accomplished kitchen that makes very few mistakes. The dining-room is calm and comfortable, the service suave and poised. There's at least one choice appetizer—raw tuna with a garnish of radish and avocado. Next comes tortellini with foraged mushrooms, wild coho salmon with pickled cabbage and navy beans, pork belly Thai-style and Alaska black cod with asparagus and lovely mashed potatoes. The wine-list may be thin on wines from France and Italy, but it's strong on wines from the Okanagan. This is not the time for a Lafite (though they have one or two). The thing to drink here is a bottle of Blasted Church or Blue Mountain.
Open Monday to Friday 11.30 am to 2.30 pm, 5.30 pm to 9.45 pm, Saturday and Sunday 5.30 pm to 9.45 pm. Licensed. Amex, Master Card, Visa. No smoking. Free valet parking.

VANCOUVER   MAP 216

DON FRANCESCO   ☆
860 Burrard Avenue   **$150**
(604) 685-7770

Don Francesco isn't crowded or noisy, like so many successful restaurants. It's quiet and well lit, with widely-
spaced tables, stiff white napkins and highly polished
glasses. The menu is, of course, Italian and it's broadly
familiar. Not that there are no surprises. The calamaretti
is one such. Calamaretti are baby squid and they're served
here with sweet capers, tomatoes and extra-virgin olive-
oil. The ruby trout with lemon, parsley and olive-oil is
another. The list of barolos—six of them, all priced at
about 150.00 a bottle—is still another. If you want to see
the kitchen at its best, ask for a bowl of wild-mushroom
soup, made with a beautiful rich stock. The pasta is all
perfect, the greens delicate and wonderfully fresh. The
fish is all simply grilled. The veal is pounded until it's fork
tender and then grilled. As for the service, it's perfect too.
*Open Monday to Friday 11.30 am to 5 pm (lunch), 5 pm to 11
pm (dinner), Saturday and Sunday 5 pm to 11 pm. Licensed.
All cards. Book ahead. No smoking.* ♿

VANCOUVER   MAP 216

FRAICHE
2240 Chippendale Road   **$185**
West Vancouver
(604) 925-7595

Fraiche isn't quite what it used to be. The menu is still
there and the view. They still serve Kusshi oysters, grilled
octopus, Qualicum Bay scallops, quinoa-crusted sweetbreads, pan-seared foie gras and wild-boar chops. But the
scallops are overcooked, the sweetbreads seriously overcooked. The oysters are good, of course, and they still
have an expansive (and expensive) wine-list. (The best
buy is the Laughing Stock pinot gris at 58.00 a bottle.)
And the view of the Lion's Gate Bridge is magnificent.
Open Monday to Friday 5 pm to 10 pm, Saturday and Sunday

10 am to 3 pm (brunch), 5 pm to 10 pm. Licensed. Amex, Master Card, Visa. No smoking. Book ahead. ♿

VANCOUVER   **MAP 216**
LA GHIANDA   ☞
2083 Alma Street   **$60**
(604) 566-9559

La Quercia (see below) is the oak, Ghianda the acorn in Italian. This is a licensed Italian deli and restaurant operating in the Point Grey district of Vancouver. The menu changes daily but always has a fine selection of soups, salads, pastas and sandwiches. For 10.00 you get your choice of three pastas, three paninis and three main dishes. Everything is authentic Italian. At noon you can have orichette with gorgonzola and walnuts, grilled fennel sausages or grilled trout. The sandwiches, served on house-made ciabatta, are rich and massive. We like the veal with tuna sauce and the lamb panini, both of which cost around 10.00. Our favourite sweet is the apple strudel and the cappuccino is wonderful. The deli offers charcuterie and an abundance of Italian cheeses.
Open Tuesday to Saturday 11 am to 9 pm. Closed on Sunday and Monday. Licensed. Master Card, Visa. No smoking.

VANCOUVER   **MAP 216**
GO FISH   ☞
1505 W 1 Avenue   **$45**
(604) 730-5040

Go Fish is a small shack on Fisherman's Wharf overlooking False Creek, within easy walking distance of Granville Island. It has outdoor seating on a heated patio, which is fine unless it rains. They serve surprisingly complex dishes like Pacific salmon with side-stripe-shrimp mayonnaise, Japanese pickled cucumber and organic greens on a fresh Tartine Bakery bun. The salmon comes with Pacific Rim coleslaw, which is one of their signature dishes. Of course there's also halibut and chips in a beer

batter with thick-cut potato fries. As for the oyster
po'boy sandwich, everybody seems to love it. When
things get really busy, the staff can sometimes be quite
rude. Pay no attention.

Open Tuesday to Sunday 11.30 am to 6.30 pm. Closed on
Monday. No liquor. Master Card, Visa. No smoking. No reser-
vations. ♿

VANCOUVER   MAP 216
HAWKSWORTH   ✩✩✩
Hotel Georgia   **$180**
801 W Georgia Street
(604) 673-7000

When he first opened at the Georgia Hotel, David
Hawksworth, in spite of all the years he spent at West,
still had things to learn. Well, he's learned them. His
restaurant now has nearly every important virtue. The
menu is lively and interesting, offering as it does things
like charred hamachi salad, caramelized squid with
chorizo, smoked salmon and saffron, pork belly with
Japanese mustard, Lois Lake steelhead trout, Pacific
halibut and sablefish with pickled shitake, crisp yam and
pea-shoots. It's true, the curried lamb doesn't compare
with the lamb stews schoolboys used to eat years ago. The
lamb isn't the same, but Hawksworth plays all the cards
in his hand—cauliflower, raita and pakoras—to make his
lamb a dazzling dish. The chef works with a remarkable
variety of textures and his flavours are all clear and
colourful. Hawksworth has a big list of open wines and
they all speak for themselves. Try the Little Farm riesling
from the Simulkameen or the Starmont chardonnay from
Napa and judge for yourself. If you're drinking by the
bottle, ask for the pinot noir from Joie Farm. It costs
98.00 but it's lovely.

Open Monday to Friday 1130 am to 2 pm, 5.30 pm to 11 pm,
Saturday and Sunday 10.30 am to 2.30 pm (brunch), 5.30 pm
to 11 pm. Licensed. All cards. No smoking. Valet parking. Book
ahead.

JAPADOG
530 Robson Street   **$25**
(604) 569-1158

The first Japadog was opened a few years ago by a Japanese couple who came to Canada with the idea of creating a street stand selling dogs Japanese-style. They started by working alone, then added one helper, then another, then several more. Eventually they had five locations in Vancouver and 30 employees. One of these, the one on Robson Street, is a full-service restaurant. The Japadogs all marry Canadian and Japanese traditions of street food. Canadian hotdogs are good, but (as we've said before) Japanese hotdogs are better. Ask for their top-of-the-line okinomi dog, which is made with a gourmet kurobuta wiener, bonita flakes, fried cabbage, Japanese mayonnaise and a special okinomiyaki sauce. Most people also like the oroshi dog, which comes with bratwurst, grated radish, green onions and soy sauce.
Open daily noon to 7.30 pm (later on weekends). No liquor, no cards. No smoking. No reservations.

KIRIN
1172 Alberni Street   **$75**
(604) 682-8833

Kirin has a smart interior, good service and an unusual menu. The specialties of the house include things like deep-fried shrimps with spicy bread-crumbs, deep-fried squid with spicy salt, deep-fried leather-jacket, spicy duck and capelin with green onions, ginger and soy. Avoid the soft-shell crab and the hot Chinese broccoli— a whole plate of half-raw broccoli leaves is not for most Canadians. Hot Gekkeikan sake is the only thing to drink.
Open daily 10 am to 2.30 pm, 5 pm to 10.30 pm. Licensed. Amex, Master Card, Visa. No smoking. ♿

VANCOUVER   **MAP 216**
LIN   ☆☆
1537 W Broadway   **$95**
(604) 733-9696

Ru Lin Zhang, who runs Lin, has never been interested in Cantonese cuisine. Instead, he cooks in the szechuan style and his restaurant has become famous for both its dumplings and its noodles. Conde Nast considers them both the best in the world. The magic here is created by Yu Miao. Under her fingers the dumpling dough turns into dainty sachets, which she places in bamboo baskets as they are made; then they are taken to the kitchen to be steamed. We always start with the cold appetizer of Shanghai greens in a sesame-oil dressing or sometimes with a spicy szechuanese won-ton in peanut sauce with garlic. Next come tan-tan noodles and prawns with a coating of honey and garlic. They do fish well here, especially the spicy fried garlic squid. The beef and broccoli is much lighter and more delicate than the same dish as it's made in most Cantonese restaurants. Recently Lin has opened a second restaurant just two blocks away at 1788 W Broadway: Suite 101 (telephone (604) 558-3989). Sen, as it's called, takes the best of Lin's northern Chinese dishes and plays with them, sometimes to brilliant effect. Their take on Lin's Xiao Long Bao, for instance, is just as good as the original, maybe better. The same is true of their buns stuffed with Shanghai greens and their sablefish in chilli with garlic. Sen is open seven days a week for lunch and dinner.
Open Monday and Wednesday to Sunday 11 am to 3 pm, 5 pm to 10 pm. Closed on Tuesday. Licensed. Master Card, Visa. No smoking. ⅃

VANCOUVER   **MAP 216**
MAENAM   ☆
1938 W 4 Avenue   **$115**
(604) 730-5579

If you usually find Thai seasoning overwhelming, come

to Maenam, where delicacy is the name of the game. At noon there's a five-course tasting menu at a very modest price. It starts with hot-and-sour soup, curried Fraser Valley duck and Mussaman curried beef (from the Islamic south of the country). For dinner you start with chicken satays in peanut sauce and go on to curried duck, pork from Sloping Hills Farm and three-flavour lingcod with Thai basil and kaffir lime. There's also a so-called Royal Thai dinner, which costs 90.00 for two. It comes with nine dishes, all based on traditional Thai recipes modified by Angus An's experience of the cuisine in a number of top Western restaurants. Critics habitually underrate Maenam; it's a first-class restaurant.

Open Monday 5 pm to 11 pm, Tuesday to Saturday noon to 2.30 pm, 5 pm to 11 pm, Sunday 5 pm to 11 pm. Licensed. Amex, Master Card, Visa. No smoking. &

VANCOUVER   MAP 216
MARKET   ☆
Shangri-La Hotel   **$175**
1115 Alberni Street
(604) 695-1115

Market made a good beginning when it opened in 2009, but since then it's lost a lot of its original polish. Try the snapper if you want to see what we mean. The fish comes in a lively broth, but it's seriously overcooked. The warm chocolate cake may be made with the best chocolate, but it's been left in the oven far too long. Overall, however, the menu is as impressive as ever. Dinner begins with Kusshi oysters on the half-shell, steelhead sashimi, beef tartar and a fine homemade soup. The grilled lamb and beef that come next are both local, which is certainly no hardship. But what you really come to Market for nowadays is the stunning wine-list, with its pages of chardonnays and cabernet sauvignons. Prices are extremely high though and you won't be drinking a Mouton-Rothschild unless you have 3000.00 in your pocket. There are some cheaper wines, of course, but not many.

Open Monday to Friday 11.30 am to 2.30 pm, 5 pm to 11 pm,

Saturday and Sunday 11 am to 3 pm (brunch), 5 pm to 11 pm.
Licensed. Amex, Master Card, Visa. No smoking. Book ahead.
&

VANCOUVER   **MAP 216**
PAPI'S
12251 No. 1 Road   **$120**
Steveston
(604) 275-8355

Papi's, a formal Italian dining-room, is owned by Ken Iaci
and Claudette Piacenza, and is managed by their partner,
Steve Ward. You can begin with an amazing tempura-
style portobello mushroom, followed by al dente penne
(with Italian sausage, say). The squid that comes next is
remarkably tender and perfectly cooked. Or you may
prefer slow-roasted leg of lamb with mint and dijon
honey-mustard. In the evening there are also seared scallops with burnt-orange butter, wild salmon crusted with
parmesan cheese and slow-roasted bison with port and
caramelized shallots. We usually end with a small lemon
tart. Papi's is well worth the drive from Vancouver.
Open Monday to Friday 11.30 am to 2 pm, 5 pm to 10 pm,
Saturday and Sunday 5 pm to 10 pm. Licensed. Amex, Master
Card, Visa. No smoking. &

VANCOUVER   **MAP 216**
PASTIS   ☆
2153 W 4 Avenue   **$140**
(604) 731-5020

Pastis is a typical bistro, and it serves both lunch and dinner. It's not cheap, and most of the appetizers sell for
nearly as much as the main courses. Still, the steak tartar
is perfect and so are the sautéed sweetbreads with pumpkin, sage and foie gras. The fish is all well prepared, especially the wild salmon and the Arctic char with barley
and black-trumpet mushrooms. The cassoulet is a great
dish, filled as it is with confit of duck, Toulouse sausage
and braised white beans. Finish with an apple tarte tatin

or a lemon crème anglaise. The wine-list is mostly French and it's very well chosen.
Open Tuesday to Friday 11.30 am to 2 pm, 5.30 pm to 10.30 pm, Saturday and Sunday 11 am to 2 pm (brunch), 5.30 pm to 10.30 pm. Closed on Monday. Licensed. Amex, Master Card, Visa. No smoking. Book ahead if you can. &

VANCOUVER   MAP 216
THE PEAR TREE   ☆
4120 E Hastings Street   **$125**
Burnaby
(604) 299-2772

The Pear Tree is elegant and full of poise, though it occupies premises in a rundown section of Burnaby that's crowded with pizza parlours. The place was opened ten or twelve years ago by Scott Jaeger and his wife, Stephanie. Since then, Jaeger has gone on to become one of the city's most celebrated chefs, while Stephanie has become highly adept at running the front of the house. Their ravioli stuffed with chanterelles may be disappointing, but their spot prawns in foam with dashi custard is a wonderful creation. Jaeger gets his lamb from Peace River country and his lamb shanks are perfect. His dry-aged beef tenderloin comes with braised short-ribs that it might do better without, but the kitchen recovers its form with its beautiful lemon tart. The wine-list still lacks any discernible point of view. There are no important clarets and none of the big wines from Napa, but there's at least one great buy, Blasted Church, by the glass.
Open Tuesday to Saturday 5 pm to 10 pm. Closed on Sunday and Monday. Licensed. All cards. No smoking. &

VANCOUVER   MAP 216
PHNOM PENH   ☜🖅
244 E Georgia Street   **$90**
(604) 682-5777

Phnom Penh is a family-run operation serving first-class Vietnamese and Cambodian food at very affordable prices. Over the years it's often been called the best Asian restaurant in the city. The tables are close together and almost always full. Chances are, you'll have to wait on the street to get a place inside. The interior is neat and trim, and if you can't wait go to the front desk and give them your order to take away. There are said to be 200 dishes on the menu, all served with such Asian spices as cilantro, lemon grass and chilli. Our favourite is the butter beef, which is the Cambodian answer to carpaccio. It comes to the table barely steamed with a soy-lime dressing and a liberal sprinkling of fried shallots and cardamom. We also like and admire the hot-and-sour soup, the garlic squid, the rolls stuffed with prawns and the papaya salad, made with papaya and carrots tossed in a spicy citrus dressing topped with peanuts, mint and cardamom The rice pudding with fruit is an exotic dish that goes well with any of the moo milkshakes.

Open daily 10 am to 10 pm. Licensed. Amex, Master Card, Visa. No smoking. No reservations.

VANCOUVER   **MAP 216**
LA QUERCIA   ☆☆
3689 W 4 Avenue   **$150**
(604) 676-1007

In 2009 this place was named the best new restaurant in Vancouver—and it was. They still have excellent service, fair prices and outstanding food. Their carpaccio of beef comes with the best shaved parmesan cheese and shredded arugula, their scallops are pan-seared in a reduction of raisin and port. Venison is either pan-seared or roasted and finished with chocolate. Their lamb's neck is a great, hearty peasant dish seldom seen outside rural Italy. There's also a tasty chicken-liver pâté and a great deboned rabbit wrapped in prosciutto and served on a bed of puréed celeriac. Toffee pudding is the best of the sweets, though some prefer the apple strudel with raisins and pine-nuts.

Open Tuesday to Sunday 5 pm to 10 pm. Closed on Monday. Licensed. Master Card, Visa. No smoking. Book ahead.

RANGOLI
1488 W 11 Avenue   **$75**
(604) 736-5711

Vij's Rangoli doubles as a market and a restaurant, selling
ready-to-eat Indian dishes and freshly roasted and ground
Indian spices, as well as eat-in dishes that are almost as
good as Vij's (see below) and a lot cheaper. There are several eat-in dishes, especially at noon: pakoras with dal,
lamb and beef kebabs with tamarind chutney, marinated
chicken with sprouts, pulled pork with sour-cream chutney and beef short-ribs in kalonji curry. They all come
with hot naan.
*Open daily 11 am to 10 pm. All cards. No smoking. No reser-
vations.* &

LA REGALADE
2232 Marine Drive   **$125**
(604) 921-2228

La Régalade went though a bad period several years ago
and we dropped it from the guide. Recently, however, it
has recovered its original form and, under Alain Raye and
his wife, Brigitte, is turning out fillets of pork with
roasted apples to packed houses every night of the week.
The place is noisy and conversation is impossible, but that
it presumably the price of success. The fillet of pork with
two apples, as they call it, is the best of the new dishes,
that or the steak tartar or the grilled prime rib with shallots, potatoes and garlic. The sweets are the work of
Raye's son, Steeve, and the lemon tart and the floating islands are both masterpieces of the genre. There's a useful
wine-list and the service (when Brigitte is on the floor) is
excellent.
*Open Tuesday to Thursday 5.30 pm to 10 pm, Friday and Sat-
urday 11.30 am to 2 pm, 5.30 pm to 10 pm, Sunday 5.30 pm
to 10 pm. Closed on Monday. Licensed. Amex, Master Card,
Visa. No smoking. Book ahead if you can.* &

SHANGHAI RIVER
7831 Westminster Highway **$85**
Richmond
(604) 233-8885

When it comes to the pork-filled dumplings known as xiao long bao, the Shanghai River runs head to head with the celebrated Lin (see above). They also make superb Peking duck, black-vinegar spare-ribs with pine-nuts and pork belly with preserved mustard greens. The service problem, however, hasn't gone away, as we once believed. It's worse.

Open daily 10.30 am to 3 pm, 5.30 pm to 10.30 pm. Licensed. Master Card, Visa. No smoking. Book ahead. &

TABLEAU ☆☆
1181 Melville Street **$125**
(604) 639-8692

If you want to find out how good the cooking at Lumière used to be, come to Tableau on Melville Street. Marc-André Choquette, who used to work at Lumière, opened the place after Lumière closed. When he first opened Tableau, it was called Voya and served as a dining-room for the Loden Hotel, an upscale boutique hotel next door. But now, with a brand-new name, the restaurant is all his own. The menu is limited but exciting, offering things like steak tartar, tuna niçoise, grilled squid, dungeness crab and Kusshi oysters on the half-shell, followed by steelhead trout with quinoa and lemon, steak frites and charcuterie with cheese. The cooking is superlative and the service is excellent. The wine-list is full of good drinking—just look for either the Pfaffenheim gewurztraminer or the barbera d'Alba from Bratiasiola. Nothing at Tableau, except the Kusshi oysters, is expensive, and that's part of the pleasure. (Lumière was very expensive indeed.)

Open Monday to Friday 11.30 am to 2.30 pm, 5 pm to mid-

night, Saturday 5 pm to midnight, Sunday 10 am to 3 pm (brunch). Licensed. Amex, Master Card, Visa. No smoking. Book ahead if you can. Valet parking. &

VANCOUVER   MAP 216
VIJ'S   ☆☆
1480 W 11 Avenue   **$150**
(604) 736-6664

Vij's is not just a restaurant; it's an experience. Vikram Vij doesn't cook Indian pure and simple. He uses Indian spices and creates every dish out of his imagination. The service is the best we can remember, and if you have to wait for a table—they take no reservations—they bring you *amuse-bouches* that help to while away the time. When you finally get to sit down, it's a good idea to ask for an appetizer of spicy pork belly and follow that with lamb popsicles, served with turmeric spinach or rice. The Rajistani goat curry is good too and so is the black cod with yogurt and tomato. There's always plenty of naan; if you want more, just ask for it. The pistachio kulfi with mango is a great way to finish any meal. There are many local wines on offer, but beer goes better with most of Vij's dishes, and of course it's cheaper.
Open daily 5.30 pm to 9.30 pm. Licensed for beer and wine only. All cards. No smoking. No reservations. &

VIBANK, Saskatchewan   (MAP 166)
THE GROTTO   ☆
101 2 Avenue   **$100**
(306) 762-2010

Friday is Mexican night at the Grotto. Cecilia Zimmerman comes from Oaxaca in Mexico and her three-course Mexican dinners cost only 27.00. They start with red-corn soup or real grasshoppers and go on to smoked pork ribs with norena chilli, beef-brisket enchiladas in mole sauce or a chorizo-and-cheese quesadilla. Everything is fresh and everything is authentic. Kevin, Cecilia's husband, comes from the deep south, and every Saturday

313

night he prepares a southern-style barbecue of smoked brisket and pork or beef short-ribs, with a German-style potato salad and fresh-baked corn bread. If you want a drink, ask for a glass of fresh-squeezed lemonade. Vibank is 30 minutes from Regina on Highway 16.

Open Tuesday 9 am to 2 pm, Wednesday and Friday 9 am to 9 pm, Saturday 5 pm to 9 pm. Closed on Sunday, Monday and Thursday. Licensed. Master Card, Visa. No smoking. You must book ahead (weeks ahead for the Mexican dinner).

VICTORIA, B.C.   MAP 218
THE BLACK OLIVE
739 Pandora Avenue   **$150**
(250) 384-6060

The Black Olive is at its best in the evening, when dinners start with sautéed calamari with tomatoes and lemon or with a wild-mushroom tart laced with a reduction of balsamic vinegar and truffle oil. Their signature dish is rack of lamb, which comes with fresh green beans and roasted fingerling potatoes in a black-olive jus. Breast of duck is served in a tomato broth filled with roasted peppers, clams and mussels. Lunch is less successful, but there's at least one fine dish, a zesty tomato-and-bean soup flavoured with chorizo and fresh herbs. After that there's a straightforward crème brûlée, plus a first-class flourless-chocolate cake.

Open Monday to Friday 11.30 am to 2.30 pm, 5 pm to 10 pm, Saturday 5 pm to 10 pm, Sunday 5 pm to 9 pm. Licensed. All cards. No smoking. ♿

VICTORIA   MAP 218
BRASSERIE L'ECOLE   ☆
1715 Government Street   **$140**
(250) 475-6260

Brasserie l'Ecole is a true bistro—small and crowded, but full of enthusiasm. Steaks, mussels and fries—everything is cooked to perfection. The steaks come in a reduction of red wine topped with a dab of roquefort butter. The fries are served with parmesan cheese, garlic, parsley and truffle oil in a house-made mayonnaise. Start your meal with either the onion soup or the chicken-liver mousse with brandy and graine de moutarde. Or you can do almost as well with either the duck confit or the roasted pork loin in a sweet-potato purée. There's a decent wine-list with a number of wines sold by the glass as well as the bottle.

Open Tuesday to Saturday 5.30 pm to 11 pm. Closed on Sunday and Monday. Licensed. Master Card, Visa. No smoking. No reservations. &

VICTORIA   MAP 218
CAFE BRIO   ☆☆
944 Fort Street   **$125**
(250) 388-0009

Café Brio is a warm and very professional restaurant. The chef came from Bis Moreno and the Pear Tree, where he worked under Scott Jaeger. Already he's attracted a considerable following here in Victoria. To enjoy him at his best, order the Family Menu, which costs 40.00 a head for six tasting dishes chosen by the chef. Our favourite at the moment is the smoked sablefish in a velouté of white wine with caramelized fennel and buckwheat dumplings, though the roasted breast of duck and the braised short-ribs both run it a close second. The french-fried potatoes come in a grainy-mustard mayonnaise and are absolutely wonderful. There's a great wine-list and excellent, well-informed wine service. *Note:* many of these dishes are offered in half-portions at reduced prices. *Open daily 5.30 pm to 10 pm. Licensed. Master Card, Visa. No smoking.* &

VICTORIA   MAP 218
CHOUX CHOUX CHARCUTERIE
830 Fort Street   **$45**
(250) 382-7572

Choux Choux has the best lunch in Victoria. It's very

small, however, and there are only two tables inside and two outside. In summer, ask for one of the tables out on the sidewalk, where you'll feel as if you were in Paris waiting for Hemingway to show up. This is the best place to buy pâtés, homemade sausages and cured meats. Most of the cured meats are made right here, using only fresh organic pork from Sloping Hill Farm in Qualicum Beach, Mill Bay rabbits, Cornish game hens, Cobble Hill lamb and Quebec foie gras. They also have a cheese cooler where they keep European *lait cru* cheeses like tomme d'abondance from France, tête de moine from Switzerland, queso de la peral from Spain, taleggio from Italy and cashel blue from Ireland. Apart from the charcuterie, Choux Choux has braised pork belly with apples and potatoes, braised lamb shanks with polenta and several hearty soups and sandwiches. Lunch dishes can all be had to take away.

Open Tuesday to Friday 10 am to 5.30 pm, Saturday 10 am to 5 pm. Closed on Sunday and Monday. No liquor, no cards. No smoking. No reservations.

VICTORIA   MAP 218
DAIDOCO
633 Courtney Street   **$40**
(250) 388-7383

Daidoco is a Japanese restaurant that offers an unusual variety of Japanese soups, salads and seafood dishes. Greens come from their own organic farm in Metchosin. Daidoco seats only about twenty people and the atmosphere is cosy. Their menu is quite limited, but everything on it is the best of its kind. The soups are wonderful, but they sell out quickly, as do their don rice bowls. The tuna sashimi and the grilled chicken are both outstanding, but come early or they too will be sold out. They do a brisk takeout business as well. Place your order by telephone and call early.

Open Monday to Friday 11 am to 2 pm. Closed on Saturday and Sunday. No liquor. Master Card, Visa. No smoking. &

VICTORIA

MAP 218

DEVOUR
762 Broughton Street   **$90**
(250) 590-3231

This small place is attracting new admirers all the time.
Breakfast, lunch or dinner, it doesn't matter. Everything
on the menu is fresh and good. Jena Stewart, who came
here from the Sooke Harbour House, uses only the best
organic produce, to which she brings her own rare talents
as a cook. At noon, she has a lovely duck-and-pork tourtière, served with a green salad in a balsamic vinaigrette
Dinner, served after 5 o'clock on Thursday and Friday
only, features Ahi tuna, pork wellington, a spicy chicken
mole and a lamb tart with chanterelles, stilton and
caramelized onions. Devour must be the smallest licensed
restaurant in Victoria, though in summer tables are laid
outside on the patio. In winter you can order from the
takeout menu by telephone.
Open Monday to Wednesday 8 am to 4 pm, Thursday and Fri-
day 8 am to 9 pm. Closed on Saturday and Sunday. Licensed.
Master Card, Visa. No smoking.

VICTORIA

MAP 218

FOO
769 Yates Street   **$45**
(250) 383-3111

Foo is at the corner of Yates and Broughton, facing a
hotel parking-lot that Foo's customers are not allowed to
use. Here they serve Asian street food at bare tables that
encircle the room. Everything is very cheap and the
counter service is very crisp. The menu is written up on
big blackboards and few things ever change. There's always some red coconut curry, butter chicken, octopus
salad with a glaze of sweet chilli, caramelized chicken,
sweet-and-sour pork and tuna tataki with soba noodles.
The last two are our favourites, but they never put a foot
wrong with any of their dishes. There are no wines or
spirits and only two beers, Driftwood ale and White Bark

wheat beer, both of them brewed locally. We usually ask for the ale, but whatever you ask for you'll be glad. We love Foo.

Open Monday to Saturday 11.30 am to 10 pm, Sunday 11.30 am to 9 pm. Licensed for beer and wine only. Master Card, Visa. No smoking. No reservations. ♿

VICTORIA   **MAP 218**
MATISSE   ☆☆☆
512 Yates Street   **$165**
(250) 480-0883

Matisse occupies a quiet dining-room on Yates Street, where everybody feels warm and comfortable. There are old-fashioned graphics on the menu and crisp, fresh table-cloths on every table. The menu is inviting. It offers things like foie gras de canard in a pineau-des-charentes jelly, sautéed Arctic char and rack of fresh Australian lamb. The lamb is about as good as it gets, and the foie gras is a lively variation on a familiar theme. Dinner usually ends with something like bavarois au citron with red fruit, a beautiful dish. The wine-list is ambitious and rises to a Mouton-Rothschild (1050.00 for a bottle of the 1985). But if you settle for a white wine, you can have a bottle of mâcon chardonnay for just 60.00. Matisse has been underrated for years. It's now time that it was taken as seriously as it deserves.

Open Wednesday to Sunday 5.30 pm to 10 pm. Closed on Monday and Tuesday. Licensed. Amex, Master Card, Visa. No smoking. ♿

VICTORIA   **MAP 218**
PRIMA STRADA   👉
2960 Bridge Street   **$90**
(250) 590-4380

Prima Strada has recently been awarded the Verace Pizza Napoletana or True Pizza of Naples award, which means they make their pizzas as they've been made in Naples for hundreds of years. Only a handful of restaurants in

Canada have won this award. We think the pizzas at this location are even better than those at 230 Cook Street (telephone (250) 590-8595). Prima Strada uses great local produce and their thin-crust pizzas are much the best in Victoria. Try the pizza funghi, which is topped with roasted mushrooms and onions, porcini cream and thyme. We think you'll agree.

Open Tuesday to Saturday 11 am to 9 pm. Closed on Sunday and Monday. Licensed. Master Card, Visa. No smoking. &

VICTORIA   **MAP 218**
RE-BAR
50 Bastion Square   **$65**
(250) 362-9223

Re-Bar was one of the first restaurants to serve organic and vegetarian dishes, but now that several years have passed it needs some new ideas. There's criticism of both the service and the cooking, which is less reliable than it used to be. We ourselves still like the huevos rancheros and the goat-cheese omelettes. The fries are all hand-cut, and locally-roasted coffee is brought to your table as soon as you sit down. They also have ten or twelve wines from the Pacific Northwest, beer from any number of micro-breweries and a remarkable assortment of fruit drinks.

Open Monday to Thursday 8.30 am to 9 pm, Friday and Saturday 8.30 am to 10 pm, Sunday 8.30 am to 3.30 pm. Licensed for beer and wine only. All cards. No smoking. No reservations.

VICTORIA   **MAP 218**
STAGE   ☆
1307 Gladstone Avenue   **$115**
(250) 388-4222

Stage is a 50-seat bistro that features small plates. It's situated in the funky neighbourhood of Fernwood, right next to the Bastion Theatre. The menu was designed by George Szasz, who came here after he closed Paprika. The menu is divided into five parts: charcuterie, vegetables, cheese, fish and meats. Each dish combines Hungarian comfort food with seasonal ingredients from local artisans. Szasz is good with salads and you shouldn't miss the crisp goat-cheese salad, dressed in raspberry, that goes with the beef carpaccio. He's good with fish too. Try his Ahi tuna, served with potatoes and a crisp fennel salad, and see for yourself. There are many good wines that are sold by the glass as well as the bottle.

Open daily 5 pm to midnight (earlier on Sunday and Monday). Licensed. Master Card, Visa. No smoking. No reservations. &

VICTORIA   MAP 218
IL TERRAZZO
555 Johnson Street   **$150**
(250) 361-0028

Il Terrazzo is hidden in Waddington Alley, right behind Willie's Bakery at No. 537. It serves northern Italian cuisine and has more than once been rated Victoria's best Italian restaurant. They start with a hearty fisherman's soup (brodetto del pescatore). If the brodetto has extinguished your appetite, go for the calamari ripieni, which means grilled baby squid stuffed with olive tapenade and served in tomato sauce. If on the other hand you're still hungry, ask for the pork tenderloin with crisp prosciutto, pine-nuts, arugula, sundried tomatoes and balsamic vinegar. There are several important main dishes on the menu, among them blackened Ahi tuna, pork tenderloin with savoy cabbage, venison with sour cherries, bison short-ribs, char-grilled lamb chops and a tenderloin steak. Or you can just settle for a wood-fired thin-crust pizza. Our favourite is the so-called Gamberi, which is topped with black tiger shrimps, roasted garlic and zucchini— but they're all pretty good.

Open Monday to Friday 11.30 am to 2 pm, 5.30 pm to 10 pm, Saturday and Sunday 5.30 pm to 10 pm. Licensed. Amex, Master Card, Visa. No smoking. &

We accept no advertisements. We accept no payment for listings. We depend entirely on you. Recommend the book to your friends.

VICTORIA

ULLA

509 Fisgard Street
(250) 590-8795

MAP 218

$110

Ulla is located in a restored building at the corner of Fisgard and Store, where skid row ends and Chinatown begins. High ceilings, arched windows and contemporary
art all give the place a gentrified air. Now in its second
year, Ulla has a menu that features ethically-raised pro-
teins, whatever that means. Presumably, albacore-tuna
tataki in ponzu sauce and short-rib steaks in black-garlic
jus. Reviewers all admire the semolina polenta, the beet
salad and the fingerling-potato soup with caramelized-
onion crackers. The kitchen takes its sweets seriously too,
especially the *sous-vide* apple cake.
Open Tuesday to Saturday 5.30 pm to 10 pm. Closed on Sunday
and Monday. Licensed. Master Card, Visa. No smoking. Book
ahead.

VICTORIA

ZAMBRI'S

820 Yates Street
(250) 360-1171

MAP 218

☆

$160

The new Zambri's is all steel and glass. The menu is Italian. It starts with tuna tartar and chilled octopus with
tomato and goes on to penne with gorgonzola, tagliatelle
with duck, shoulder of pork, lamb shanks and panna
cotta with (too little) grappa. The cooking is country-
style Italian. The flavours are bold, the helpings large. At
times the cooking is brilliant, and the chilled octopus
with fresh tomatoes is certainly a brilliant dish. The same
is true of the thin-crust pizzas. At other times, however,
Zambri is merely pedestrian. The Cornish game hen, dry
and thin on flavour, is such a dish. The veal is really
young beef—milkfed veal is hard to find anywhere except in Montreal. The beef tenderloin with gorgonzola
is a much better choice. There's a decent list of Italian
wines, and they have an appealing chianti classico from

Castello di Bossi for 60.00 a bottle.
Open daily 11 am to 3 pm, 5 pm to 10 pm. Licensed. Amex, Master Card, Visa. No smoking. No reservations for lunch. ♿

VICTORIA
See also SALT SPRING ISLAND, SIDNEY, SOOKE.

VICTORIA-BY-THE-SEA, P.E.I.   (MAP 43)
ISLAND CHOCOLATE COMPANY
Main Street
(902) 658-2320

This old general store has been completely renovated. The machines that produce the chocolates have been moved to the back and the front opened up for more tables. The chocolates are made with Belgian chocolate stuffed with fresh fruit—strawberries, raspberries and cranberries, each in their season. We first heard of Linda Gilbert as a baker and she still bakes a lot of muffins, brownies and flourless tortes. She has espresso and cappuccino as well, both made from beans roasted right here on the Island. Three years ago the Gilberts organized a chocolate festival that's since become an annual event. It takes place on the third Saturday in September.
Open Monday to Saturday 10 am to 8 pm, Sunday noon to 6 pm from mid-June until early October. No liquor. Master Card, Visa. No smoking. ♿

VICTORIA-BY-THE-SEA   (MAP 43)
THE LANDMARK CAFE
12 Main Street   **$80**
(902) 658-2286

The Landmark is a fixture in the village of Victoria-by-the-Sea. The opening night in June is sold our every year; regulars come to celebrate the return from abroad of Eugene Sauvé and his family. Eugene himself has been here for 25 years and his son, Oliver, and his daughter, Rachel, now help in the kitchen. Not that Eugene needs help—he's as strong as a horse. He's a relaxed and friendly man and he cooks well. His menu seldom changes, though the specials vary with the seasons. Our favourites are the lobster roll packed with sweet, fresh lobster and the meat pies, which can be superb. The only complaint we've ever had was that Eugene doesn't put enough vegetables on the plate. But, vegetables or no vegetables, the Landmark is always fun.

Open daily 11.30 am to 8 pm from 1 June until Thanksgiving. Licensed. Master Card, Visa. No smoking. Book ahead. &

WAINWRIGHT, Alberta   MAP 220
THE HONEY-POT
823 2 Avenue   **$95**
(780) 842-4094

We discovered the Honey-Pot in 1989. It had opened ten years earlier, when it began offering meals to the soldiers of Western Command. The soldiers were lucky to find such a place in a small Prairie town like Wainwright. The Honey-Pot has now been owned and operated by three generations of one family. Alex Heath is running the place today, with the help of his daughter, Michele. Alberta beef is what the kitchen does best. They tried ranch-raised elk a few years ago, but found the quality of the meat wasn't always up to scratch. The fish and chips, however, are surprisingly good and so is the Caesar salad. The vegetables are always fresh and there's a different homemade soup every day of the week except Sunday. All the sweets are made in the kitchen, even the vanilla pudding called Foggy Bottom. The local Ribstone Creek beer is on tap and that's usually the thing to drink.

Open Monday to Saturday 11 am to 9.30 pm. Closed on Sunday. Licensed. Amex, Master Card, Visa. No smoking. &

WATERLOO, Ontario   (MAP 100)
MASALA BAY   ☆
3B Regina Street N   **$85**
(519) 747-2763

Waterloo is the high-tech capital of Canada, home of the

University of Waterloo, the Perimeter Institute of Theoretical Physics and the Steven Hawking Institute. Masala Bay is a small Indian restaurant where Dr. Hawking has been photographed with the proprietors. This is not surprising, because the food is good and very cheap. The best things come from the tandoor oven and the naan is superb. People write to us about the tikka and the aloo gobi. Actually, our favourite is the bhoona gosht or beef curry. There's a good buffet at noon, but the evening helpings are too large for comfort.

Open Monday to Thursday noon to 2 pm, 5 pm to 10 pm, Friday 11 am to 2 pm, 5 pm to 10.30 pm, Saturday 11.30 am to 2 pm, 5 pm to 10.30 pm, Sunday 6 pm to 9 pm. Licensed. All cards. No smoking. &

WATERLOO (MAP 100)
NICK & NAT'S UPTOWN 21 ★★
21 King Street N **$150**
(519) 883-1100

Nick is the chef, Nat the waiter. If you take a seat at the bar, you can watch them both at work. Every day they put on a *prix-fixe* dinner where you can have shiitake-mushroom soup, any one of a number of salads made with local greens and foie gras with salty peanuts. There's also an à la carte that offers local trout, Ontario lamb and beef cheeks with homemade pickles. For vegetarians there's great ravioli, stuffed with a variety of seasonal ingredients. Then there's always some fresh fish. Nick smokes his own sausages and serves them with pork chops braised in white wine. There's a decent wine-list that majors in wines from the Niagara Region.

Open Tuesday to Saturday 5 pm to 9 pm. Closed on Sunday and Monday. Licensed. All cards. No smoking.

This is a guide to Canadian restaurants from coast to coast—the first ever published and the only one of its kind on the market today. We accept no advertisements. Nobody can buy his way into this guide and nobody can buy his way out.

WATERLOO (MAP 100)
SOLE ☆
83 Erb Street W: Building 2 **$140**
(519) 747-5622

Lunch at Sole features Kobe-beef burgers and wienerschnitzel. In the evening they add rack of lamb with
honey and pommery mustard, Arctic char and bouillabaisse. The char is sometimes overcooked, but the lamb
and the wienerschnitzel, both of which come with
braised fennel, mashed potato and sour cream, are always
carefully prepared. The sweets are all made in-house, and
the vanilla-bean crème brûlée is unusually good. The
wine-list majors in wines from the Niagara Region, but
there are many important wines from the Old World as
well.
*Open Monday to Thursday 11.30 am to 11 pm, Friday 11.30
am to midnight, Saturday 11 am to midnight, Sunday 11 am to
9 pm. Licensed. All cards. No smoking.* &

WELLINGTON, Ontario (MAP 150)
EAST & MAIN
270 Main Street **$150**
(613) 399-5420

East & Main is a relative newcomer in this area, but already it's packed at all hours, and you should book ahead.
There are good reasons for its success. The cooking is
good, the portions ample, the service attentive. The
wine-list offers twenty local whites and twenty local reds.
You can start dinner with gravlax cured in vodka and go
on to braised lamb shanks with zinfandel or cider-brined
pork tenderloin with red cabbage The best of the sweets
is either the chocolate torte or the blueberry streusel cake.
*Open Monday and Thursday to Sunday noon to 2.30 pm, 5.30
pm to 9.30 pm. Closed on Tuesday and Wednesday. Licensed.
Master Card, Visa. No smoking. Book ahead.*

Our website is at www.oberonpress.ca. Readers wishing
to use e-mail should address us at oberon@sympatico.ca.

WHISTLER, B.C.

MAP 223

ARAXI

☆☆

422 Village Square

$200

(604) 932-4540

Gordon Ramsay called Araxi Canada's best restaurant. This is hardly true, but the place certainly has its virtues. James Walt's carefully crafted menu touches all the important bases. For instance, his Raw Bar serves six varieties of oyster and five sushis. There are 9000 bottles of wine in the cellar, many of them priced within the means of the average diner. Most things on the menu are fairly priced too. For instance, grilled red tuna can be had for just 29.50, which is cheap for Whistler. Almost everything on the menu (with the exception of the lobster and some of the cheeses) is grown locally. This includes the dungeness crab and the breast of duck, which comes from Yarrow Farms. The steaks are as good as any in the province. The short list of sweets offers poached Okanagan pears and valhrona chocolate. The best of the cheeses come from Salt Spring Island.

Open daily 11 am to 11 pm from 1 June until 30 September, daily 5 pm to 11 pm from 1 October until 31 May. Licensed. All cards. No smoking. Book ahead if you can. ♿

WHISTLER

MAP 223

BEARFOOT BISTRO

☆☆

4121 Village Green

$350

(604) 932-3433

The Bearfoot Bistro gets a lot of bad press. We, however, have never found anything to criticize. The service is no slower than one would expect for dishes that require so much last-minute attention. Prices are high, of course, but cooking of this quality always costs money. André St.-Jacques runs a very tight ship and he makes very few mistakes. In Melissa Craig he has the best chef in the business. Never mind the multi-course tasting menu. If instead you ask for the three-course table d'hôte you'll get a superb meal. There's yellowfin tuna with a beautiful grilled-squid salad. There's truffled cauliflower with a porcini soufflé. There's Alberta beef tenderloin, which is probably as good as the Wagyu beef and 50.00 cheaper. Melissa Craig cooks complicated dishes, but they all work as they're meant to work. We never order her nitro ice cream, which costs 20.00 extra; instead we ask for one of the fruit sweets—coconut, pineapple, apple and caramel. In the wine-cellar there are no fewer than 1100 labels. There's plenty to enjoy here. Enjoy yourself, but look before you leap.

Open daily 5.30 pm to 10 pm. Licensed. All cards. No smoking. Book ahead. &

WHISTLER   **MAP 223**
RIMROCK CAFE   ☆☆
Highland Lodge   **$200**
2117 Whistler Road
(877) 932-5589

The Rimrock needs redecorating, but that's not likely to happen, if only because the customers are happy with the place as it is, so long as Rolf Gunther is in the kitchen. The Highland Lodge isn't easy to find, but once you're seated at your favourite table you'll be happy too. The Rimrock has the friendliest staff, the best service and (many people think) the best cooking in Whistler. Seafood has always been the kitchen's strong suit, though in recent years Rolf Gunther has become interested also in game, especially caribou. Fish and shellfish (including lobster) come in regularly by truck from Vancouver. The seafood trio of halibut, prawns and tuna is always cooked to perfection, and so are the beef and the lamb. The sablefish is elaborately crusted with pecans and macadamia nuts and then roasted in the oven. There's a three-course *prix-fixe* that covers most of the à la carte, and it's a pretty good buy. If you want a sweet, you won't do better than the sticky-toffee pudding. The wines are well chosen but very expensive.

Open daily 5 pm to 9.30 pm. Licensed. All cards. No smoking. Book ahead if you can.

WHISTLER

MAP 223

SPLITZ GRILL
4369 Main Street: Unit 104   **$55**
(604) 938-9300

This is one of the few informal restaurants in Whistler.
They have a children's menu offering hamburgers, hotdogs and chicken fingers for about 6.00. For grown-ups
there are chicken, turkey, ham, lamb, salmon and bison
burgers, each with at least twenty different toppings—
garlic, hummus, baba ganoush, and satziki, as well as
mustard and relish. Recently they've added a spicy lentil
burger for vegetarians. There's also a huge selection of
ice creams. The banana splits are great and the chocolate
milkshakes absolutely wonderful. The service is cafeteria-style, but you can take your meal away with you if
you like. You'll find Splitz in the Alpenglow Hotel, not
far from the centre of the village.
Open daily 11 am to 9 pm from 1 May until 30 November, daily
11 am to 10 pm from 1 December until 30 April. Licensed for
beer and wine only. Master Card, Visa. No smoking.

WHITBY, Ontario   (MAP 209)

NICE BISTRO   ☆
117 Brock Street N   **$110**
(905) 668-8839

It's almost twenty years since Bernard Alberigo and his
wife, Manon, opened this bistro in Whitby. They've
worked hard and kept their standards high, and we've seldom heard a word of criticism. The menu aims to marry
Canadian produce like maple syrup with French recipes.
You'll find some of the best things among the specials on
the chalkboard—the soup of the day, the country-style
pâté and the snails in garlic butter. Of course, they also
have steak frites, mussels marinière and steak au poivre.
Nice isn't far from Italy and so it's no surprise to find
tortellini stuffed with spinach and figs on the menu. On
Tuesday night they offer all the mussels you can eat. The
rest of the week there's a four-course table d'hôte for

30.00 a head (39.99 on jazz nights). The cheeseboard is ambitious and well maintained. Manon is in charge of the sweets, and the wine-list is always full of good things. *Open Tuesday to Saturday 11.30 am to 3 pm, 5.30 pm to 10 pm. Closed on Sunday and Monday. Licensed. Amex, Master Card, Visa. No smoking.* &

WHITEHORSE, Yukon   MAP 225

We don't know of any really good restaurants in Whitehorse, but there are several places that you should know about. The Sanchez Cantina at 211 Hanson Street (telephone (867) 668-5858) claims to have the only authentic Mexican cooking in the Yukon. Otelina Sanchez knows how to cook and she makes a lot of things from scratch, among them guacamole, enchiladas, adobos, chilli rellenos and mole poblanos. Don't expect big helpings and don't order the chicken or any of the daily specials. The Cantina is open for lunch and dinner every day but Sunday, has a licence and takes Master Card and Visa. The Burnt Toast Café at 2112 2 Avenue (telephone (867) 393-2605) is very popular in spite of its name, which is almost as bad as that of a café we know of called Cold Coffee. It's a quirky little place with quite good cooking. There are tapas nights and several vegetarian dishes. The current owners are young and very much into fresh regional cuisine. They're open every day but Monday for lunch and every day but Sunday and Monday for dinner. They have a licence and take Amex, Master Card and Visa. One of the hottest spots in town right now is a bakery called Baked at 100 Main Street (telephone (867) 633-6291). It's a terrific place for breakfast, and at noon they have big, healthy sandwiches. Baked is open every day for lunch, has a licence and takes Master Card and Visa.

WHITE LAKE, Ontario   MAP 226
CASTLEGARTH   ☆
90 Burnstown Road   **$150**
(613) 623-3472

Matthew and Jennifer Brearley make the best of their unlikely location—Castlegarth is an hour's drive from Ottawa, the nearest city. But the two chefs (both graduates of the Stratford Chefs School) have stayed true to their belief that everything should come straight from the garden to the table. (The family farm down the road makes it possible to serve tomatoes on the vine and just-picked beans.) The house, which is right in the middle of the village, has no frills, but it seats 30 people in comfort. The menu changes frequently, and during the year there are some special occasions. Not long ago, Robbie Burns Day brought a salad of brussels sprouts with haggis and rabbit sausage with pickled rutabaga. At other times they offer things like seared quail with butter-braised cabbage, wild-rice pancakes and onions with hawthorn honey. The coffee is marvellous.

Open Wednesday to Sunday 5.30 pm to 10 pm. Closed on Monday and Tuesday. Licensed. Master Card, Visa. No smoking. &

WINDSOR, Ontario   MAP 227
TOSCANA
3891 Dougall Avenue   **$100**
(519) 972-5699

Gino Parco keeps appearing and disappearing from the Windsor restaurant scene. Luckily, the last time this happened he left behind Jonathan Reaume, an old partner, at Toscana. Smoked salmon on a potato pancake is still always on the menu, as well as a number of daily specials. Reaume likes to say that his cuisine is contemporary Italian with Asian grace notes. Certainly, he never overcooks his fish or any of his pasta. The soup of the day is usually a better buy than either the carpaccio or the portobello mushrooms. There's a sushi menu as well, but it's basically just a list of ceviches. The wine-list has a number of upscale wines, among them a Caymus Conundrum, which costs only 58.00 a bottle. Toasted Head chardonnay is also sold quite cheaply by the glass.

Open Monday to Friday 11 am to 2 pm, 5 pm to 10 pm, Saturday 5 pm to 10 pm. Closed on Sunday. Licensed. Amex, Master Card, Visa. No smoking. &

WINNIPEG, Manitoba   MAP 228
BISTRO DANSK   🖾
63 Sherbrook Street   **$90**
(204) 775-5662

Josef Vocadlo started the Bistro Dansk many years ago; nowadays the place is run by Josef's son, Paul. The restaurant hasn't changed much since it opened, and it still has its Danish menu, with a few Czech dishes to give it variety. Start with the herring and go on to the frikadeller, the kylling (half roasted chicken stuffed with apricots and walnuts), the veal tenderloin stuffed with ham and cheese, the pan-fried rainbow trout or the pork tenderloin sautéed in garlic with sweet-and-sour cabbage. With your dinner, ask for a bottle of Mondavi Woodbridge, which costs almost nothing. Indeed, everything at Bistro Dansk is spectacularly cheap.

Open Tuesday to Saturday 11 am to 2.30 pm, 5 pm to 9 pm. Closed on Sunday and Monday. Licensed. All cards. No smoking. Book ahead.

WINNIPEG   MAP 228
EAST INDIA COMPANY   ☆
349 York Avenue   **$75**
(204) 947-3097

This is one Indian restaurant where nobody has to apologize for the décor or, for that matter, for anything else. The dining-room is bright and cheerful. It has a big buffet table that starts with salads and yogurts, goes on to tandoori chicken and such things as mussels, shrimps and whole fish. There are vindaloos on order and a variety of vegetarian dishes. The dessert table has a number of custards, of which we think the mango is the best. There are a few wines on offer and a couple of Indian beers. When it comes to value for money, no restaurant in the city can compare with the East India Company.

Open Monday to Friday 11 am to 2 pm, 5 pm to 10 pm, Saturday 5 pm to 10 pm, Sunday noon to 8 pm. Licensed. Amex, Master Card, Visa. No smoking. Book ahead if you can. ♿

WINNIPEG   **MAP 228**
THE LOBBY
295 York Avenue   **$160**
(204) 896-7275

Dale and Barb Yuell are no longer at the Lobby. Shan
Shuwera is in charge now. Prices are still quite high and
the rib steak now costs 55.00. It's a big steak, however,
and if you have an appetite to match perhaps it's worth
it. The chocolate torte is still as good as ever and so is the
wine-list. The Lobby is basically an upscale steak house,
with plenty of the best wines, all the right cocktails and
first-class service. One thing it doesn't have, however, is
off-street parking, so you just have to take your chances.
*Open Tuesday to Saturday 5 pm to 10 pm. Closed on Sunday
and Monday. Licensed. All cards. No smoking. Book ahead.* &

WINNIPEG   **MAP 228**
NORTH GARDEN
33 University Crescent: Unit 6   **$60**
(204) 275-2591

The North Garden is actually in south Winnipeg and it
has no garden. But it's popular with Chinese students and
faculty from the nearby University of Manitoba, and
rightly so because they have a great variety of authentic
szechuan and cantonese dishes. Dim sum is offered in
steamer baskets every day until 3.30 pm. This is by far
the best dim sum to be had in Winnipeg. They also have
lobster and crab at market prices, and the place is crowded
every evening during the school year. After about 9 o'-
clock, however, things become quieter and the service
improves.
*Open Monday to Thursday 10 am to midnight, Friday and Sat-
urday 9 am to 1 am, Sunday 10 am to midnight. Licensed. All
cards. No smoking. Book ahead if you can.* &

We accept no advertisements. We accept no payment for
listings. We depend entirely on you. Recommend the
book to your friends.

WINNIPEG   **MAP 228**
THE PALM ROOM   ☆
Fort Garry Hotel   **$125**
222 Broadway Avenue
(204) 942-8251

The Fort Garry Hotel was built in 1913. Later taken over
by the C.N.R., it was eventually allowed to fall into dis-
repair. A few years ago, it was restored by Richard Bel
and Ida Albo and turned into a grand hotel with a period
dining-room. The menu at the Palm Room, as it's called,
is that of a road-house, presented in high style. In the
evening you dine on gravlax, roast chicken and pecan pie,
all to the gentle music of a string quartet. On Sunday
they put on a magnificent buffet costing 50.00 (40.00 for
seniors and children under twelve). There's a massive
array of eggs, pancakes, roasts, pastries, tarts and tortes,
as well as a fine selection of whiskies. If you want to recover from all this excess, the hotel operates a Turkish-
style spa.
Open Monday to Thursday 11 am to midnight, Friday and Sat-
urday 11 am to 1 am, Sunday 9 am to 2 pm (brunch), 3 pm to
11 pm. Licensed. All cards. No smoking. Book ahead for Sunday
brunch. ♿

WINNIPEG   **MAP 228**
PEASANT COOKERY   ☜
283 Bannatyne Avenue: Unit 100   **$90**
(204) 989-7700

Oui has now been renamed Peasant Cookery. Oui, in
turn, was a cheaper version of the extravagant 529 steak
house. The name raises some important questions. It
could be intended to suggest either a rural truck-stop or
a minimalist, perhaps also an inexpensive, restaurant. Or
it could be just an up-market joke. As it happens, there
are some wonderful things to be had here as well as things
to avoid. The dining-room is large and the tables generously spaced. The service is efficient and in summer you
can dine *al fresco* and listen to the bands playing in the park

333

across the street. Everything at the Peasant Cookery is surprisingly cheap. A huge slice of tourtière, for instance, costs less than 20.00. There's a charcuterie platter, which is available all day for 15.00. Poutine is on every day at lunchtime, mussels at dinnertime. If you want to go really downmarket, there's bangers and mash and (wonderful) short-ribs. But be sure to avoid the french fries.

Open Monday to Saturday 11.30 am to 10 pm, Sunday 5 pm to 9 pm. Licensed. All cards. No smoking. &

WINNIPEG   MAP 228
RAE & JERRY'S
1405 Portage Avenue   **$100**
(204) 783-6155

Rae & Jerry's takes you back more than 50 years to 1957, the year the place opened. Very little has changed since then. They still have thick red carpets on the floor and deeply cushioned booths. The bar still treats martinis as if they were a fashionable cocktail. The kitchen still caters to people—of all ages and incomes—who want roast beef or beefsteak. The steaks are all good—surprisingly good. There's a fine pecan pie, as well as a coconut-cream pie and bread pudding. They have some good cabernets from Australia and several good malbecs from Argentina. The wines are all fairly priced and so is the food.

Open Monday to Saturday 11 am to 11 pm, Sunday 11 am to 8.30 pm. Licensed. Amex, Master Card, Visa. No smoking. Book ahead if you can. &

WINNIPEG   MAP 228
LA SCALA
725 Corydon Avenue   **$125**
(204) 474-2750

Perry Scaletta has run La Scala for twenty years and more. It's always had an Italian menu with touches here and there of fusion cuisine. But to enjoy the place to the full you have to know what to order. That means dumplings, which are Chinese in concept but ethereal on your plate.

It means seafood linguine and penne with spicy sausage. Best of all, it means penne with garlic and tomatoes, chillies and red and green peppers. Main dishes run from osso buco and cioppino to veal scaloppine and rib steak with black beans. The wine-list is large and features cabernets from Italy and Australia. The service is competent, the prices reasonable.

Open Monday to Friday 11.30 am to 1.30 pm, 5 pm to 11 pm, Saturday and Sunday 5 pm to 10 pm from 1 May until 31 August, Monday to Saturday 5 pm to 10 pm from 1 September until 30 April. Closed on Sunday in winter. Licensed. All cards. No smoking.

WINNIPEG   MAP 228
SYDNEY'S AT THE FORKS   ★★
1 Forks Market Road   **$175**
(204) 942-6075

There's no more elegant restaurant in Winnipeg than Sydney's at the Forks. True, to get there you have to make your way through the schmaltz that the Forks Market has become. But it's worth it—Sydney's is an island of calm and good taste. The menu is at once imaginative and clever, the service perfect. Dinner costs 55.00 a head, plus wine, tip and taxes. For that they give you a lovely soup, an appetizer (cured salmon, say), followed by masterly versions of chicken confit or pork chops with apple, ending with crème brûlée or pumpkin pudding. The wine-list offers everything from an old barolo to a Pétrus priced at only 342.00, which (believe it or not) is cheap for what it is. Lunch is much the same, though cheaper, featuring linguine with scallops and prawns, which at 19.00 is actually a very good buy. Sydney's treats everybody as a somebody and, in spite of its high prices, always offers fair value for money. In other words, it's expensive but worth it.

Open Monday 5 pm to 9 pm, Tuesday to Friday 11.30 am to 2 pm, 5 pm to 9 pm, Saturday 5 pm to 9 pm. Closed on Sunday. Licensed. All cards. No smoking. Book ahead. &

WINNIPEG
MAP 228
TRE VISI
173 McDermot Avenue   **$110**
(204) 949-9032

The original Tre Visi is in a shabby district, but inside
everything is warm and comfortable. The creation of the
chef-owner, Giacomo Appice, it has the best Italian
kitchen in Winnipeg. They have a variety of cured meats
and marinated vegetables. They have some amazing pastas—just try the capellini with roasted red peppers and
saffron cream. They do a fine piccata of veal in white
wine as well, and their saltimbocca of pork has few
equals. If you don't feel like another zabaglione marsala,
ask for the chocolate ganache instead. Recently, Tre Visi
has opened a second restaurant at 926 Grosvenor Avenue
(telephone (204) 475-4447). It has a similar but smaller
menu that emphasizes pasta, but they don't take reservations.
Open Monday to Friday 11,30 am to 2.30 pm, 5 pm to 9 pm,
Saturday 5 pm to 10 pm. Closed on Sunday. Licensed. All cards.
No smoking. Book ahead. ♿

WOLFVILLE, N.S.
MAP 229
BLOMIDON INN   ☆☆
195 Main Street   **$150 ($325)**
(800) 565-2291

The Blomidon Inn has a number of handsome bedrooms
and a dining-room of mid-Victorian splendour. The
place is run by two of Jim and Donna Laceby's sons. Sean
is in charge of the kitchen; his brother, Michael, is the
sommelier. At the moment, Michael has the advantage, because he has several Benjamin Bridge wines on offer. Best
of all, he has a few bottles of the Benjamin Bridge
sparkling wine, which is much the best of its kind ever
produced in Nova Scotia. It's a celebrated wine and hard
to find elsewhere, even at the going price of 125.00 or
more a bottle. Sean's menu is conservative—lobster tails,
grilled lamb, filet mignon—but everything is prepared

exactly as it should be. Some things—the maple-cured salmon is one—are brilliant. Laceby has his own smoke-house, where he smokes his own chicken, his own bacon and his own salmon. The service is formal but relaxed, and the prices are surprisingly low. The maple-cured salmon costs only 9.95, and it's worth twice that.

Open Monday to Friday 11.30 am to 2 pm, 5 pm to 9.30 pm, Saturday and Sunday 10 am to 3 pm (brunch), 5 pm to 9.30 pm. Licensed. Master Card, Visa. No smoking.

WOLFVILLE   MAP 229
CELLAR DOOR
Luckett Vineyards   **$50**
1293 Grand Pré Road
(902) 542-2600

Pete Luckett made an instant success of his grocery stores, which he calls Pete's Frootiques. He then opened a vine-yard called Luckett's. That was in 2010 and the Luckett Vineyards were rated the top tourist attraction in Wolfville just two years later. The wines are still young, of course, but the restaurant offers spectacular views of Minas Basin and Cape Blomidon. The Cellar Door itself is reserved for private parties, but the outside patio has seating for ordinary travellers. Here you can have a soup, a sandwich (Italian ham with figs, say) and a salad (patty-pan squash with chanterelles, perhaps). They also have cheese-and-charcuterie platters, as well as one or two ex-cellent sweets. The German tasting varietal, Ortega, is the best of the wines on offer, though it's often sold out. Good news—they have a red telephone booth from which you can call anyone in North America free of charge.

Open daily 10 am to 5 pm from 1 June until 31 October. Li-censed. Amex, Master Card, Visa. No smoking. Book ahead if you can.

Every restaurant in this guide has been personally tested. Our reporters are not allowed to identify themselves or to accept free meals.

FRONT & CENTRAL
117 Front Street   **$130**
(866) 542-0588

Michael Howell was a leading proponent, perhaps the leading proponent, of the slow-food movement in Nova Scotia. And located as he was in Wolfville, he was able to say (with truth) that most of what he served came from the Annapolis Valley. Illness, however, has forced him to sell Tempest to his chef de cuisine, Dave Smart. Smart has renamed the restaurant Front & Central. He has a good reputation, but the new menu was not available when this edition went to press. Further reports needed. *Open Tuesday and Wednesday 5 pm to 9 pm, Thursday to Sunday 11.30 am to 2.30 pm, 5 pm to 9 pm. Closed on Monday. Licensed. All cards. No smoking.* &

WOLFVILLE
See also GRAND PRE.

WOODSTOCK, N.B.   MAP 230
HEINO'S
John Gyles Motor Inn   **$75**
Highway 165
(866) 381-8800

To get to Heino's, which is no longer right on the Trans Canada Highway, take Exit 200 a few miles south of Woodstock, turn left at two stop signs and proceed a few hundred yards to the north. The John Gyles is at the top of a hill on the west side of the road. Heino Toedler cooks in the German style, which means sauerbraten, schnitzels and several kinds of sausage—bratwurst, debreziner, knackwurst and weisswurst. He also makes such things as butterfly shrimps and deep-fried scallops, but it's usually best to stick to a schnitzel or one of the sausages. (Actually, our favourite dish is the potato pancake.) There's only one (indifferent) German wine by the glass, and it's a good idea to ask for a beer instead. Heino's is trim and neat inside and out and always very well served. Everybody seems to like the place.

Open Monday to Saturday 5 pm to 9 pm, Sunday 5 pm to 8 pm. Licensed. Amex, Master Card, Visa. No smoking. &

WOODY POINT, Newfoundland   (MAP 170)
THE OLD LOFT
Water Street   **$75**
(709) 453-2294

The Old Loft is a success because they took the trouble to find the best suppliers of local fresh produce. Another reason for their success is, of course, that Clarice Bursey is a good cook and a keen baker, turning out multi-grain bread, bake-apple cheesecake and all kinds of fresh berry pies. When it comes to the cooking, she turns out a lot of traditional Newfoundland dishes. Clam chowder is always on the menu, as are salmon, halibut and capelin. All the fish is pan-fried and nothing is ever overcooked. The vegetables are steamed and the french-fried potatoes are made right on the premises. Woody Point is on the south arm of Bonne Bay in Gros Morne National Park. The town was settled more than a hundred years ago and the big old houses with their lovely gardens have been cared for lovingly ever since. The Old Loft occupies one of these and it's been completely restored. To get here, leave Highway 431 on the road to Trout River. The Old Loft is right on the highway.

Open daily 11.30 am to 9 pm from Victoria Day until Thanksgiving. Licensed for beer and wine only. Amex, Master Card, Visa. No smoking.

YARMOUTH, N.S.   MAP 232
OLD WORLD BAKERY
232 Main Street   **$40**
(902) 742-2181

In spite of the recent cancellation of ferry sailings between Yarmouth and Bar Harbour, Tony and Nova Papadogiorgakis are carrying on at the bakery as if nothing had happened. Their breads and pastries are as good as ever. Their huge muffins are good enough to take home. (They come with cheese, cranberry, lemon, blueberry, bran, cinnamon, dates, apples and oranges.) They make rye, whole-grain, sourdough and sweet-potato bread. There's also a homemade soup every day and big, filling sandwiches, of which our favourite is the smoked lamb. (The lamb, like the turkey and the sausages, is smoked on the premises.) The coffee is fairly traded and it's always great.

Open Tuesday to Friday 7 am to 6 pm, Saturday 7 am to 5 pm. Closed on Sunday and Monday. No liquor, no cards. No smoking. &

YARMOUTH
See also MIDDLE WEST PUBNICO.

YELLOWKNIFE, N.W.T.   MAP 233
BULLOCK'S BISTRO   ☆
3534 Weaver Drive   **$130**
(867) 873-3474

Everybody likes Bullock's. It used to be a working fish shack, and it's always been here—small, crowded, noisy and expensive. The chairs are rickety, the tables carved with old initials, the service easy-come, easy-go. But the fish is about as fresh as it gets. Most of it comes from Great Slave Lake—whitefish, cod, pickerel and trout are always on the menu. Renata serves all the fish grilled, pan-fried, poached, blackened Cajun-style or deep-fried in a beer batter. Meals all come with warm sourdough bread and a slab of butter. If you want something to drink, help yourself from the cooler—there's always plenty of beer and a couple of wines in there.

Open Monday to Saturday 11.30 am to 9 pm. Closed on Sunday. Licensed. Master Card, Visa. No smoking. Book ahead if you can.

If you use an out-of-date edition and find it inaccurate, don't blame us. Buy a new edition.

YELLOWKNIFE
FROLIC
5019 49 Street
(867) 669-9852

MAP 233
★★★
$220

The recession of 2008-09 wiped out Pierre LePage's dream of a grand restaurant in Yellowknife. He shouldered his loss and promptly turned Frolic into an elegant restaurant operating on two floors. Downstairs they offer fondues and on Wednesday mussels and beer as well. Upstairs the menu is much more ambitious, the wine-list astonishing. Pierre LePage is a culinary gold medallist who's travelled the world, studying the food and wine of many countries. Wild game and fresh fish are his specialties, but he adds his signature to every dish, whether it's halibut or char, bison or caribou. Every evening he offers two main dishes. One might be halibut poached with vermouth, another might be Barren Lands caribou with maple, cranberry and port wine. Appetizers include pâté, snow crab, Malpèque oysters and prawns en croûte. Sweets don't much interest him, but he always has a fresh-fruit tart on his menu. Pierre LePage also holds the lease on the Wildcat Café in the old town. But they're working on the foundations there and the Wildcat won't be open until next year.

Open Monday to Saturday 3 pm to 1 am. Closed on Sunday. Licensed. All cards. No smoking. Book ahead if you can.

We will soon be preparing the next edition of this guide. To do that, we need the help of our readers, many of whom routinely send us information and comments on restaurants that interest them, whether or not they are already in the guide. Please address us by mail at 145 Spruce Street: Suite 205, Ottawa, Ontario K1R 6P1, by fax at (613) 238-3275 or by e-mail at oberon@sympatico.ca

We acknowledge the support of the Government of Canada through the Canada Book Fund for our publishing activities.

First published July 1971. Reprinted September 1971, November 1971, January 1972. Second edition published June 1972. Reprinted July 1972. Third edition published June 1973. Reprinted July 1973. Fourth edition published June 1974. Fifth edition published June 1975. Book-of-the-Month Club edition published July 1975. Sixth edition published June 1976. Seventh edition published June 1977. Eighth edition published June 1978. Ninth edition published June 1979. Tenth edition published June 1980. Eleventh edition published June 1981. Twelfth edition published June 1982. Thirteenth edition published June 1983. Fourteenth edition published June 1984. Fifteenth edition published June 1985. Sixteenth edition published June 1986. Seventeenth edition published June 1987. Eighteenth edition published June 1988. Nineteenth edition published June 1989. Twentieth edition published June 1990. Twenty-first edition published June 1991. Twenty-second edition published June 1992. Twenty-third edition published June 1993. Twenty-fourth edition published June 1994. Twenty-fifth edition published June 1995. Twenty-sixth edition published June 1996. Twenty-seventh edition published June 1997. Twenty-eighth edition published June 1998. Twenty-ninth edition published June 1999. Thirtieth edition published June 2000. Thirty-first edition published June 2001. Thirty-second edition published June 2002. Thirty-third edition published June 2003. Thirty-fourth edition published June 2004. Thirty-fifth edition published June 2005. Thirty-sixth edition published June 2006. Thirty-seventh edition published June 2007. Thirty-eighth edition published June 2008. Thirty-ninth edition published June 2009. Fortieth edition published June 2010. Forty-first edition published June 2011. Forty-second edition published June 2012. Forty-third edition published June 2013.